*To the widows and widowers described herein*

# *Contents*

# Introduction

Bereavement, the loss by death of someone loved, is the most severe psychological trauma most people will encounter in the course of their lives. Nor are its effects easily overcome. It has long been a topic of literary examination, philosophical speculation, and psychological study; yet, as Shakespeare said, "Everyone can cure a grief but he who has it."

Some recover from grief unscathed, or even strengthened, while others suffer lasting damage to body, mind, and spirit. This book gives an account of a systematic attempt to discover the roots of recovery. How is it that there is so wide a variety of patterns of response to bereavement? Why do some people recover spontaneously from the awfulness of loss, others only with help, and still others not at all? And, if help is to be provided, what form should it take, and to whom should it be offered?

This book is based in large part on the Harvard Bereavement Study. It is now over ten years since the collection of data for that study was completed. One book and several scientific papers have already been published. The book, *The First Year of Bereavement* (Glick, Weiss, and Parkes 1974), relates how our sample of Boston widows and widowers under forty-five years of age coped with their bereavements. It describes the experiences of grief, the processes of mourning, and the special ways in which family and friends helped our respondents get through the first year. Several papers then appeared. They contain the basic scientific findings of the study and were published in scientific journals and books for specialist readers. The first of these, "Health after Bereavement" (Parkes and Brown 1972), measures the effects of bereavement on health by comparing our sample of bereaved people with a control group of married people of the same age. (Further details of this comparison are given in chapter 2.) The second paper, "Determinants of Outcome Following Bereavement" (Parkes 1976), attempts to ascertain whether there is any way of predicting, at the time of bereavement, who will develop problems in physical and emotional adjustment within a few years and who will come through relatively unscathed. We will restate and develop our findings on this issue in several parts of this book.

Several other aspects of the project were taken up by one or the other of us in further work. Loneliness, so much a part of the experience of widows and widowers, was examined by Weiss (1973), who also undertook a study of that other basis for the ending of marriages, separation and divorce (1975). Parkes made use of the predictive data from the Harvard study to select bereaved people in need of support by the staff of the Bereavement Service at St. Christopher's Hospice, near London, the first of the new type of "hospices" for terminal cancer care (1979). His evaluation of recent developments in this approach is given in chapter 10. He also compared reactions to the loss of a limb with those to the loss of a person, and from his work with these varied conditions discussed the importance of psychosocial transitions as a general framework for understanding reactions to major changes, be they losses or gains (1971, 1972c, and 1975).

It is clear that the Harvard Bereavement Study has given rise to productive investigation in a variety of settings. But throughout our work we have found ourselves returning again and again to puzzle over certain questions. In our earlier book we had described the processes of mourning and recovery among respondents, taking the respondents as a group. We had noted, dutifully, that some respondents did much less well than others. But we did not deal at all adequately with the question of why this might have been so. Why did people who had suffered sudden, unexpected bereavement find it so hard to recover? How could the occasional reaction of intense pining or intense anger or intense guilt be explained, and why were such reactions associated with lasting difficulties in adjustment? Until we had dealt with these issues we would not have met our initial aim of providing understanding of pathological grief as well as of the normal and typical grief process.

The questions we had were of more than academic interest. Only if we could understand why some people responded so badly to bereavement would we be able to prevent, or at least ameliorate, similar failures to recover. With such understanding we might be able to give direction to doctors, nurses, clergy, and others who are at hand when people are approaching death and who want to help the husbands, wives, and children soon to be bereaved. Further, with such understanding we might be able to inform the efforts of the general practitioners or social workers who are often called on by the bereaved months, perhaps years, after the loss for help with psychological difficulties.

There was a further justification for our pursuing the investigation. The information and ideas that derive from the work of social scientists and psychiatrists become the common property of the society in which we all live. It is reasonable to suppose that neighbors, friends, and relatives of the bereaved, as well as many of the bereaved themselves, will gain from a study that helps clarify the difference between healthy and unhealthy ways of grieving.

The Harvard Bereavement Study was initiated by Gerald Caplan working with Peggy Golde and Len Baler. The fruitfulness of the study is testimony to Professor Caplan's vision and leadership. We want again to acknowledge the invaluable contributions of our interviewers, research assistants, and secretaries, all named in the introduction to our first book. We want

*Introduction*

also to acknowledge the many contributions, ranging from the development of case materials to editing, made by Carolyn Bruse, who joined us for this second book. Funding for our project came from the National Institute of Mental Health, Grant No. 5 R01 MH12042, "Mental Health Implications of Conjugal Bereavement," and Grant No. 2R12 MH09214, "Study of Community Mental Health Methods." Robert Weiss's work on this volume has been supported by a fellowship for the study of attachment in adult life from the John Simon Guggenheim Foundation. The dedication to this book expresses our continued gratitude to the widows and widowers who worked with us.

# Recovery from Bereavement

# Chapter 1

---

# *The Study of*
# *Bereavement*

---

"I had heard that expression, 'heartache,'
and I had read it, but this is the only time I
really knew what it feels like. It is pain
inside me, physical pain, all the way up. It's
very tight and I get very hurt. It's inside
the heart that I hurt."

Widow, aged thirty,
three weeks after
bereavement

Is grief an illness? It has been persuasively argued that it is a
sickness and should be treated as such (Engel 1961). After all,
grief is a very painful condition that impairs the ability of the
afflicted individual to function effectively in everyday activities. It produces a range of somatic symptoms: heaviness in
the limbs, sighing, restless apathy, loss of appetite and weight,
sleeplessness and languor, with pangs of acute distress. It is
the occasion for sympathetic relatives to gather round and
speak in hushed tones just as they do at the bedside of the
seriously ill. Yet there are also grounds for regarding grief as
the "normal" accompaniment of a major loss. Indeed, the *ab-*

*sence* of grief in such a situation has been regarded as a sickness (Deutsch 1937).

An analogy can be drawn to the effects of physical trauma. We could say that the nausea and vomiting which follow the ingestion of an irritant poison is a form of sickness, but it is also a "normal reaction" without which the individual might become very much more sick. Many of the symptoms of illness are consequences of the body's normal defensive reactions to abnormal conditions. An inflammatory reaction to a wound may mean that the wound has become infected, but it also means that the body's defenses against infection are functioning normally. The absence of inflammation may mean that there is no infection, but it may also mean that the body's defenses are inoperative.

Can we view grief, the "normal" reaction to bereavement, as being a similar defense against psychological trauma? This notion certainly seems implicit in Freud's concept of "grief work" (1917). In "Mourning and Melancholia," Freud suggests that "mourning"[1] is the process by which libido (sexual energy) is withdrawn from a loved object. But since no one willingly abandons a "libido position," this leads to an internal struggle, and the object may be clung to as an "hallucinatory wish psychosis" until each memory that bound the libido to it has been brought up and "hypercathected." When this process has been completed, said Freud, the ego is once again free and uninhibited.

Freud's theory has been criticized on the grounds that his "libido," which he thought of as a kind of relational energy, is a confusing concept. However, even if we omit libido from the formulation we are still left with the notion of grief as a struggle between opposing impulses, one tending toward realization of the loss and the other toward retention of the object.

Another view has been proposed by Bowlby and Parkes

[1]We prefer to reserve the term "mourning" for the observable expression of grief and to use "grief" as the term for the overall reaction to loss.

(1970) on the basis of investigations that reflect earlier work by Charles Darwin (1872). Fundamental to this view is recognition of the similarity between the mourning behavior of human adults and that of young children and, to go much farther afield, of other social animals. There is a clearly discernible tendency among many adults who are separated from those they love to cry out, to search restlessly for the lost person, to attack anything or anybody who impedes the search, and to find some way of "keeping alive" memories of the person they have lost. A similar tendency to search is regularly observed in nonhuman social animals when separated from their young or from other members of the same species to whom they are attached. In the case of domestic animals, separation from the human beings who care for them induces similar behavior. The biological function of this behavior is not withdrawal from the lost object; it is, rather, reunion. Only in the statistically rare event of irreversible separation (as by death) is the biological function of the behavior defeated.

But grief is not simply an atavistic remnant of behavior which is now of no value. It still has an important role to play in situations of reversible separation and, as Bowlby has described so persuasively in his book *Attachment* (1969), the separation anxiety, pining, and restlessness that are such striking features of grief are very important parts of the set of reciprocal feeling and behavior patterns which bind a child to its mother and spouses to each other.

Crying, of course, is a signal to other members of the same species. It may call back the lost one or evoke sympathetic and protective action in others. Similarly, all aspects of the expression of grief, whatever their original function, have an additional function of signifying to others the distress of the grieving individual. The bereaved person by this means establishes a social situation in which the normal laws of competitive behavior are suspended. Even outbursts of anger, which would normally produce reciprocal aggressive behavior, are treated

3

with sympathy and respect. For a time, the bereaved person is treated as would be a sick and wounded member of the species, as an object of special care, a precious and vulnerable possession in need of protection, and so as a catalyst of collaborative social action.

It would seem from this analysis that there are, in fact, good biological reasons for classing the social situation of the newly bereaved alongside that of the sick and wounded. Both are distressed, both are in need of care and protection, and both arouse anxiety in others.

The last consideration needs to be looked at more closely. The loss of a member of a social unit may affect one or two members of that unit more than others, but it also affects the whole unit. Not only do all those who are attached to the lost individual react directly to the loss, but their expressions of anguish affect other members of the unit by contagion. The whole group becomes anxious, restless, and defensive. Anxiety may be transmitted to neighboring social groups in communication with the immediately affected individuals. The size of the total unit affected by a given loss will depend upon the status of the lost individual, the number of affectional ties that have been made to that person, the level of anxiety already prevailing in the group, and the range over which signals of distress can be perceived, but quite regularly it will extend some distance outward from an individual's closest ties.

In most animal communities the range of perception of distress signals is not likely to be very large: the "lost call" of a young rhesus monkey cannot be heard farther than about a mile away. But the means of communication available to human adults can sometimes give rise to a situation in which the loss of a single important person can affect millions of others all over the world. It is now possible for an entire nation to become "sick with grief" within the space of a few hours. In our time the death of a president, or even a single Vietnamese peasant, can be witnessed and reacted to almost simultaneously around the world. Processes of grief can be set in train which may affect the decisions of voters, politicians, and military strategists.

If conditions are wrong, the death of one can lead to the death of ten, the death of ten to that of a hundred, and the death of a hundred to the kind of escalation whose effects already mar the history of mankind. But reactions may be of another sort entirely, including insistence that help be extended to the suffering, that killing end, that there be a stop to the making of victims. Out of the distress created in us by death and by grief may spring a discontent whose consequences are creative rather than destructive.

Bereavement, like all else, has its good and bad effects, and among the bad some are worse and more persistent than others. Good/bad, healthy/sick, adaptive/maladaptive—all of these polarities have been used to express some evaluation of reaction to bereavement. How shall we decide, in a given instance, what is nearer the one end and what nearer the other?

If the "normal" reaction to bereavement is a period of grieving during which those most affected are distressed, are unable to function at the same level as before the loss, and become the objects of sympathetic care and protection, it is also "normal" for this grief to decline gradually in intensity and for the affected individuals to "recover" in the sense that they replan their lives and achieve a new and independent level of functioning. If, for any reason, this "recovery" fails to take place, we might say the reaction is "abnormal."

Comparing once again the reaction to bereavement with the reaction to physical trauma, we would say that normally a person with a broken arm can expect the bone to heal within six weeks. If, at the end of six weeks the bone is still unjoined, then healing is abnormal, and we speak of "complications" having set in. In much the same way we might regard the abnormal persistence of grief as a "complication" of the normal picture.

We see grief as a normal reaction to overwhelming loss, albeit

5

a reaction in which normal functioning no longer holds, and we think it important to spare the bereaved from the stigma that attaches to all forms of mental illness and the helplessness that such attributions evoke in those who adopt a "sick role." We accept, however, that grief may be complicated by pre-existing psychological and somatic circumstances so that it takes an abnormal course and that there are kinds of loss which may produce long-lasting distortions of individuals' abilities to function. Here it might be appropriate to invoke the concept of "illness," although it may not always be necessary or useful.

## Effects of Bereavement on Health

What "illnesses" may follow bereavement? Researchers have attempted to answer this question in two ways. One is to study a group of bereaved people in order to find out how many of them become sick; the other is to study a group of sick people in order to find out how many have been bereaved. In either case, a comparison group is needed if we are to be confident that the incidence of sickness in the bereaved group or of bereavement in the sick group is excessive.

### ILLNESS IN BEREAVED PEOPLE

Studies of the illnesses of bereaved people have gone on over many years, and it is unnecessary to discuss all of them here. (See reviews of such work by Parkes 1972b and by Lynch 1977.) Suffice it to say that bereaved people often report that their "general health" has been worse following bereavement; they tend to consult doctors more frequently than nonbereaved controls and to report a higher prevalence of symptoms of ill health. Maddison and Walker's (1967) and Maddison and Viola's (1968) studies showed that 21 percent of Boston widows and 32 percent of those in Sydney, Australia, suffered a "marked deterioration in health" during the first year of bereavement, and when these figures are compared with the health assessment of married controls (among whom 7 percent in Boston and 2 percent in Sydney showed similar deterioration), it is obvious that conjugal bereavement constitutes a threat to health. Similar findings have been made by other studies, including our own.

Some difficulty arises when we try to distinguish physical health from mental health, for there are many symptoms (for example, loss of appetite or weight) that are likely to be affected by either. In fact, the more we study the subject the more uncertain we become of the distinction between the two. The autonomic nervous system determines how the body responds to a person's state of mind. Symptoms such as palpitations, sweating, indigestion, dizziness, and blurring of vision can all be produced by the action of the autonomic nervous system. They might, perhaps, be characterized as physical manifestations of mental states. In any event, all of these symptoms were reported more frequently in newly bereaved widows than in married controls. However, only a minority of widows tend to report these symptoms, so they cannot be regarded as essential components of normal grieving.

INCIDENCE OF BEREAVEMENT IN SICK PEOPLE

When we examine the incidence of bereavement in people who come to the attention of doctors, it becomes clear that loss increases the risk of serious illness and death. There is clear evidence from several studies of an increase in the death rate following bereavement (Young, Benjamin, and Wallis 1963; Parkes, Benjamin, and Fitzgerald 1969; Rees and Lutkins 1967; and for a succinct review, Stroebe et al. 1981). This increase is largely confined to the first six months of bereavement and is usually attributable to deaths from coronary thrombosis and arteriosclerotic heart disease. Nobody knows just how bereavement can kill. It certainly seems unlikely that bereavement causes arteriosclerosis since that condition takes many years to develop, but it seems very likely that a person who already has arteriosclerosis affecting his or her heart is at special risk after bereavement. The added burden of bereavement on that heart may be sufficient to produce a myocardial infarction and to reduce the person's chances of surviving an infarction should one occur.

In the same way, some people may be vulnerable to psychiatric ill health. It should come as no surprise to find increased rates of bereavement among people admitted to a psychiatric clinic. The greatest reported increase is in people diagnosed as suffering from "reactive depression" (Parkes 1965; Stein and Susser 1969). Clayton's observation of an increased frequency of depressive symptoms among bereaved people is confirmed by increased rates of bereavement among psychiatrically depressed people (Clayton et al. 1973).

Much research has been conducted in recent years into the life events that precede the onset of a wide range of physical and mental illnesses. Brown and Harris have proposed a method of assessing the frequency of such "life events." The publication of their results (1978) stirred up a storm of controversy that has not yet abated. Although this is not the place to argue the minutiae of the scientific methods involved, we may note that most of the "life events" identified by these workers can be viewed as losses of one sort or another. These include, for example, the departure of a confidant or the loss of a job. Some of Brown and Harris's major findings appear supported by research into the one major life event of bereavement. While no final conclusions can be drawn from these studies, there does seem to be much evidence that bereavement is not the only event that can precipitate physical and mental illness.

Some of the milder conditions that bring bereaved people into the care of their general practitioners seem to reflect the psychological and physiological effects of typical grief. Further studies are needed to confirm these findings and to discover how long the effects of bereavement are likely to persist. As far as life-threatening physical illnesses are concerned, we can only speculate.

## Pathological Grief

When we come to look at the mental illnesses that follow bereavement, the situation is a little clearer. A number of detailed studies of bereaved psychiatric patients have shown that most of them are suffering from atypical forms of grief. That is to say, the symptoms that have brought them into psychiatric care are part of an overall clinical picture which has the form of distorted or abnormally persistent and severe forms of grief. Because "grief" is not a recognized clinical diagnosis, the bereaved psychiatric patient is likely to be diagnosed as suffering from "reactive depression" or from some similar condition, the particular diagnosis to an extent depending on the symptom that predominates at the time the patient first seeks help. However, there are grounds for regarding pathological forms of grief as separate conditions in their own right, having distinctive etiology, psychopathology, symptomatology, and prognosis.

Psychoanalysts were the first to attempt to explain the link between bereavement and mental illness. The first attack on the problem was made in *Studies in Hysteria* (1893), in which Breuer and Freud attempted to explain and treat the hysterical symptoms developed by Anna O. during and after the terminal illness of her father. This case, they believed, confirmed Charcot's theory, which supposed that in cases of hysteria a precipitating psychological trauma had occurred in a state of altered consciousness: "Chains of coincidences set up pathological associations and sensory motor disturbances. . . ." This theory was subsequently abandoned, but interest in the traumatic effects of bereavement persisted, and in 1917 Freud made a serious attempt to examine the resemblance between depressive illness and grief in his ingenious and influential paper, "Mourning and Melancholia." Both mourning and melancholia, said Freud, are caused by the loss of a love object: in melancholia (depressive illness), however, the loss is usually unconscious, the duration is greater than it is in mourning (grief), and there is a marked loss of self-esteem.

Freud claimed that the terms of abuse which melancholic patients use against themselves always fit the love object rather than the patient. Hence, he concluded, melancholia results from disappointment with a love object, withdrawal of libido from the object onto the ego, and identification of the ego with the object: "the shadow of the object fell upon the ego." By identifying with the object, the patient's connection to the object can be retained despite the patient's ambivalence. The patient can punish the love object through the illness without openly expressing hostility.

Freud himself was careful to point out that empirical evidence for his elaborate theory was slight, but some aspects of the theory have since been corroborated. The studies described above have established that object loss by bereavement may be followed by depressive illness, and comparisons between the grief of bereaved psychiatric patients and that of unselected widows have confirmed expectations that many pathological reactions to bereavement are characterized by excessive guilt and self-reproach (Parkes 1965). Whether or not ambivalence is critical to these reactions, however, remains to be seen; and even if it can be demonstrated that conscious or unconscious loss of a love object is a cause of depressive illness, it is unlikely that it will be found to be the only cause.

Other psychoanalysts have developed and modified Freud's theory of the psychopathology of melancholia. Abraham (1924) provided some evidence for the correctness of Freud's assertion that the self-accusations of melancholics refer properly to the lost object rather than to themselves. He described a patient, whose father had just been sent to prison for theft, who had an attack of depression with delusions of being a thief. He also speculated that the wish to regain a lost object might be expressed in fantasies of oral incorporation by eating food that had come to symbolize the lost person. According to his theory, the mourner has the task of reinstating the lost object internally; if, due to ambivalence toward the object, this can not be done successfully, manic-depressive illness may result. This viewpoint was further elaborated by Klein (1940). She asserted that not only are the good and bad aspects of lost objects reinstated by the mourner, but the whole inner world that was associated with them as well, including the parent figures whom the object had come to replace. It is for this reason, she said, that adult mourning may be impaired or complicated by the revival of difficulties which originally arose during childhood, particularly those that arose at weaning. Klein believed that the newly weaned child mourned the loss of the breast, a phenomenon she called "the infantile depressive position."

Bowlby (1960) shared Klein's view that childhood losses were the precursors of later losses, but disagreed with her respecting the significance of weaning as *the* "primal loss." "It is my thesis," he said, "that the significance of loss of breast has been exaggerated, that when it appears to be of consequence it is often because it occurs contemporaneously with separation or loss of close contact with mother. . . . My view is that a principal trauma which is potentially present in the life of a young child is loss of mother, or loss of her love, and that the processes connected with the depressive position . . . are spread out over a long period, beginning at about the sixth month and continuing into and beyond the fourth year." This view he supported by copious evidence from direct observations of the effects of separation from the mother upon young children and the young of other species.

One of the first systematic accounts of pathological development after bereavement was given by Deutsch in 1937. She described four adult patients, each of whose psychiatric symptoms she traced to the loss by death or divorce of a parent during the patient's childhood. It appeared that each of the patients had expressed little or no grief at the time of bereavement. She concluded that, "Death of a beloved person *must* produce reactive expression of feeling in the normal course of events," and "unmanifested grief will be found expressed to the full in some way or another."

This conclusion found ample support in the classical study by Lindemann (1944) of 101 bereaved persons who attended a bereavement clinic he set up after the disastrous fire in Boston's Coconut Grove night club. Lindemann described the typical reaction to bereavement and then delineated what he believed to be pathological forms of grief. What he called "delayed" grief was in his view "the most striking and most frequent reaction of this sort. If the bereavement occurs at a time when the patient is confronted with important tasks and when there is necessity for maintaining the morale of others, he may show little or no reaction for weeks or even much longer." During the period of delay, the bereaved person may behave quite normally or show symptoms that Lindemann regarded as distorted forms of grief. These include overactivity without a sense of loss, the acquisition of symptoms belonging to the last illness of the deceased, progressive isolation from friends and relatives, hostility toward specific persons (usually people who can in some way be held responsible for the death or suffering of the deceased), wooden formality hiding intense anger, enduring loss of patterns of social interaction with inability to initiate or maintain any activity, protracted self-punitive behavior (such as excessive generosity), and in a small proportion of cases, agitated depression with tension, insomnia, and feelings of worthlessness. According to Lindemann, reactions such as these can usually be transformed into normal reactions, which then follow their usual course toward resolution by means of a form of psychotherapy in which the therapist "shares the grief work." Occasionally, he believed, sedative or stimulant drugs may be needed.

Lindemann's work was a milestone in the development of our ideas about bereavement. In this one paper he provided us with a clear description of the syndrome of normal grief, an account of the atypical forms which it may take, and some eminently practical guidelines for intervention which would help to prevent these pathological forms from persisting. It is no exaggeration to say that his work has colored all subsequent thinking about reaction to loss and has pointed the way to the prevention of mental illness by intervention services for people who have undergone a major loss.

Lindemann's work can be criticized on the grounds that he gave no figures to indicate the frequency of the various atypical forms of grief which he described or the effectiveness of his method of preventive intervention. His claim that, using his method of treatment over a period of four to six weeks, "It was normally possible to settle an uncomplicated and undistorted grief reaction," has caused many to assume that grief is a very much more transient phenomenon than later investigators have found it to be. (This point was elaborated in our earlier book.) In addition, others have discovered several major omissions in his list of the atypical forms that grief may take. Yet as a frame of reference and guideline without which most subsequent work might not have taken place, the importance of Lindemann's pioneering paper cannot be denied.

It was Anderson, working at Sutton Hospital in Sutton, England, from 1944 to 1947, who carried out the first large study of pathological grief (published in 1949). He found "morbid grief reactions" among 9 percent of psychiatric patients. Unfortunately, he did not make clear exactly what he meant by this term. Anderson's descriptions of these reactions are unsystematic and difficult to evaluate. He made an important contri-

13

bution, however, in pointing out the large part played by anxiety as opposed to depression in pathological grief. Furthermore, he most effectively described the syndrome of "chronic grief," a morbid illness in which anxiety, tension, restlessness, and insomnia predominate, and self-reproachful ideas and angry outbursts are common.

Parkes carried out a statistical comparison between 94 bereaved patients at the Bethem Royal and Maudsley Hospitals in England and 3,151 nonbereaved patients (1965). Although "reactive depression" was the most common diagnosis given the bereaved patients, 72 percent of the bereaved patients received other diagnoses. This suggests that either bereavement can cause a variety of clinical conditions or that traditional psychiatric diagnoses do not adequately characterize loss reactions.

Parkes subsequently went on to interview twenty-one bereaved psychiatric patients. Among the twenty-one he found only one whose reaction to bereavement corresponded to the typical picture of grief which had been provided by Lindemann (1944) and Marris (1958). In eight patients the onset of grieving had been delayed for over two weeks. These resembled the "delayed reaction" described by Lindemann. But more common than the "delayed reaction" was the "chronic grief" syndrome described by Anderson. Twelve patients showed abnormal prolongation of grief, usually in intense form, and, in five of these, this reaction was accompanied by "identification symptoms," symptoms resembling those suffered in the course of his or her last illness by the person who had subsequently died.

Common in both types of reaction were persisting ideas of self-blame. This was prominent in fourteen of the twenty-one patients. Other studies (Marris 1958; Parkes 1970) have shown that this is a feature that is much less likely to be present in unselected bereaved persons. Less common, but also a problem in six cases, were intense feelings of panic and distress produced by reminders of the death, loneliness, or loss of support. Also

14

reported were attacks of breathlessness and "choking sensations" at the time of day when the spouse—the husband in all instances—had formerly returned from work.

Linking this study with other studies of the psychological reaction to bereavement, bereavement reactions have been classified as: (1) typical grief; (2) chronic grief; (3) inhibited grief (with some partial or distorted expression of grief); and (4) delayed grief. In addition a variety of nonspecific reactions (such as psychosomatic disorders) may also be found in populations exposed to bereavement as well as to other forms of stress.

This empirically derived classification, while simpler than Lindemann's, includes one reaction he omitted: chronic grief. Lindemann, concentrating on what he characterized as "acute grief," failed to describe what several investigators have found to be the most common pathological reaction to bereavement, its indefinite prolongation. (For example, see Wahl 1970; and Volkan 1970).

THE CAUSES OF PATHOLOGICAL GRIEF

The foregoing studies have shown quite clearly that bereavement can affect physical and mental health. How it does this remains a matter for speculation. Although practically every psychiatrist and psychoanalyst who has written about grief has provided his or her own explanation, there is very little real evidence on which to build.

One thing is apparent from the work reported in the scientific literature on bereavement: most of the psychological symptoms that bring bereaved persons into the care of their doctors can be seen as distortions or exaggerations of the normal process of grieving. It is this observation that causes us to look more closely at the day-to-day factors that normally influence the course of grief. Granted that the intensity, duration, and form of grief vary greatly from one individual to another and that most of these variations are within the range of normality, it may well be that the pathological variations are no more than

15

extreme forms that appear in response to particularly unfavorable circumstances.

Looked at in this way, there are a host of demographic and other variables which might be thought to play a part in shaping the overall outcome of bereavement. There is no shortage of claims for attaching importance to age, sex, social class, personality, and many other factors. Unfortunately, the research findings are far from consistent, and each person who has studied the subject seems to have come up with a different list of determinants of grief. Many of the sweeping generalizations which seemed justified by early research in this field are now being called into question. The determination of the outcome of bereavement is more complex than was, at first, believed.

For those who are familiar with research in the social and psychological sciences this will come as no surprise. Human beings are complex animals, and there are few mental disorders and distresses whose causes are simple. In fact, psychiatrists and social workers devote much of their working lives to attempts at unraveling the complex interactions of circumstances and events which explain why a particular person has "broken down," "gone mad," "attempted suicide," "acted out," "cried for help," or in some other way come to the end of his or her tether at a particular moment.

Nevertheless, some general conclusions can be drawn that do seem to have been confirmed in a variety of studies. They explain some of the inconsistencies in findings among different populations of bereaved people studied in various parts of the world.

Most investigators would probably agree that two major groups of factors are likely to complicate the course of grief. On the one hand, there are factors that discourage the expression of grief. On the other hand, there are factors that discourage the ending of grief. On the face of it these two types of factors might be thought to cancel each other out. But if we accept that grief is a process which takes place over time and that it has a "normal course," then it may be that the first group of factors, those governing the expression of grief, are important in determining the onset of grief and the second group of factors in determining its ending.

Factors thought to influence the onset of grief include the mode of the death itself, the types of social support which are available, and the predisposition of the bereaved. Each of these may act to facilitate the expression of grief or to block it.

Sudden and untimely deaths are often thought to interfere with the course of grieving because of the shock that they produce and the psychological defenses that this evokes. Volkan (1970), in his study of twenty-three psychiatric patients with "pathological grief," claimed that all had experienced the death as sudden, either because it in fact occurred suddenly or because, for some other reason, the respondent was not prepared for it. Although this claim has not gone unchallenged, much evidence, which we shall examine in more detail in chapter 4, does seem to confirm the negative impact of unforewarned loss on the course of grieving.

Social influences were given great weight by Maddison and Walker (1967) and by many other researchers. These investigators proposed that the immediate family may encourage or discourage the bereaved to express or inhibit grief and so foster typical or atypical grieving. Society at large may also influence grieving through religious and other rituals, which may provide social sanction for mourning or may withhold it.

Gorer (1965) claimed that the contemporary decline in accepted ritual and religious guidance after bereavement is responsible for "a very considerable amount of maladaptive behavior." He provided detailed descriptive evidence that seems to indicate that failure to engage in guided mourning is likely to be followed by lasting depression, impaired relationships, and irrational attitudes toward death and destruction. Some confirmation of Gorer's thesis came from a study by Parkes (1970) of seven widows who expressed very little distress during the first week of bereavement, did not wear mourning dress, and failed to visit their husbands' graves. This group was significantly more disturbed three months later than were eighteen other widows who had expressed grief and mourned actively from the start. Thereafter the differences between the groups grew less, but as the anniversary of the death approached it was again the group who had not reacted emotionally in the first week who became more disturbed.

It seems likely that societies which expect the bereaved to engage in the overt expression of grief will go some way to counteract delayed or avoided grief reactions. Yet in Western societies, where women are more free to cry than are men, we might expect that women would consequently have fewer problems arising out of the repression of grief. This makes it surprising to find that women constitute the majority of the clients who seek help from bereavement services (Stern, Williams, and Prados 1951; Wretmark 1959). But there are other factors that may help explain this finding. First, in Western society, women are more likely than men to feel free to ask for help. And second, there is a preponderance of women among those who suffer conjugal bereavement because men die at a younger age than women do and also tend to marry women younger than themselves. In order to discover which sex is the more vulnerable to pathological grief we would have to take these factors into account.

Age is another demographic factor that has been said to influence the expression of grief (Maddison and Walker 1967). Widows and widowers under forty seem to be at greater risk of pathological development than are older widows and widowers when both groups are compared with still married age-mates. One possible explanation is that older people in Western society come from a generation in which, much more than is now true, mourning was not only socially acceptable but an obligation to the dead. In recent years, however, some reversal of this trend has become apparent, and young people today may be rediscovering the importance of permitting themselves to express grief.

Of course, even quite sudden deaths are not untimely in the elderly age group, and this factor, too, may explain the higher rates of psychological disturbance which have been reported in younger bereaved people. Cumming and Henry (1961) found a "mutual severing of ties between a person and others in his society" at around the age of sixty-five in a random sample of 279 men and women over the age of fifty in Kansas. Their theory of natural disengagement has been criticized as misinterpreting a withdrawal imposed on the elderly, but if they are correct that the withdrawal is voluntary, then one possible explanation for it is that with age comes expectation of loss, an expectation that is reinforced each time a death occurs. Similar reactions have been witnessed by Parkes among relatively young patients in a terminal cancer ward. After a time such patients may withdraw from contact with other patients in order to avoid the pain that would result if they allowed themselves to become attached to people who are soon to leave them by dying.

Factors thought to influence the perpetuation of grief include the nature of the relationship with the person who has died, the personality of the survivor, and the surrounding social circumstances. Grief is not only a psychological reaction to bereavement; it is also a duty to the dead. Some people may feel compelled to engage in perpetual mourning as a tribute to the dead or to make restitution for some failure or sense of guilt arising out of the bereavement. The psychiatric literature on grief is replete with anecdotal accounts of pathological griefs attributed to ambivalent relationships, with the grief serving as both penance and reparation. There is some confirming evidence from systematic studies that both ambivalence and overdependence predispose individuals to chronic grief.

In Parkes's (1962) study of ninety-eight bereaved psychiatric patients, mixed feelings of fondness and hostility toward the dead person were reported by 21 percent of those whose illness was evidently a pathological form of grief, but by only 6 percent of those who showed little evidence of problematic grief at the time of admission. Interestingly, situations in which the deceased had been "dependent" upon the survivor were also more common in the pathological grievers than those whose grief had been normal; dependency may be a two-way transaction.

If ambivalence and dependency are characteristics of certain types of relationships, they also reflect the personalities of the individuals who form those relationships. Some individuals simply have difficulty in forming entirely satisfactory relationships. Those who have difficulty in establishing satisfactory relationships may then have special difficulty in severing the relationships they do make because such relationships are more nearly irreplaceable. "If one can learn how to live with the living, then one can manage to live with the dead" (Krupp 1962).

The tendency to cling to others has been postulated by Bowlby (1969) as one consequence of excessive separation from mother in childhood, and it might be expected that this would give rise to one type of "grief-prone person." But no statistical research on this hypothesis has been reported and only general assertions, such as the claim that patients with pathological grief have been made more sensitive to separation by previous separation in childhood (Volkan 1970), can be cited in its support.

That multiple bereavements in adult life may make the survivors more vulnerable to further losses is suggested by Janis (1962), who described the "old sergeant's syndrome," which is said to occur in fighting troops who suffer casualties over a long period of time. There is a build-up of depression with a loss of interest in daily life and preoccupation with grief. The soldier becomes afraid to make new relationships for fear that they, too, will be disrupted.

Whatever the contribution of such factors it does seem that the personality and previous life experience of the individual are likely to be important determinants of the reaction to bereavement. It is hardly surprising that a high incidence of previous depressive illness among bereaved psychiatric patients has been found (Parkes 1962). Bereavement may also cause exacerbation of antecedent neurotic symptoms (Wahl 1970). Still, Lindemann thought that a history of previous neurotic illness is comparatively unimportant in determining prognosis after bereavement.

Social circumstances may play a role in the relinquishing of grief. Direct pressures may be placed upon a bereaved person by family and friends to come out of mourning although grief continues, perhaps in the belief that ending the one will end the other, or to continue mourning even though the psychological need has begun to abate. Children may resent any attempt on the part of a bereaved parent to enter into new heterosexual relationships. Some widows and widowers report that their families continue to treat them as if they were permanently disabled by grief.

More important are the indirect influences of social isolation and lack of support which cause some bereaved people to hide their grief for fear of ostracism, while encouraging others to cling to a fantasy relationship with the dead person as the one meaningful connection they retain. The fact that society does permit bereaved people temporarily to withdraw, with assured support, from social and occupational responsibilities, may encourage some to suppress grief and others to remain withdrawn, just as some physically ill people refuse to admit to their illnesses and others remain disabled long after their health has begun to improve.

The loneliness of the widow is often reported. Kay, Roth, and Hopkins (1955), in discussing the causes of depressive illnesses in old age, placed "loneliness" and "physical disability" as the two principal factors. Wahl (1970) remarked that widows who develop neurotic grief are often "unable to make any displacement of their emotional needs onto any contiguous person." Hence, they become "progressively more withdrawn and self-engrossed." The fact that social withdrawal is itself a feature of grief probably tends to perpetuate a vicious cycle among those widows who lack a close, supportive family. The quarrels and splits that commonly result from the ill-directed expression of anger during the acute stage of grief may lead to lasting antipathy between family members and loss of support at a time when it is most needed.

# Chapter 2

# *The Method of Study*

The principal aim of the Harvard Bereavement Study was to identify the factors that determine the course of grief over the first years of bereavement in a sample of relatively young American widows and widowers. It seemed to us that the factors that determined the course of grief in this sample might well prove to be the same factors that were responsible for the more extreme reactions found in psychiatric clinics and that can only be studied retrospectively in those settings. In addition, we hoped to learn more about the nature of recovery from bereavement among people who do not seek psychiatric help and about the forms taken by failure to recover.

Other studies had shown that the reaction to conjugal bereavement is age-related. In one study (Maddison and Walker 1967) young age was so strong a factor in determining the reaction that it outweighed all other possible determinants. Another study found evidence that the death of a husband or wife caused more psychiatric illness than did the death of other family members (Parkes 1964). We decided that we would maximize the likelihood of encountering troubled recoveries by selecting for study widows and widowers under the age of forty-six. We expected that the sample, as a whole, would show evidence of a decline in health, at least during the first year or so of bereavement, but that some members of the sample would display much more serious declines in well-being than would others.

We conducted a series of four main interviews with each of our respondents. We held the first interview about three weeks after the death of the spouse, the second interview about five weeks later, and the third interview about thirteen months after the spouse's death so that we would not trigger anniversary reactions but might learn about them if they had occurred. These were the only interviews we initially planned to conduct, but after completing them we decided to return for a single follow-up interview. Depending on when we had first contacted the respondents, this follow-up interview took place shortly after the second, third, or fourth anniversary of the death of the spouse.

## The Sample

To recruit respondents we arranged for the Office of Vital Statistics in Boston to inform us when there had been a death of an individual from natural causes or from accident whose spouse was aged forty-five or younger. We excluded those dead from suicide or homicide. We sent the new widow or widower a letter describing our study and saying that we would soon call. Then by telephone or in a home visit we asked the new widow or widower whether we could visit to talk about the loss and its effects. If we met any resistance to the idea, we apologized for our intrusion and let the matter drop. We did not want to do anything that might increase the distress of the people we had contacted.

We received a total of 231 names of widows and 118 names of widowers from the Office of Vital Statistics. About one widow in five and about one widower in three had moved or could not be found at home despite repeated telephone calls. Of the 191 widows and 83 widowers whom we contacted, nearly three–fifths agreed to be interviewed. Some of these were found to be unsuitable for our study because they had been separated at the time of the spouse's death, because the death had been by suicide or homicide (even though this did not appear on the death certificate), or because they spoke so little English that interviewing them would have been difficult. It also turned out that a few of the respondents who had agreed to a first interview refused to be interviewed a second or third time. A total of 49 widows and 19 widowers completed all three initially scheduled interviews, and 43 widows and 16 widowers were interviewed in the follow-up.

About two years after the beginning of the study, an experienced social worker telephoned a small sample of those who had declined participation to ask what had been their feelings about the study, as well as they could remember. Most said that they had been unwilling to talk with a stranger at a time when they were so upset. We cannot say why some people felt this way and others did not. There is some indication that widows and widowers who ranked lower on the socio-economic scale may more frequently have been willing to work with us, but the association, if it exists, is not strong.[1]

Despite our having sent potential respondents a letter whose intent was to prepare them for a call from a representative of the study, when one of us actually did call, the letter had often been forgotten. In any event, in our call we described in some detail the study we hoped to do and asked the recently bereaved man or woman whether he or she would participate. Some agreed to participate because they thought the study might help others. Some were pleased to have a stranger to talk to. But some said that they could not give their minds and energies to anything except their grief and their need to keep going. And sometimes, when we telephoned or went to the home, we en-

[1]Further description of our sample is provided in Glick, Weiss, and Parkes 1974.

countered not the new widow or widower, but a protective family member who would then turn us away.

On occasion, we were treated in this first contact as people who might just possibly provide help. One man, for example, told us that his home was in chaos and that he desperately needed a housekeeper. We provided him with the names of a few agencies and called one on his behalf.

Most respondents who consented to be interviewed said later that they were glad they had had the opportunity to talk. One widow said, "You have to get it off your chest. You've got to talk about it." It is possible that our interviewing may have provided enough support to have reduced the incidence of long-term detrimental effects on health and psychosocial adjustment. To the extent that this occurred, we may have been led to underestimate the likelihood of continuing distress as a consequence of bereavement. However, our primary research aim was to learn what facilitated recovery or impeded it, and there is no reason to suppose that interchange with our interviewers significantly altered our results in this respect.

## The Interviews

The first interview with our respondents, held three weeks after their loss, and the second, held about five weeks later, were both intended to provide us with systematic information about the nature of the marriage that had preceded the spouse's death, about the circumstances of that death, and about the current circumstances of the respondent's life. All these matters seemed to us likely to have some influence on later outcome.

The first interview explored issues having to do with the

events leading up to the death, the circumstances of the death itself, and the way the death was dealt with by the respondent and those close to the respondent. Respondents were asked about how they had felt at various times—when the spouse was admitted to the hospital, when they learned of the spouse's death, when they arranged for the funeral and the burial, and when they actually took part in these ceremonies —and about what others had done that had helped or failed to help. They were asked what the marital relationship had been like, and what disagreements they might have had. They were also asked to respond to a checklist of thirty items, each of them a thought or feeling that bereaved people commonly report. The list began with "I get tired so easily" and "I'm so irritable and quick to lose my patience" and continued on to "I wouldn't care if I died tomorrow" and "I can't get myself to do things." This first interview concluded with a medical history of the respondent and a review of the problems that seemed to be most pressing.

The second interview, held eight weeks after the death of the spouse, explored the ways in which the widow or widower was coping with the early weeks of loss. Among the issues discussed in the interview were how the respondents were managing the jobs that had formerly been carried out by their spouses, what were the financial problems the respondents might be encountering, and again, who was helping and in what ways. A good many questions were asked about the respondents' feelings and how those feelings were being managed. Questions were asked about whether the respondents saw friends or had entered into a period of seclusion. The widows and widowers were again asked to respond to a checklist of beliefs and feelings, differently phrased, but for the most part covering the same ground as the checklist in the first interview.

The third interview took place about thirteen months after the respondent's bereavement. The aim of this interview was to assess the respondent's progress toward recovery. Respondents were asked to describe how their lives had gone since the previous interview, to give a picture of a typical day, to rate their own efficiency and mood. They were asked whether they still thought regularly about their spouses, whether they dreamed of their spouses, how they now understood the loss of their spouses. And again, as before, they were asked what had helped them and how. Their feelings of sadness, remorse, and grief were explored at length. They were also asked how they had gone about reestablishing their lives and whether they had in any way moved toward finding someone new. They were asked about their children, about work, about friends and relatives. Again they were asked to respond to a checklist repeating items that had occurred in earlier checklists.

As a further check on the reliability of our interviewers' assessments, each respondent was revisited a week of so after this interview by a different interviewer who knew nothing of the previous interviews. This interviewer asked for replies to a series of structured questions covering: (1) onset or changes in the autonomic symptoms that commonly accompany anxiety and tension (palpitations, sweating, and so forth); (2) other physical symptoms; (3) changes in consumption of drugs, alcohol, and tobacco; (4) frequency of consultations with doctors or admissions to the hospital; (5) persistence of feelings of depression, loneliness, and so forth; (6) a checklist of common worries; (7) frequency of seeking help with emotional problems; and (8) a series of questions intended to assess personality characteristics. This health questionnaire constituted the second part of the third interview. (The questionnaire is given in full in appendix 1.) The final interview, the fourth, was held between two and four years after the respondent's bereavement. It covered the same ground as the third interview and included a shortened form of the health questionnaire.

## The Assessment of Outcome

Much of what we report here is based on codings of respondents' rich and complex descriptions. Our interviewers had a fixed set of issues they were required to explore with respondents, but respondents were to be encouraged to talk in a free, relatively uninterrupted, fashion. To reduce this material to categories of responses, we prepared a coding manual in which detailed directions were given for interpreting and classifying interview materials. We then had two coders independently rate the tape recording of the first three interviews from twenty-nine respondents on all the items we had developed. We excluded or modified items on which coders did not agree 90 percent of the time.

Unfortunately, among the items we were forced to discard because its coding reliability seemed inadequate was "overall outcome." We had asked our coders to assess how outcome in a particular case compared with the outcome that might be expected in the average situation. We found that both our coders tended to appraise more outcomes as "better than average" than as "average" or "worse than average," a phenomenon often encountered when individuals are asked to rate themselves, but a surprise for us in this context. What made the coding unusable, however, was that our coders had frequent disagreements about whether a particular outcome was "better than average" or simply "average."

The problem was not simply that of making assessments on the basis of extensive conversational responses to only partially standardized questions. The coders showed a high level of agreement when assessing discrete feeling states, such as guilt and anger. "Outcome" turned out to be peculiarly difficult to assess because it embraced so many different issues. The problem, fundamentally, was in our conceptualization. What do we mean by a "good outcome" to the mourning process? A return of feelings of well-being, a regained capacity to cope with problems of everyday life, or a decline in preoccupation with grief? The three will often correspond to each other, but they need not. If they do not, how should we decide between them?

Clearly there are many ways of deciding what should be taken as establishing recovery, and it is difficult *a priori* to choose one above another. Nor is this the end of the problem. Whatever way of indicating recovery we agree to, we have to decide whether our assessment will be based on the respondent's self-evaluation or on more objective indicators. Do we give greater weight to a respondent's report that there are no real problems or to our interviewer's belief that the respondent is barely fending off depression?

In addition, we must recognize that physical, emotional, and social recovery do not necessarily proceed at the same rate. Many respondents returned to full social participation while continuing to grieve in private. Some respondents were entirely free of physical symptoms, though emotionally distressed or socially withdrawn. A few respondents reported physical symptoms but were managing well in other respects.

On one thing we were decided: we wanted to know about the outcome that could be expected once recovery was well under way, that is, a fairly long-term outcome. We were less concerned with whether pain and grief had subsided after six weeks than we were with whether they had subsided after a year.

It might be thought that the best time to measure outcome would be many years later. But life is never static, and even within the four years of the follow-up phase of the study many of our respondents had suffered further losses or undergone major changes in their lives which could have influenced their physical and mental health. Changes of employment and of home environment, separation from significant family members, sickness, financial setbacks—all occurred and took their toll. Some of these events were themselves indirect consequences of the bereavement, but the longer the time interval between the bereavement and the assessment of outcome, the more difficult it would be to be sure that the latter was in any way a result of the former.

We were also less concerned with a respondent's absolute level of well-being a year or so after bereavement than we were with the relative degree of recovery in comparison with the previous state. Some respondents might have been badly off at the time of their bereavement. To find that they were badly off a year later would not indicate that they had failed to recover from the effects of the bereavement. And so we had to consider what might be thought of as each respondent's expectable level of well-being.

Given all these issues, it may be no wonder that the coders could not reliably assess ultimate outcome. And yet, listening to tapes and reading the transcripts, we could discern some individuals who very clearly had been disabled by the bereavement and others who seemed to have returned to effective functioning by almost any criterion. In addition, it appeared that by thirteen months the trajectory of recovery or failure to recover was evident. We felt that widows and widowers who were at that time still intensely grief-stricken or otherwise distraught were unlikely to improve greatly in the short term and, although gradual diminution in their disturbance could be expected, those who were judged "most disturbed" at thirteen months were likely to remain "most disturbed" for some time to come. Our follow-up study confirmed this. In a few cases respondents did move from a less disturbed to a more disturbed position between the thirteenth-month interview and the follow-up interview, but in virtually every case, this was a consequence of an intervening life event, such as a serious illness.

At this point it appeared to us that although the coders could not establish a satisfactory level of agreement when rating outcome overall, partly because the concept of recovery was unclear, there were clearly discernible differences among respondents in *aspects* of recovery—the subsiding of grief or the return to social life, for example. We therefore decided to set the coders the task of evaluating, not overall outcome, but rather facets of outcome. When we considered what these might be, we found we could draw up a very long list. Our final code included: sixty-eight aspects of the persistence and form of features of grief, including items regarding the way grief was experienced and was expressed, the times it was experienced and expressed, its intensity, and the ways it had changed since the first weeks; forty-nine items dealing with financial problems and handling of property; twelve dealing with occupational adjustment; seven with handling of domestic affairs; nine with depression and loneliness; thirty-one with anxiety; seventeen with anger and irritability; twenty-six with guilt and self-reproach; eighteen with tiredness, restlessness, difficulty in concentration, and similar symptoms.[2]

THE CODERS' ASSESSMENT SCORE

Two coders were asked to rate each respondent on all 250 characteristics. The coders used tape recordings of thirteenth-month interviews together with the transcripts of these interviews so that they could better judge the meaning of respondents' words. The coders also made overall ratings of respondents on inclusive issues. Any of these general assessments that did not prove reliable were excluded from further use. Ten general assessments seemed to us to capture all the various facets of recovery. They were:

1. *Level of functioning in comparison with pre-bereavement level.*
2. *Movement toward solution of outstanding problems.*
3. *Acceptance of the loss.* This aspect had three subaspects, and re-

[2]The coding system was developed by Dr. Peggy Golde, who was the project's first director.

spondents' scores in these subaspects were combined to give an overall score for the aspect. The subaspects were:

   a. Absence of distortion: The respondent demonstrated no expectation of return or difficulty in believing the death had occurred, no undue idealization or denigration of the deceased.

   b. Access of the grief to dissipation through interchange. The respondent was not prevented by distress from talking or thinking of the dead person or the events associated with the death, and showed an increasing comfort in talking about these matters.

   c. Integration of the event into the respondent's worldview. The respondent had worked out an acceptable, rational explanation for the death which did not involve distortion of reality or marked departure from beliefs normal in the respondent's culture.

4. *Socializing.* The respondent had reentered social life and was as active and effective socially as before the bereavement.

5. *Attitude toward the future.* The respondent's attitude toward the future was positive and included realistic plans. In addition, the respondent displayed ability to think through problems of remarriage, of sexual life, of children, in an attitude of reasonable optimism and hope.

6. *Health.* The respondent's current health was as good as it had been before bereavement. There was no evidence of general disturbance such as insomnia, weight loss, tension, or tremors.

7. *Anxiety or depression.* General level.

8. *Guilt or anger.* General level.

9. *Evaluation of self.* General level of self-esteem.

10. *Resilience.* The respondent's apparent ability to cope with future loss.

We asked the coders to rate each of these aspects of recovery on a scale from one to five. We then added together the scores respondents received on each of the ten measures to give an overall score of respondents' recoveries, which we termed the "Coders' Assessment Score."

## The Comparison Group

Despite the code book's detailed description of code categories, the coders' assessments were, of course, dependent on the respondents' reports and the coders' interpretations of them. We felt that outcome assessed in this way should be checked by a more objective assessment of outcome. We therefore sought to assess the extent to which individuals reported specific, concrete difficulties associated with bereavement thirteen months after the bereavement had occurred. To learn what might be such consequences of bereavement, we compared our entire sample of bereaved individuals with a matched sample of still-married men and women.

For each bereaved individual participating in our study we chose six potential comparison individuals from a directory of the neighborhood in which the bereaved individual lived. Such directories have long been maintained by the Boston Police Department as a basis for establishing eligibility to vote and simply as an information file. They list individuals by blocks and give for every address the names of people living there and their occupations. Each of the comparison individuals was in a similar occupation and lived within a few blocks of the bereaved individual, but, in contrast to the bereaved respondent, was still married. We sent a letter to each of the six saying that we were interested in the health status of members of the community and that we particularly wanted to talk with individuals of particular ages. We then telephoned to ask whether he or she would participate in the study. About 75 percent of those we contacted agreed to participate. We selected the individuals most closely matched in age with our bereaved respondents and, when we had several individuals of about the same age as our bereaved respondents, we selected those who were also matched in religion. We then interviewed them in their homes using the same health questionnaire that we used to measure changes in health in the bereaved sample (appendix 1) and obtaining basic information about their life circumstances as well.

Our married comparison group, taken together, did not differ from our bereaved group in age, occupational class, religion, church attendance, country of birth, ethnicity, number of children at home, number of relatives living in Boston, education, or incidence of having been orphaned while growing up. However, there was a difference in current income between the comparison group and the bereaved group, despite their shared neighborhoods, in consequence of the decline in income among our widows. Over 40 percent of our widows, compared with only 15 percent of women in the comparison sample, said that their incomes were now less than they had been a year earlier.

## Differences between Bereaved and Nonbereaved

Our bereaved group, thirteen months after the loss of their spouses, did differ from the comparison married group in many ways. In brief, we found that our bereaved subjects exceeded the comparison sample in the proportion who reported physical, emotional, and social difficulties.

The bereaved sample reported more ill health than the comparison sample. They more often reported having experienced an acute illness or a physical disability during the year preceding the interview. They were especially likely to report symptoms associated with functioning of the autonomic nervous system.

35

AUTONOMIC SYMPTOMS

The autonomic nervous system is the system referred to by individuals when they speak of "nervous tension." It is the system, ordinarily not under voluntary control, that readies the body for fight or flight and that is triggered by situations of apparent danger. Expressions of autonomic functioning include trembling or twitching, nervousness, pain in the chest, sweating without cause, a persistent lump in the throat, dizziness or fainting, and palpitation.

We counted a symptom of autonomic functioning as present if a respondent reported that it either had come on for the first time in the preceding year or had gotten worse during the preceding year. We found that widows reported 50 percent more autonomic symptoms than the women in the comparison group, and widowers displayed fully four times as many autonomic symptoms as married men! This is not to say that widowers were more likely than widows to display autonomic symptomatology: quite the reverse. Widows averaged 1.8 autonomic symptoms while widowers averaged only about half as many. But while married women reported an average of about one autonomic symptom each, married men rarely reported any autonomic symptoms at all: only one symptom was reported, on the average, for every five married men. Thus autonomic symptomatology is quite unusual among married men but fairly frequent among bereaved men. Among women, autonomic symptomatology is frequent among married women, and even more frequent among one-year bereaved widows.[3]

HOSPITAL ADMISSIONS

Twelve bereaved individuals, ten widows and two widowers, had been admitted to the hospital during the year after their loss. This compares with only four members of the comparison

[3]The statistical details of the comparison are given in appendix 2.

sample—all women—who had been in the hospital in the year preceding the interview. On a case by case review it appeared that the conditions for which the bereaved sample received hospital admission were more serious than the conditions reported by the comparison sample. In the comparison sample one woman was admitted for a dilatation and curettage, one for oral surgery, one for surgical treatment of varicose veins, and one for an investigation of recurrent headache. Among the widows, two were admitted for surgical treatment of cancer—in one case a cancer of the breast which had been discovered before the widow's bereavement, in the other a cancer of the uterus which had not been discovered until afterward. A third widow had a hysterectomy; a fourth had benign ovarian cysts removed; a fifth received treatment for a duodenal ulcer; a sixth for pneumonia; and a seventh for what was described as "neurological seizures." Two widows were also admitted for two of the conditions represented within the comparison sample: one for the gynecological condition requiring dilatation and curettage, the other for a condition requiring oral surgery. Finally, one widow was admitted with what was diagnosed as a manic-depressive illness (see page 11). Two widowers were admitted for, respectively, rheumatoid arthritis (of seven years' duration) and retention of urine.

It is difficult to say to what extent bereavement contributed to any one of the particular conditions from which our bereaved respondents suffered. Yet the much greater incidence of medical problems among the bereaved is far above chance levels. It does seem likely that bereavement exacerbated, if it did not actually produce, much of the disability reported.

EMOTIONAL DISTRESS

The bereaved sample also displayed a greater incidence of emotional distress. Emotional distress can, of course, express itself in many ways: in anxiety, restlessness, feelings of strain or depression, sleep disturbances and disturbances in appetite, or an increase in the use of drugs intended to combat distress.

We asked two questions about feelings of tension and stress. The first question asked respondents whether or not they would agree that: "During the past year I have had periods of such great restlessness that I couldn't sit long in a chair." Half the bereaved sample said that this had been true for them; less than a fourth of the comparison group did. The item dealing with stress asked whether it was true that: "Life is often a strain for me." More than a third of the bereaved sample agreed; only about a sixth of the comparison sample did.

Our measure of depression was a set of 18 items from the health questionnaire which tended to occur together (on factor analysis), each of which seemed to reflect depression or unhappiness. The bereaved sample on the average said that about 6 of the 18 "depression" items were currently true for them. The comparison sample on the average said that about 4 of the 18 items were true for them. Widows were more likely than widowers to report indicators of depression: widows reported as true for them an average of 6.6 indicators of depression, compared to 4.9 for the widowers. In the comparison sample married women reported as true for them an average of 4.6 items, compared to the married men's 2.8. Not the focus of our study, but still worth noting, is a tendency of married women, more than married men, to report a certain number of indicators of depression. That the bereaved are likely to be more depressed than the married should not be taken as indication that the lives of the married are entirely happy.

Not all the "depression items" turned out to be equally discriminating between the bereaved and the married groups. On careful examination, just five items seemed to discriminate significantly. These five "most sensitive" items were:

1. "You sometimes can't help wondering whether anything is worthwhile any more." (This was agreed with by 50 percent of the bereaved sample and 26 percent of the comparison sample.)

2. "Taken all together, how would you say things are these days: very happy, pretty happy, or not too happy?" ("Not too happy" was reported by 19 percent of the bereaved sample and 6 percent of the comparison sample.)
3. "Would you tell me whether loneliness is something that worries you often, sometimes, or never?" ("Often" and "sometimes" were reported by 65 percent of the bereaved sample and 25 percent of the comparison sample.)
4. "Think of how your life is going now. Do you want it to continue in much the same way? Do you wish you could change some parts of it? Or do you wish you could change many parts of it?" ("Wish to change many parts" was reported by 22 percent of the bereaved sample and 7 percent of the comparison sample.)
5. "During the past few weeks did you ever feel depressed or very unhappy?" ("Yes" was the reply of 49 percent of the bereaved sample and 29 percent of the comparison sample.)

Insomnia is a common symptom of the distress associated with loss. Not quite a third of the bereaved sample reported having had difficulty falling asleep, and about 40 percent reported awakening in the middle of the night. Widowers and widows reported sleep difficulties in very similar proportions. In the comparison sample 12 percent of married women and 5 percent of married men reported sleep difficulties.

The bereaved sample also reported changes in appetite and in weight more often than did the comparison sample. About a third of the bereaved sample reported weighing less than they had a year earlier, compared with about a quarter of the comparison sample. There did not seem to be marked differences in the experiences of men and women here.

DRUG CONSUMPTION

Among the most dramatic differences between the bereaved sample and the comparison sample was the report of increased drug use within the bereaved sample. Twenty-eight percent of the sixty-eight widows and widowers reported an increase in smoking, 28 percent reported an increase in consumption of alcohol, and 26 percent had either begun taking tranquilizers or had increased their use of tranquilizers. There had been virtually no increase in drug use in the married sample, except for an unexplained increase in smoking among about a fifth of married men. That a significant proportion of the widows and widowers relied on drugs in order to manage their distress seems to us to be both understandable and regrettable. Starting to take tranquilizers was particularly likely to be reported by widows (31 percent compared with 16 percent of widowers, 6 percent of married women, and no married men). Increase in smoking was particularly likely to be reported by widowers (37 percent compared with 25 percent of widows, 21 percent of married men, and 4 percent of married women). Increased use of alcohol was reported by both widowers and widows (32 percent of widowers, 27 percent of widows, 11 percent of married men, and no married women).

### HELP SEEKING

Finally, we find that about a third of the widows and widowers reported consulting a professional for help with an emotional problem during the year preceding our third interview, while only one in fourteen of our comparison sample had done so. A somewhat greater proportion of widows than widowers had consulted professionals (40 percent compared with 21 percent). A good many of the professionals consulted were physicians; their response, in many cases, may have been a prescription for tranquilizers.

### SOCIAL DIFFICULTIES

About a third of bereaved respondents reported that they felt apart or remote even among friends, a suggestion of withdrawal from social life. A response of this sort was made by about one respondent in six in the comparison sample. Almost two-thirds of the bereaved sample reported worry about loneliness, an entirely understandable reaction to the loss of their closest tie.

It is worth noting at this point that in our two-to-four year follow-up of bereaved respondents we found the movement toward social withdrawal to have progressed quite far in a good many cases. Fully two thirds of the sixty bereaved individuals who provided a follow-up interview agreed at that point with the statement, "Most of the time I don't care what others think of me." Only 28 percent of the matched members of the comparison sample agreed with this statement. In addition, eleven of the sixty bereaved respondents said "Yes" when asked, "When you go out, do you usually prefer to go by yourself?" Only one in the matched comparison sample responded in the same way to this statement.

It seems generally to have been the case among our bereaved respondents that they were both troubled by loneliness and experiencing some tendency toward social withdrawal. A degree of distancing from others seemed to be fairly typical among the bereaved respondents as time went on. For a small number of bereaved respondents, disengagement from others seemed to have proceeded quite far.

In general, comparison of our bereaved respondents with the sample of married individuals matched for sex, age, neighborhood of residence, occupation of the husband, and in most cases, religion, demonstrated that the bereaved sample, one year after the loss, was significantly worse in incidence of physical symptoms, in depression, in feelings of stress, and in social withdrawal. Our problem now was to use these observations as a basis for assessing recovery from loss among particular bereaved individuals.

## Overall Outcome

Among the many questions in the health questionnaire, there were ten that best distinguished bereaved from nonbereaved respondents. It seemed reasonable to lump these together to form a single measure of outcome which we termed the "Ten Best Questions Scale" (marked B.Q. in appendix 1). These included the five questions from the depression scale listed on pages 38–39, three questions revealing increases in the consumption of tranquilizers, alcohol, and tobacco, one question about the respondent having sought help for an emotional problem, and two general questions, "Do you agree, 'Life is often a strain to me,' and 'It's safer not to fall in love' "?

The Coders' Assessment Score had provided us with a first instrument for assessing outcome. We now had a second basis, entirely independent of the coders' judgments. Whereas the Coders' Assessment Score was based on many subjective appraisals, each using all the interview material, the Ten Best Questions Score of outcome was more nearly objective and based on responses to just ten items. We now sought to combine information from our two approaches to outcome assessment.

To achieve maximum correlation between the scores we adopted arbitrary cut-off points for both scores in such a way that the top eighteen individuals were characterized as "good" outcomes, the middle thirty-one individuals as "intermediate" outcomes, and the bottom nineteen as "bad" outcomes. Having done this we found thirty-nine instances in which the Coders' Assessment and the Ten Best Questions scores gave identical ratings, twenty-seven instances in which individuals were rated as having a "good" or "bad" outcome by one approach and an "intermediate" outcome by the other, and two instances in which individuals were rated as having a "good" outcome by one approach and a "bad" outcome by the other. In each of the two anomalies the individual had been rated by the coders as having a good outcome but had received a low score on the Ten Best Questions Scale.

Where the coders' rating and the scale score agreed, individuals were given the agreed-on rating as their outcome rating. Where either the coders' rating or the scale rating was "intermediate ," and the respondent was rated by the other approach as having an outcome that was "good" or "bad," the respondent was characterized as having the more extreme outcome. We included the two anomalies among the indifferent outcomes. We ended with twenty-seven respondents characterized as having "good" outcomes, eighteen as having "intermediate" outcomes, and twenty-three as having "bad" outcomes.

Outcome, as rated by this approach, corresponded well to the judgments we came to on reading summaries of the four interviews we had had with respondents. It was with some confidence in our outcome ratings that we turned to our next task, identifying the determinants of outcome.

# Chapter 3

---

# *The Identification of Patterns of Grieving*

We devote this chapter to a discussion of the factors initiating three main types of pathological grief, patterns of grief associated with failure to recover from the bereavement. We shall call each of these types a "syndrome," for each comprises a cluster of symptoms similar to the syndromes that characterize most mental illnesses. Yet insofar as the term "syndrome" suggests a mental illness it is misleading, for these syndromes are not to be counted as illnesses in their own right. Rather, we regard them as unpromising patterns of response to particular circumstances. They signal an increased vulnerability to mental illness; in a way they are precursors. They are thus analogous to "accident proneness," which is a recognizable state of increased risk yet not, in itself, an illness.

In later chapters we shall consider the likely forms of the illness associated with each of these grief syndromes. In this chapter our attention is given to the conditions that may bring each syndrome into being.

## The Best Predictors

On completion of the coding of our first two interviews we had available to us information on a forbiddingly large number of variables that might have played some role in deciding the outcome of the grieving process. These included demographic variables, such as age, income, and number of children, and variables having to do with the quality of the marriage, the nature of the illness, the kind and length of time of forewarning, where the death occurred, what were the early reactions of the widow and widower, and so on.

To reduce the large quantity of data from the first two interviews to a manageable number of variables, we used our judgment to produce a medium and a short list of reliable measures which would reflect the main types of predictive variables. We were guided in our choice of variables by our sense of the data and our anticipations of what might prove to be useful findings. We attempted to select as diverse a range of variables as possible. The medium list contained 166 variables: 55 "demographic and other antecedent variables," which could be assumed to have been present before bereavement, 52 "early reaction variables" covering the first three to four weeks of bereavement, and 58 "later reaction variables" covering the period between the first and second interviews (three to eight weeks). The short list included 18 variables: 10 "demographic and antecedent variables" and 8 "early reaction variables." We did not include any measures of the later reaction in our short list.

PREDICTORS FROM THE SHORT LIST

The starting point for our analysis was to carry out a discriminant function analysis of the eighteen predictive variables from our "short list." Discriminant function analysis is a multivariate statistical technique that designates the cluster of independent variables which most effectively predicts to which category of a dependent variable each member of a set of cases belongs. We used this technique to identify the independent variables that together would best predict "good" or "bad" outcome, omitting the intermediate group whose outcome was neither good nor bad. Full details of this analysis are given in appendix 2.

Eight of the eighteen variables together gave a satisfactory prediction of outcome. These, in order of significance, were:

1. Coders' Prediction of Outcome
   Scored 1 to 5, with 5 as the worst outcome. This was an educated guess based on criteria listed on pages 32–33.
2. Respondent's Level of Yearning (3 to 4 weeks after bereavement)
   1 = Never pines
   2 = Seldom misses deceased
   3 = Pines only when reminded
   4 = Frequent pining when inactive
   5 = Able to take mind off pining for brief periods
   6 = Constant pining interferes with other thinking
3. Respondent's Attitude Toward Own Death
   1 = Does not wish to die
   2 = Does not care
   3 = Would welcome death but for children
   4 = Would welcome death
   5 = Has attempted suicide
4. Duration of Terminal Illness
   1 = 6 months or more
   2 = 2 to 5 months
   3 = 3 to 30 days
   4 = 1 to 2 days
   5 = 24 hours
   6 = Instantaneous
5. Social Class
   1 = Professional and top level executive
   2 = Semi-professional, intermediate managerial, highly special-
       ized sales
   3 = Small shop proprietor, manager with few subordinates,
       office and clerical
   4 = Skilled manual

     5 = Semiskilled manual
     6 = Unskilled manual
  6. Years of Marriage
  7. Respondent's Level of Anger (3 to 4 weeks after loss)
     1 = None other than normal irritation
     2 = Mild—rather more irritable than usual or episodic outbursts
     3 = Moderate—occasional severe or continuous mild aggressive
         feelings
     4 = Severe—hostility paramount, affect leading to impaired so-
         cial relations
     5 = Extreme—chronically bitter, paranoid, or resentful
  8. Respondent's Level of Self-Reproach (3 to 4 weeks after loss)
     1 = None evident
     2 = Mild—occasional ideas of self-reproach in vague or general-
         ized way
     3 = Moderate—intermittent ideas of self-reproach, not exceed-
         ing other affects
     4 = Severe—preoccupied with ideas of guilt, exceeding other
         affects but short of clear conviction; some interference by
         ideas of guilt with thought or action
     5 = Extreme—constant preoccupation with clearly held convic-
         tion of guilt, interferring with thought or action

Leaving aside the first predictor, "The Coders' Prediction," which will be discussed in chapter 9, we have seven predictive variables, three of them antecedent variables and four early reaction variables, which contributed to outcome independently of each other. Most of them make sense in terms of our expectations, but some require explanation, and in all cases we must look more closely at the other symptoms and antecedents that are associated with them before we can say with confidence what each of them means.

The second predictor, "Yearning," is the single most typical feature of grief. We might suppose that people who avoid or repress grief are the most likely to become disturbed a year later, yet this is not the case; on the contrary, intense yearning was our second best predictor of poor outcome. The reasons for this became clear when we looked more closely at the way these widows and widowers described their marriages. Many of the respondents with high scores on "Yearning" at the first interview saw themselves as having been unduly dependent on the dead person, and it would seem to be this antecedent factor of dependency which explained both the immediate reaction of intense grieving and the longer-term failure of these grief reactions to resolve. This pattern of grieving (or "chronic grief syndrome") will be examined in more detail in chapter 6.

No such simple explanation was found for our third most powerful predictor, "Respondent's Attitude Toward Own Death." The expression, at the first interview, of a wish for one's own death seemed to arise in a variety of circumstances and was not associated with any particular antecedent or outcome factor. In other words, although it has predictive value, the wish for one's own death appears to be equally an expression of several different syndromes of pathological grief.

On the other hand, our fourth predictor, "Duration of Terminal Illness," turned out to be closely associated with the particular syndrome of unanticipated grief, which we describe in chapter 4. It also had strong conceptual affinities with predictors of outcome not included in our short list.

PREDICTORS FROM THE MEDIUM LIST

Among the fifty-five antecedent variables from our *medium list*, nine were found to correlate with outcome score thirteen months after bereavement. These are listed in table 3.1, with positive correlation indicating that the variable tended to be followed by a bad outcome.

Included in the list are "Short Duration of Terminal Illness," "Cause of Death *Not* Cancer," and "No Opportunity to Discuss Impending Death with the Spouse." Each of these can be seen as reflecting bereavements that were relatively sudden and unexpected. Further confirmation of the importance of unexpected deaths came at a later stage of analysis when we looked at another antecedent variable that had not been included in our

TABLE 3.1

*Antecedent Variables That Correlate with Later Outcome*

|  | $r^a$ | $p^b$ |
|---|---|---|
| Short Duration of Terminal Illness | 0.29 | $<0.05$ |
| Low Social Class | 0.28 | $<0.05$ |
| Cause of Death *Not* Cancer | 0.27 | $<0.05$ |
| Small Number of Sisters | 0.26 | $<0.05$ |
| No Opportunity to Discuss the Impending Death with the Spouse | 0.25 | $<0.05$ |
| Infidelity | 0.44 | $<0.01$ |
| Divorce | 0.27 | $<0.05$ |
| Pregnancy | 0.25 | $<0.05$ |
| Job Loss | 0.25 | $<0.05$ |

[a]product-moment correlation coefficient
[b]probability, if the null hypothesis were the case

original list, "Place of Death." The relationship of this variable to outcome is shown in table 3.2.

TABLE 3.2

*Place of Death as a Factor Determining Adjustment in the Spouse*

| | | Outcome | |
|---|---|---|---|
| Place of Death | Good | Intermediate | Bad |
| Hospital | 20 | 13 | 13 |
| Home | 4 | 4 | 2 |
| Other | 3 | 1 | 7 |

Seven of the eleven spouses of patients who had died in places other than home or hospital (for example, at work or in the street) had a bad outcome. Further analysis showed that six of these seven bad outcome cases had received little or no warning of the probable death of their partners. Examination of the subsequent course of the reaction to bereavement among those who suffered unexpected and untimely losses showed it to be quite distinctive. It can justifiably be said to constitute a "grief syndrome."

Our fifth predictor, "Social Class," presents serious analytic problems. "Low social class" indicates a life setting in which there may be special stresses, combined with a deficiency of resources. It may also indicate a history of life difficulties with a tendency to drift down the ladder of success. We have no means of knowing which of these factors explains the association between low social class and poor outcome following bereavement.

Furthermore, we expected to find that if social class affected the outcome of bereavement it would also affect the course of grief. But when we came to examine the reactions of our bereaved respondents at the time of the first and second interviews (three to four and six to eight weeks after bereavement), we found that the respondents of lower socio-economic status had grieved in much the same way as those of higher status. It seemed that social class—or whatever social class served as an indicator for—affected outcome without affecting the course of grief. Perhaps it was not so much the loss of a husband or wife *per se* which was poorly tolerated by the lower socioeconomic status group but rather the life situation that had been brought about by the loss.

Further shaking our confidence in this variable was the observation that whereas "Social Class" (which had educational and occupational components as well as an income component) did correlate with outcome, poor financial status and low income did not correlate with outcome. Income might well have been reduced in those situations where there had been a long terminal illness. In this way, lower income could have become associated with situations of forewarning and (as is discussed in the next chapter) of better outcome. In other studies it has been found that there is a quite consistent association between low socioeconomic status and mental ill health (see Dohrenwend and Dohrenwend 1969, for instance), and it is not unreasonable to suppose that the members of society with fewest resources will find the greatest difficulty in coping with the problems of loss. In the situation of the bereaved, however, the relationship between the income component of socioeconomic status and recovery may be quite complex.

Long "Duration of Marriage" reached statistical significance as a predictor of poor outcome only at borderline levels. Its importance could be evaluated only in the light of other evidence. A small number of respondents had been attached to each other for so short a time that they found it relatively easy to return to their unattached state. However, we concluded that while brief marriages may be easier to give up than longer marriages, there is no reason to regard long marriage as itself a major cause of pathological bereavement. This conclusion is borne out by the findings of studies of older widows and widowers who appear, if anything, less vulnerable to the effects of conjugal bereavement than do younger couples with shorter marriages.

Respondent's levels of "Anger" and "Self-Reproach," although also associated with poor outcome only at borderline levels of significance, are of particular interest for several reasons. Both have been found with undue frequency among bereaved psychiatric patients (Parkes 1965) and have often been blamed by clinicians for the pathological grief reactions that are met with in psychiatric practice (Volkan 1970). Anger and self-reproach may reflect ambivalent marriages, and it came as no surprise to us to find that respondents who reported having quarreled more than others with their spouses also had worse outcomes than those who said that they had had fewer disagreements.

Assessments of the quality of the marriage, like assessments

51

of the degree of dependence, had not been included in either the short or the medium lists of predictive variables. But there was at least one antecedent variable highly relevant to these issues. Table 3.1 shows that an antecedent variable that strongly predicted a poor "combined outcome" was "Infidelity" ( < .01). (In this rating, "infidelity" referred to any occurrence reported by the respondent: the respondent's own or the spouse's.) When we came to examine the pattern of grief among those whose marriages had been ambivalent, we found a distinctive type of response which fully justifies our treating these reactions as a separate syndrome. This will be described in chapter 5.

Finally, three other antecedent variables from the medium list were associated with poor outcome, although we have no sure means of knowing how seriously to take these associations. "Job loss" and "Pregnancy" both faced the respondent with new challenges at a time when his or her capacity to cope was likely to be at a low ebb. "Small Number of Sisters" suggests the usefulness of sisters, in particular, as sources of help and understanding.

All in all, three major determinants of pathological grief syndromes emerged from this phase of the analysis, and they comprise the starting point for the designation of the syndromes:

1. Sudden, unexpected bereavements were a major precursor of poor outcome.
2. Reactions of anger and/or self-reproach, often associated with ambivalence toward the former partner, were associated with poor outcome.
3. Reactions of intense yearning, often associated with a supposedly dependent relationship with the former partner, were also associated with poor outcome.

The further exploration of these three syndromes will occupy the next three chapters.

We turn now to consider some of the negative findings. All of the variables on the short list had been selected because it seemed likely that they would have some influence, good or bad, on the outcome of bereavement. In our data this does not seem to have been the case. The following antecedent variables showed zero to close-to-zero correlations with outcomes: age, number at home, religion (Catholic/non-Catholic), alcohol consumption, siblings living near, race (White/non-White).

*Age.* Since the study was restricted to a narrow age range with no respondent over forty-five and 82 percent between thirty and forty-five years of age, it was unlikely that age would emerge as a major predictor of outcome. Other studies have indicated that when a wider age range is included it is found that widows in their sixties and seventies tend to show less evidence of lasting emotional disturbance and deterioration in health than do their younger counterparts. But even this finding has been called into question by Maddison and Viola's work in Sydney, Australia (1968), which implied that in that city, at any rate, there was no close correlation between health deterioration and young age at bereavement.

*Number at home.* Although widows and widowers who had more children did somewhat better on the whole than the remainder of the sample, the difference was not statistically significant. Nor did simply having others in the home—other adults as well as children—make for better recoveries. It appears that the burden of coping with children unaided nearly matches the support that having children can provide, and that sharing a home with other adults is also at once help and hindrance in recovery.

*Religion.* There was no difference in outcome between respondents of the Roman Catholic faith and other religious faiths. Neither was there a difference between those who said they believed the death was "God's will" and those who did not. We did not learn how intensely involved each respondent was with the church that he or she espoused. Few of our respondents were prepared to declare themselves "agnostic" or "atheist," and the number who did were too few for separate analysis. Likewise, it was not practicable to break down the "other religious faiths," which were numerous and which individually had too few adherents to justify separate study. All that can be said is that respondents who called themselves Catholics were no more or less likely to have a poor overall outcome after bereavement than members of other (mostly Protestant) faiths.

*Alcohol consumption.* Alcohol is the most popular tranquilizer, and one that is often used by bereaved people as a night sedative or a means of controlling excessive tension. As such, it may have some beneficial effects. Unfortunately, like other drugs, it is also liable to be abused. Use of alcohol, taking our respondents as a group and relying entirely on respondents' estimates to judge the extent of their use of alcohol, appeared neither helpful nor harmful. However, among respondents whose outcomes were unsatisfactory, several appeared to have developed alcohol addictions. (See chapter 8 for further discussion of these issues.)

*Siblings living near.* The proximity of brothers and sisters constitutes a potential source of support, and we had anticipated that their proximity would be associated with better outcome. In fact this was not the case, and we can only speculate as to the reason. One possible explanation is that there is an inverse association between, on the one hand, mobility—and having few relatives nearby—and, on the other, social class. That is, those from lower occupational class are less mobile and more likely to have siblings living near. Since low social class was associated with poorer outcome, this may have balanced the benefits of proximity. There is another possibility, too: it may not be proximity to potentially supportive others that is important so much as the ability to maintain good relationships with them. We say more about this later.

*Race.* Although, taken overall, our black respondents had poorer outcome scores than our white respondents, race did not turn out to be a better predictor of outcome than socioeconomic status. The poorer outcome scores of black respondents may be attributable to their low socioeconomic status rather than to their race.

Turning now to the early reactions to bereavement as observed in our three-week and six-week interviews, is there any general aspect of these reactions that foreshadows outcome a year later? Among fifty-two assessments made at the three-to-four–week interview, fourteen were significantly correlated with combined outcome, and among fifty-eight assessments from the six-to-eight-week interviews, seventeen were significant predictors. The details of these correlations add little to the findings of the discriminant functions analysis of the predictive variables on the short list described above. Further discussion of them will be reserved for later chapters. One negative finding, however, is worth mentioning: among the early reaction variables included in the short list of predictors was "Numbness at Interview I." "Numbness" is frequently reported as part of the immediate reaction to bereavement. Although it has been interpreted as a sign of psychic defense and therefore, by inference, predisposing to mental illness, we found no evidence that it is an unhealthy reaction. Blocking of sensation as a defense against what would otherwise be overwhelming pain would seem to be entirely normal. We agree with other observers that the form of the immediate reaction to loss bears little relation to subsequent adjustment.

# Chapter 4

---

# *Unanticipated Grief*

"A great philosopher says that moderate afflictions permit the heart to sigh and the mouth to lament, but that very extraordinary, terrible and fatal accidents fill the soul with a stupor, which renders the lips mute and prevents the action of the senses." So wrote Father Cyprien de Gamache after breaking the unexpected news of King Charles I's execution to his wife, Queen Henrietta Maria. He continued: "Such was the state to which our Queen was reduced. The arguments that we employed to rouse her, found her deaf and insensible. At last, in awe, we were obliged to desist and remain grouped about her in profound silence."

For the next two days she shut herself away, and, when seen by Madame de Motteville on the second morning, her conversation, which was "feverishly repetitive," was interrupted by "wild bursts of weeping. . . . Wringing my hand with renewed tenderness and sorrow, she said that she had lost in the King a husband and a friend for whom she could never weep enough, and that the rest of her life must be unrelieved torment."

The queen retired to a convent where, a few weeks later, she received a letter that her husband had written to her after sentence of death had been passed upon him. After reading a few lines, she fell fainting into the arms of two nuns. She emerged from the convent wearing deep mourning, a form of dress which she continued to wear for the rest of her life. Mme. de Motteville wrote: "She wore a perpetual widow's mourning for him on her person and in her heart. This lasting sadness, those who knew her were well aware, was a great change from her natural disposition, which inclined to gaiety rather than seriousness" (Oman 1936, pp. 181–85).

## Preparation for Loss

Is it possible to prepare oneself for bereavement? Will anticipation in any measure lessen its impact and, if so, how? It has been suggested that people who are suddenly and unexpectedly bereaved will react more severely than those whose bereavement was anticipated because the latter started their grieving earlier than did the former. Their grief, according to this theory, is already past its peak by the time the bereavement actually occurs. The overall effect of loss is the same whichever mode of death occurs; if the widow or widower who anticipated the bereavement seems to be doing better, it is only because of an earlier start.

Our findings contradict this picture. We found that recovery from anticipated bereavement and from unanticipated bereavement took quite different courses. Individuals informed of the unexpected death of a husband or wife did not disbelieve what they were told, but they were unable to grasp its full implications. They seemed to be warding off unbearable mental pain. As they came to accept the reality of their loss, they entered into intense, deep grief. There was, then, in many cases, a stubborn persistence of this grieving, as though it would not be relinquished.

The person who was warned of a coming bereavement responded differently. There was, indeed, a sharp increase in anxiety and tension on being told of the seriousness of the spouse's condition and some attempt to avoid accepting the facts of the situation. (This, we must add, is a perfectly reasonable reaction in this circumstance, where there may still be much that can be done and so something less than certainty that death must ensue.) This anticipatory reaction was not nearly as severe as the reaction of the unexpectedly bereaved. Nor, as described to us, did the reaction appear to be one of grief with its attendant sense of loss and utter desolation. Rather it seemed to be one of intense separation anxiety, of fear.

The emotional reaction to threat of loss is different from the emotional reaction to loss itself. Evoked by each, to be sure, is separation anxiety. It is the emotional expression of the urge to stay close to or search for a person to whom an individual is attached. (Systematic studies have shown that searching plays an important role in the early stages of bereavement [Parkes 1970b].) However, after actual loss, the intensity of the separation anxiety begins to diminish and the struggle to regain the lost object is usually replaced by a period of despair and a conscious relinquishing or "giving up." Only then does the bereaved person become free to initiate new relationships and to discover a new place in the world. Thus, after actual loss, searching is followed by acceptance and acceptance, in turn, by recovery.

It is these later components of grief that are rarely found before bereavement, no matter how early the forewarning is given. Indeed, anticipation of loss intensifies attachment. Couples who have drifted apart often come together at such times and there is a resurgence of feelings of closeness, of wanting each other, and of tenderness toward each other. Only in exceptional circumstances do people become detached from a dying person.

Anticipated and unanticipated losses have different emotional implications. But the difference is not due to anticipatory grief. Furthermore, while it may not be possible to say that the one kind of loss is more painful then the other, the trauma of unanticipated loss is clearly the more disabling. To show the different consequences of anticipated and unanticipated loss, we first report our statistical materials and then present detailed accounts of the experiences of loss of two widows, one of whom lost her husband after a long terminal illness while the other lost her husband without any forewarning whatsoever.

## Differences in Forewarning

To examine the effects of forewarning or its absence, we divided our widows and widowers into two groups. In the first, which we called the Brief Forewarning Group, we included twenty-four of our respondents who said that they had had less than two weeks' warning that their spouses were fatally ill and less than three days' warning that their spouses' deaths were imminent.

These were the widows and widowers whose husbands or wives had died accidentally, or as a result of heart attacks (with no previously diagnosed heart condition), or of illnesses that were not, until just before their deaths, recognized as fatal. About half of these widows and widowers had had no fore-warning whatsoever. (It should be recalled that we worked with widowers and widows themselves aged forty-five or younger at the time of their spouses' deaths. This is an age group in which accident looms comparatively large as a cause of death, and fatal heart attacks, if they come, are likely not to have had a long history.)

In our second group, the Long Forewarning Group, we included forty-four widows and widowers who had had longer than two weeks—most of them very much longer—to prepare themselves for bereavement. Many of their husbands and wives had died of cancer or other conditions in which there had been knowledge of the illness for a year or more.

EFFECTS OF FOREWARNING: THE FIRST THREE WEEKS

Data obtained in our first interview, held three or four weeks after the loss, enabled us to examine the early reaction to bereavement in the two groups (see table 4.1). Only statistically significant differences are shown.[1]

The immediate reaction to bereavement in the Brief Forewarning Group is most often one of partial disbelief: almost two thirds agreed with the statement from a checklist, "I can't believe it's true," in comparison with only a quarter in the Long Forewarning Group. Death after a long, clearly terminal illness could be understood and to an extent accepted. Death out of the blue could not; a gap opened between the intellectual awareness, "My spouse is dead," and the understanding of the emotional meaning of that event. This dissociation was experienced as what Lifton (1967) calls "psychic numbing."

But disbelief did not prevent anxiety and dismay. Nearly half of the Brief Forewarning Group were thought by the interviewers to be moderately or severely anxious, compared with 18 percent of the Long Forewarning group. Agreement with the remarks, "How could he or she leave me?" and "I wouldn't care if I died tomorrow," were almost confined to the Brief Forewarning Group.

The finding that two thirds of the Brief Forewarning Group

[1]We present in table 4.1 the items in relation to which members of the two groups were significantly different. Because these items were chosen on the basis of statistical significance from a much larger pool of items, we do not list the probabilities of such differences occurring in two samples taken from the same population. It seems to us that if we did so, we would be implying a hypothesis-testing mode that we did not in fact use. In other tables in the book where, as was the case here, statistical significance was for us a criterion for *choosing* differences to report, we again do not give "probability on the null hypothesis" because if we did we would be implying that the differences themselves constitute grounds for asserting that one group is essentially different from another. However, where we are in fact testing an implication of an argument developed on other grounds, we do present "significance levels."

expressed feelings of guilt or self-reproach during this early period is of particular interest. Such feelings were reported by only a third of the Long Forewarning Group. This seems to confirm the clinical observation that a long terminal illness often helps husbands and wives to round off their relationships with their spouses. Some may, indeed, make restitution for real or imagined acts or omissions that might have spoiled their earlier relationships by expressing regrets and by mutual investment and devotion.

Some of those in the Brief Forewarning Group complained, during our interviews with them, that they had had no opportunity to make good deficiencies in their marital relationship: to reconsider plans, to resolve quarrels. Here, for example, is a comment made at four weeks by a young woman whose husband had been killed in an auto accident after they had had a minor argument:

Usually when you have an argument, afterward if he's wrong and he knows he's wrong, he'll tell me. If I'm wrong, and I know I'm wrong, I'll tell him. And that'll be the end of it. But I never got a chance to say [anything] . . . and he never got a chance to tell me either.

In contrast, a widow whose husband had died of lung cancer after a six-month's illness felt that she had done and said all she could before her husband had died:

If it had been a sudden death where I didn't have a chance to say what I wanted to say, it would have been more difficult. But we had said it all before lots of times. We understood each other perfectly. I knew what was on his mind. He knew what was on my mind. I knew how he felt about the children. He knew how I felt. There was nothing that I wish I did that I didn't do. . . . In these little talks that my husband and I had, we said our good-byes several times, over and over.

61

TABLE 4.1

*Reactions to Bereavement Three Weeks after Loss According
to Length of Forewarning*

|  | Long Forewarning N=46[a] | Brief or No Forewarning N=24[a] |
|---|---|---|
| **Acceptance of Death** | | |
| Respondent's immediate reaction included disbelief regarding death. | 11 (24%) | 15 (63%) |
| **Emotional State** | | |
| Respondent appeared moderately or severely upset or disturbed. | 9 (20%) | 10 (43%) |
| Respondent appeared moderately or severely anxious. | 8 (18%) | 10 (43%) |
| Some degree of self-reproach expressed in interview. | 17 (37%) | 16 (69%) |
| Respondent indicated feelings of abandonment: agreed that "How could he/she leave me?" expressed respondent's feelings. | 3 ( 7%) | 7 (33%)[b] |
| Respondent agreed with the statement: "I wouldn't care if I died tomorrow." | 3 ( 7%) | 7 (30%) |

[a]Includes one respondent who did not complete the third interview.
[b]This item was inadvertently omitted during interviews with three Brief Forewarning respondents.

Some in the Long Forewarning Group were able to take comfort from the awareness that they had been available to their husbands or wives. Here is a comment made by a widower whose wife had died of cancer:

She always said that she needed me in her illness. She always said, "Whenever you come, I feel better." So I felt she was really leaning on me, and I wanted to stay as good as I could. So I really did it for both of us.

Members of the Brief Forewarning Group three weeks after their loss already showed three ominous features that would complicate their grief: inability to acknowledge the reality of the loss (as distinguished from normally transitory avoidance), guilt, and anger. Each of these responses to loss has been shown to characterize the grief of bereaved people who subsequently sought psychiatric help (Parkes 1965). Reflecting difficulties in acceptance, self-punitive tendencies, and alienation, each response made it more difficult for the person to begin to find new ways of functioning effectively.

### EFFECTS OF FOREWARNING: SIX TO EIGHT WEEKS AFTER BEREAVEMENT

At the time of the second interview, six to eight weeks after bereavement, overall anxiety was still moderate to severe in over half of the Brief Forewarning Group and a sizeable proportion appeared depressed (see table 4.2). About half indicated that they would not find death unwelcome, although some qualified this by adding, "if it wasn't for the children." None actually attempted suicide.

Those in the Brief Forewarning Group were less likely to initiate or accept invitations to be with others than those who had had a chance to prepare for bereavement. Whether this reflected a tendency to social withdrawal on their part or indicated that others were less inclined to invite them is not evident, but in either case, those in the Brief Forewarning Group were more isolated.

Members of the Brief Forewarning Group were also less likely than members of the Long Forewarning Group to visit the grave of the husband or wife. This may, perhaps, have been part

TABLE 4.2

*Reactions to Bereavement Six to Eight Weeks after Loss According to Length of Forewarning*

|  | Long Forewarning $N=46^a$ | Brief or No Forewarning $N=24^a$ |
|---|---|---|
| **Acceptance of Death** | | |
| Respondent had visited grave. | 32 (70%) | 10 (43%) |
| **Emotional State** | | |
| Respondent appeared moderately to severely anxious. | 13 (28%) | 13 (54%) |
| Indicator of depression: respondent indicated that own death would be welcome or at least not unwelcome. | 9 (20%) | 10 (52%) |
| Indicator of depression: respondent agreed with statement, "I don't seem to laugh any more." | 6 (14%) | 8 (42%) |
| **Social Behavior** | | |
| Respondent initiated and accepted social invitations. | 30 (65%) | 9 (38%) |

[a]Includes one respondent who did not complete the third interview.

of a general tendency to shut themselves away and avoid leaving the relative security of the home. But it may also reflect the fact that many of the Brief Forewarning widows and widowers were still trying to avoid the painful reality of their bereavement. They could not give credit to their awareness that the grave had taken their husbands or wives. Nor could they yet manage the pain that such acceptance of reality would bring.

One widow, whose husband had died unexpectedly of a

cerebral hemorrhage, said she avoided visiting her husband's grave because the upset such a visit would produce was unmanageable:

> About a month afterward I had to sign papers up there so then I drove by. I had planned to go more often, but I noticed I was upset when I came home, so I thought I should let a few months go by until I can more or less take it easier when I do get there.

EFFECTS OF FOREWARNING: THIRTEEN MONTHS AFTER BEREAVEMENT

Thirteen months after bereavement, differences between members of the Brief Forewarning Group and members of the Long Forewarning Group persisted. A third of the Brief Forewarning Group broke down and cried during the interview, compared with only a few of the Long Forewarning Group (see table 4.3). Self-reproach for having in some way contributed to the spouse's death was confessed to by many more of those who had had little forewarning than by those who had had adequate forewarning. These self-reproaches seemed quite unjustified. Those with little forewarning were more likely to have continued their initial withdrawal from social participation. Most significant of all, only two of the twenty-three in the Brief Forewarning Group showed a good recovery, whereas in 56 percent of those in the Long Forewarning group a good outcome was apparent.

EFFECTS OF FOREWARNING: TWO TO FOUR YEARS AFTER BEREAVEMENT

Two to four years after their losses, about half of the members in the Brief Forewarning Group continued to have difficulty in fully accepting the reality of the deaths of their husbands and wives (as indicated in replies to the first four questions in table 4.4). The death remained inexplicable for eleven of the eighteen. (By the time of the follow-up we had

TABLE 4.3

*Reactions to Bereavement Thirteen Months after Loss According to Length of Forewarning*

|  | Long Forewarning N=45 | Brief or No Forewarning N=23 |
| --- | --- | --- |
| **Acceptance of Death** | | |
| Respondent had visited the grave three or more times. | 27 (60%) | 8 (35%) |
| **Emotional State** | | |
| Respondent was tearful during interview. | 4 ( 9%) | 9 (39%) |
| Respondent was self-reproaching during interview. | 8 (18%) | 10 (43%) |
| **Social Behavior** | | |
| Respondent was not working outside the home. | 9 (20%) | 11 (48%) |
| Apparent increase in respondent's social activity from beginning of bereavement (Coder Rating). | 26 (56%) | 5 (22%) |
| **Outcome Rating** | | |
| Proportion rated as "good" outcomes. | 25 (56%) | 2 (9%)[a] |

[a]Significant at .001 level Chi-square test.

lost from our sample six members of the Brief Forewarning Group and five from the Long Forewarning Group: most because they had moved, a few because they preferred not to take part in another interview.) We were saddened to find that the

TABLE 4.4

*Reactions to Bereavement Two to Four Years after Loss According to Length of Forewarning*

|  | Long Forewarning n=41 | Brief or No Forewarning N=18 |
|---|---|---|
| **Acceptance of Death** | | |
| Respondent occasionally or always sensed the presence of the dead person. | 8 (20%) | 11 (61%) |
| Respondent agreed with the statement, "It's not real; I feel that I'll wake up and it won't be true." | 6 (15%) | 8 (44%) |
| Interviewer assessed respondent's acceptance of death as "good" or "very good." | 35 (85%) | 9 (50%) |
| Indicator of death as inexplicable: respondent agreed with statement, "I still ask myself why it happened." | 12 (29%) | 11 (61%) |
| **Emotional State** | | |
| Respondent appeared moderately to severely anxious. | 13 (32%) | 13 (72%) |
| Respondent appeared moderately to severely upset or disturbed. | 13 (32%) | 12 (67%) |
| Indicator of depression: respondent agreed with statement, "Deep down I wouldn't care if I died tomorrow." | 6 (15%) | 8 (44%) |

TABLE 4.4 *(continued)*

|  | Long Forewarning n=41 | Brief or No Forewarning N=18 |
|---|---|---|
| Indicator of self-reproach: respondent agreed with statement, "I feel as if I could have done something to prevent his/her death." | 6 (15%) | 8 (44%) |
| Indicator of continued linkage to deceased: respondent agreed with statement, "I try to behave as he/she would want me to." | 18 (44%) | 15 (83%) |
| Respondent reported often or always lonely. | 6 (15%) | 8 (44%) |
| **Social Behavior** | | |
| Social recovery appraised by coders as fair or poor. | 8 (20%) | 9 (50%) |
| Respondent refused to consider dating. | 4 (10%) | 8 (44%) |
| Respondent displayed concern regarding functioning as spouse, parent, or worker. | 14 (34%) | 13 (72%) |
| Respondent displayed much concern regarding finances. | 12 (29%) | 14 (78%) |
| Outcome Indicators | | |
| Respondent's attitude toward the future was good or very good. | 28 (68%) | 5 (28%) |
| Coders felt things were going well or very well. | 26 (63%) | 1 ( 6%) |

emotional state of many members of this group remained as unsettled and tense as it had been at the time of the third interview. More than half the group were still anxious or upset; almost half reported that they were often or always lonely; and a similar proportion indicated that they were depressed and self-reproachful. All these proportions were significantly higher than those in the Long Forewarning Group, among whom a third were anxious or upset and only a sixth described themselves as depressed or self-reproachful.

All but three of those in the Brief Forewarning Group continued to feel some sense of obligation to the dead spouse, to "behave as he or she would want me to." This was agreed to by only about half of the Long Forewarning Group (although the level of continued feelings of obligation to the deceased spouse even in the Long Forewarning Group is noteworthy). Socially, members of the Brief Forewarning Group were more likely to be withdrawn, to refuse dating, and to be concerned about the management of their various social roles.

It is striking that the coders felt they could say "Things are going well" or "very well" for almost two-thirds of the Long Forewarning Group, but could say this for only *one* member of the Brief Forewarning Group! This was a young man, married only a little more than a year, whose wife and new child had died during childbirth. After his wife's death he returned to his parents' home, where he again became the cherished son. When we saw him three years after his wife's death, he was happily remarried. It is possible to question the extent to which the first marriage had "taken" at the time of the loss, that is, to question whether the marriage had yet become fully part of the respondent's life.

## A Possible Explanation

In order to attempt an explanation for the long-lasting failure to recover in the Brief Forewarning Group it is necessary to consider the sheer magnitude of the psychological change which must result from any conjugal bereavement. The death of a spouse invalidates a multitude of assumptions about the world that, up to that time, have been taken for granted. These affect almost every area of mental functioning—habits of thought which have been built up over many years of interaction, plans and routines that involve the other person, hopes or wishes that can no longer be realized. Sooner or later every chain of thought seems to lead to a blank wall; the dead person is everywhere and nowhere. People who have gotten used to thinking in terms of "we" have to learn to think in terms of "I." Life seems to have lost all meaning.

Bereavements are one type of psychosocial transition (Parkes 1971; Weiss 1976). These are defined as situations in which a person is faced with the need, over a relatively short period of time, to give up one view of the world and develop another. Such changes always require the individual to discover the discrepancies between the world that is now being faced and the world that, up to now, has been taken for granted. The amputee has to learn not to step on a foot that is not there, the nearly blind must learn that it is useless to look toward the source of a noise, and, in like manner, the bereaved must stop including the dead person in their plans, thoughts, and conversations. This process of learning is inevitably painful and time consuming. Time and again the amputee gets out of bed in the morning only to find himself sprawling on the floor, the blind person repeatedly peers through sightless eyes, and the widow or widower again and again forgets that the dead partner is gone forever.

Each time a mistake of this kind is made (and they are very

common at first), the person is brought up short. A pang of grief is experienced, a stab of frustration, a sense of alarm—for if we cannot rely on our assumptions about the world, what can we rely on? For a while it feels as if time is out of joint; there is a rent in the fabric of reality; nothing makes sense any more. Lacking a clear understanding of what has been lost and what assumptions have got to change, the person in transition loses confidence in his or her grasp of reality.

Each one of us maintains an internal assumptive world, a schema of the nature of our reality. We can only recognize the world that we meet and behave appropriately within it because we have formed models to interpret our perceptions and guide our behaviors. We recognize chairs, tables, doors, and windows because our internal world contains memories of all these things on the basis of which we make reliable assumptions about them. We walk through doors with confidence because we have learned at the deepest levels of our mental processes that doors set off one region of solid footing from another region of solid footing. Fortunately for us it is unlikely that we shall meet a door that looks like any other door but leads into an elevator shaft or an empty space where a now-demolished floor once existed. The new widow or widower, however, repeatedly encounters empty space where security once was.

Even quite major modifications of our assumptive world can be made without much difficulty if the changes are gradual or there has been plenty of time to anticipate them. The man or woman who plans to get married or to train for a particular job may create a new set of expectations and assumptions that will enable the transition into the new life situation to proceed relatively smoothly. This is particularly likely to occur if the anticipated event is wanted. But we do not "look forward" to events that are unwanted. It follows that events that are unwanted, and that invalidate a large part of our assumptive worlds, are likely to prove difficult for us to assimilate. Where

71

there is an absence of forewarning, the difficulty is compounded.

There are still other reasons for unexpected loss to be especially disabling. Unexpected loss shows the world to be unpredictable. Within it there is a potential for devastation that may at any time be manifested. Those who have witnessed one unforeshadowed disaster cannot be confident that another will not occur at any moment. They withdraw from risk, including the risk of new commitment. Furthermore, in the absence of an emotionally persuasive explanation for how a husband or wife could suddenly be gone, widows and widowers can easily feel themselves somehow to have been at fault, to have contributed in some way. This feeling seemed to be fairly common among those in our Brief Forewarning Group and may have encouraged them to make reparation by devoting themselves to the memories of their husbands or wives and by setting out to grieve for them forever.

Of critical importance, in conjugal bereavement, is the nature of the relationship that was lost. A marital partner is a life companion, a partner in the management of a home and family, a friend who has pledged that he or she will love and cherish us no matter what. But, important as all these are, a marital partner is still more. Marriage seems quite regularly to foster feelings of being somehow secure, augmented, extended, or completed by another which make it possible, when the marital partner is present or at least accessible, to be comfortable, relaxed, and so able to give attention to other matters. By the same token, feelings of insecurity, depletion, restlessness, and anxiety arise when the marital partner is inexplicably absent. In this sense the marital partner is an attachment figure, just as a parent is for a child—although, of course, the relationship is in other respects entirely different. Loss of an attachment figure, for a married person just as for a child, means loss of a critical security-fostering figure. It brings about a sense of being alone, beleaguered, vulnerable.

In the normal course of events, those who are confronted with sudden disaster tend to turn for help to the people to whom they are attached. But if the disaster is conjugal bereavement, the person to whom the individual would normally turn is the very person who has been lost. And so the anxiety continues unabated.

This discussion applies to any conjugal bereavement. But now consider how sudden, unanticipated loss of a spouse may complicate the situation. Faced with awareness of a sudden massive gap between the world that is and the world that should be, and with the sudden loss of the security-fostering figure, those in the Brief Forewarning Group were required to deal with a truly overwhelming threat. The ally to whom they would normally turn, the augmenting attachment figure, was not now available nor ever again to be available. So overwhelming can be the fear and pain brought about that many in the Brief Forewarning Group seemed to choose to deny the reality of some aspect of their loss as a desperate means of self-defense. In order to maintain some sense of stability under the threat of chaos they clung to the fantasy of a continuing relationship with the dead person. In this way they kept their levels of anxiety within bounds.

However, defenses that fend off reality can only be maintained if situations are avoided that would force recognition of reality. As we have noted, those in the Brief Forewarning Group, much more than those in the Long Forewarning Group, avoided visiting the grave. They also shut themselves away from people and situations that might have required that they acknowledge the loss. But by doing so they avoided the very people and situations that could have helped them to establish the new understanding, new engagement with the world, and acceptance of the loss that would be necessary for their recovery.

There can be a sense of sudden, unexpected conjugal loss as wrong, unjustifiable, and outrageous. This can be an impediment to acceptance. If other women with healthy husbands, other men with healthy wives, continue to have their husbands and wives, how can the widow or widower whose situation only a few weeks ago was identical to theirs accept being so singled out for injury? How can one accept the unacceptable?

All of this may be made more vivid by comparing the accounts of two widows, one of whom was subjected to anticipated loss, the other to unanticipated loss.

## Mrs. Goodwin: An Anticipated Loss

Mrs. Goodwin, thirty-four years old, with three children, knew for three years that her husband was dying. She first learned of the severity of his illness when he was hospitalized after a heart attack:

This one night he woke up in the middle of the night and complained of a terrible pain in his chest. I called the doctor. The doctor told me he was having a heart attack, to get him to the hospital immediately. I called the neighbor to stay with the children. Being the type of person that doesn't call for help, I got him into the car myself, which I never should have done. . . . But I did finally get him over to the hospital and they took tests of him and took X-rays and led me to believe that it was a slight heart condition.

They had taken cardiograms for a week and he had taken all kinds of tests and X-rays, and in the meantime I noticed that it was getting to be a daily thing to take quite a bit of blood from him, that they were doing extensive tests on his blood and they had oxygen on him all the time. For two weeks I called or talked to those doctors and they would tell me nothing. Finally I went to one of them and I said, "I want to know exactly what is wrong and you have to tell me." And after I said, "Do you suspect cancer?" he said, "Yes, we do."

The tentative diagnosis was confirmed: Mr. Goodwin had leukemia. Mr. Goodwin's doctors suggested to Mrs. Goodwin that her husband be kept uninformed regarding his condition. But dissimulation put Mrs. Goodwin under enormous strain, since she was required to deal with her distress without her husband's help and to hide her anxiety and concern when she was with him.

Mrs. Goodwin asked a friend to stay with her:

My girl friend came to stay with me for a few days. But I was almost in a state of shock, really, I would say. I never cried. I never let go at all—which I later realized was not a good thing—but I kept it all in and went to the hospital every day and saw him.

Mr. Goodwin returned home and for a month Mrs. Goodwin maintained her silence regarding his condition. With the help of her friend and her own doctor, her level of distress diminished. Then her husband broke through the evasions with which he had been surrounded:

One night Jack said to me, "Kitty, I have something to talk to you about," and I said, "What? Are you feeling all right?" And he said, "Yeah, I'm feeling fine. But I think I'm much more seriously ill than the doctors have said." And I said, "Why?" "Because I read an article in the paper today," he said, "I think I have leukemia." So I said, "Oh, Jack," I said, "you don't know this." And he said, "Have the doctors talked to you and told you this?" I said, "No, they told me you were ill." And I didn't know whether to tell him, and I just said to him, "Well, why don't we wait until you go for your checkup, and we'll discuss it with your doctor."

Mrs. Goodwin warned the doctor that her husband suspected his condition. Nevertheless, the doctor was not prepared when Mr. Goodwin confronted him:

When he got through examining him, Jack walked back into the office and he said, "I know I have leukemia. I don't want you to fool me. I want to know exactly what is wrong, what I have coming in front of me, and how long I have." The doctor just looked at him. He was floored. And he sat us down, and then he said, "Yes, Jack, you do."

Mrs. Goodwin began to rearrange her life. As her husband's ability to do things decreased, Mrs. Goodwin did more. She became less dependent. For a year and a half after learning he had leukemia, Mr. Goodwin continued in his business, but then he had to withdraw from it. More and more, Mrs. Goodwin looked after him.

Progressively he got so very weak that he just could not work, he could not do anything, it was an effort for him just to walk up and down the stairs. He just got worse every single day, progressively worse.

Mr. Goodwin went into the hospital. After a few weeks his disease went into remission, and he left. Then he went in again, and left again. During his last stay at home Mrs. Goodwin devoted herself totally to his care:

I had him home here for ten days, and at this point I neither slept day or night. And I got to a point where I would forget what pills I had given him and what I hadn't given him. And I called the doctor and said that it was really getting to be too much for me. He said, "You've got to get your sleep," and I said, "Well, he won't go back in the hospital." But then he got so bad that I could not care for him and carry him, wash him, feed him, and take care of three children too. And he had no patience with the children at all. And I was constantly trying to keep the children quiet and do for him and run up and down the stairs. It wore on my nerves after a while, and I thought I might just have a nervous breakdown, because I got to the point where I really didn't know what I was doing at times. If I ever were going to crack, I would have cracked then. And I felt that if I had come through that, well, I could go through anything.

Finally, Mr. Goodwin died. Mrs. Goodwin thought she was prepared for his death and, indeed, she was. But her grief was nevertheless intense.

76

The last time he went in, I had gone to the doctor and I said to him, "How bad is he?" He said, "He is very bad. The leukemia cells have gone into everywhere in his body." He said, "He will either go in two weeks or a month." His legs had swollen up and when we saw this, of course, knowing as much about the disease as we did, each symptom that he got, we knew what it was.

When it finally came, I had left him an hour before. He was conscious while I was there, and we talked and he said, "Gee, it's not going to be so long." And I said, "No, Jack, I don't think so." He was in an awful lot of pain, and I had gone out to the nurse and said to her, "Please, he's in terrible pain, could you give him a shot?" And she said, "I've just given him pills two hours before." "Well, he's very bad," I said, and she told me to see if I can talk to him to see if he can wait a half an hour. So I went in and we were talking and discussing things. He was very weak. I said to him, "How about my shaving you?" "Oh, I don't feel like getting a shave," he said. Well, I shaved him, because it would take up the time. And I washed him. His legs and hands had become very black. And then she came in and she gave him the shot. He went off to sleep for a little while, and I went out and I said to her, "He's not going to come through the night." She said, "Oh, you've seen him this bad for a week." I said, "No, he's going to go tonight. I don't want to go home. Would you call my aunt," because the children were at my aunt's. And she said, "No, I want you to go home." She must have known that he was dying and didn't want me to be there. And I said, "Well, let me stay until he falls asleep." So I held his hand and we'd talk every once in a while. Finally he just went out, completely, to sleep. And he never regained consciousness from then on. He just went to sleep and died in his sleep.

I didn't realize he was dead. I went home and picked up the children and didn't realize he was dead. And then when they called, the doctor said he had died.

Even though she had known her husband was dying, indeed had expected him to die that night, and even though she had several times in desperation prayed that he would be released from his pain, Mrs. Goodwin was dazed by the news. She called her husband's brother, and the two together returned to the hospital. Her husband had not yet been moved from his room.

I went over to him. I remember my brother-in-law taking me away from him because he said I kept holding on to him and patting his head. I cried my heart out. But I remember my brother-in-law coming to me and taking me away from him. And he said, "That's enough, Kitty." And the nurse took me out of the room and she said, "Kitty," she said, "You know he's much better off than the way that he was." And I said, "I know that. I would be a hypocrite if I said I wished he had gone on living, because the last two months I prayed that he'd die." I had prayed that he would die. And he'd said, "Kitty, pray that I go soon. I can't take any more."

Mrs. Goodwin, with the help of her brother-in-law, notified the rest of the family and a few friends. They arranged for the funeral and the burial.

The long illness and the constant awareness that it must end in Mr. Goodwin's death made it easier for Mrs. Goodwin to acknowledge emotionally and cognitively that her husband had died. Acceptance was difficult. But by three weeks after her husband's death, Mrs. Goodwin was beginning to accept the loss.

In this past week I've really come to the realization that this is final, that I'm really by myself. Even though he wasn't home this past year, he was still in the hospital and I could discuss things with him and talk to him every day. And even though the children weren't close to him—they haven't had their father at home for a year—I still saw him every day. And now the realization that he's really gone, that I am by myself, and I have to just do and think for myself, that's come in this past week. I don't know why it didn't hit me before. I suppose I was so busy before, doing things, and right now there's not that much more for me to do.

I talk about my husband a great deal like he hasn't died. The children have picked me up on it. I said to my daughter, "If your father ever sees you doing a thing like that . . . ," and my daughter, who is five, just looked at me and said, "Mommy, Daddy's dead." And I was shopping with my older daughter, who is nine, and I went to buy sour cream and I said to her, "Daddy loves this," and she just looked at me and she didn't say anything, but she took it out of the cart and she put it back on the shelf.

I have often thought, well, he's in the hospital, I can go see him. And I think this past week it's finally come to the realization, well, he's not in the hospital. He's not where I can see him, and this is it.

Having had her husband's help in considering what would happen after her husband's death proved valuable to Mrs. Goodwin as she turned to the problems of her future. She had worked out with him that she would mourn, although he had tried to discourage her from wearing mourning costume. They had agreed that she would try to reestablish her life and eventually remarry.

Jack and I discussed a lot of things, which, I think, a lot of people that have a death that is right away don't have a chance to discuss. He did not believe in mourning or wearing black for a year. He said to me that if I went around in black for a year, he would kill me. But I said to him I would wear black, if I went out, for a few months, for my own peace of mind. He didn't agree with this. But for the way that I feel, I feel that I should.

Jack said that he wouldn't want me to be by myself and he would not want the children to be brought up without any family life, because he had been through it with no mother and I with no father and it was just not a normal way. And he said that as long as it was someone that I respected and the children could respect, that he would want me to do this.

At this early point in her grieving, Mrs. Goodwin, when alone, was sometimes overwhelmed by feelings of isolation and loneliness.

I have been very lonely for the past year that he's been in the hospital, especially at night, after the children are in bed. I have found being by myself to be very lonesome and depressing. And I just have more of the same to look forward to. The other night I was sitting here, and I filled up and had a good cry to myself. It builds up inside you. It's a very empty feeling. If I didn't have the children I'd really feel empty, but I feel that I have them and they're young and they take up a lot of my time. But it is a very empty feeling.

79

Four weeks later, we saw Mrs. Goodwin again. Expressions of deep grief remained: sleeplessness, edginess, weight loss, crying spells.

Yesterday my mother said to me, "Good Lord, you're getting thin." And I said, "I'm eating." I don't know why I keep losing weight. But I put on five pounds and I take it right back off again.

My sleeping is off and on. The thing is, I have to get myself overtired and really go to bed and sleep. I do have sleeping pills, and I took them before Jack died, and I got to rely on them. I couldn't sleep at all without them. But I do find myself staying up until two and three o'clock in the morning doing things and then going to bed exhausted. I'd love to be able to just go to bed at eleven and just sleep, but I just don't seem to be able to.

I'm overenergetic. Like, I just got through painting the living room. And I did the hallway and then I laid down the carpeting one night. I overdo. I shouldn't, probably, but it keeps me busy.

And I've been just terrible, crying. I think it's because of the holidays coming on. I find myself sitting at night, probably because I'm just lonesome, and I will find myself starting to cry. I never cry in front of the children, but if I'm by myself at night I find myself crying.

And, for really no good reason at all, I find myself getting short with the children for small things. And I get into, well, not really a mood, but I can find myself getting very depressed. Then I get, not bad tempered, but very quick. I've never really ever done this before. I'm a very calm person usually. What people will tell me is that I'm mostly always in the same frame of mind and mood. But I do think I've getting very short.

Although Mrs. Goodwin had been lonesome when her husband was in the hospital, as she noted in our earlier interview, her husband's complete loss had made the lonesomeness more acute. It continued at this six week's point:

My days are pretty well taken up. I find a lot to do at night too: I sew, I iron, or do this or that. But it is very lonesome. I was lonesome when he was in the hospital for so long, but there would be the idea that, well, I would see him tomorrow. And now that I don't have the constant running and going, at night I am very lonely. There's an emptiness really. I don't really know how to explain it. I mean, before, I had a lot of company in and out. Now, after all, my friends have their own families to take care of, and constantly being alone every night, I find myself watching TV and I get bored with that, or I read. Or I'll go down and throw a wash in the machine that doesn't need to be done.

I don't know how to explain it. There is a terrible loneliness. And I miss him terribly. I need to cry. All the time he was sick in the hospital I very rarely cried and now I find, if I'm talking about him on the phone, I start to cry.

No longer was Mrs. Goodwin partnered, assured of the concern of another person so intricately allied with her that the two formed a corporate whole. Now she felt herself painfully alone. The other person with whom her world had been shared had been taken from her. As a result, she herself had been changed.

Loss of her husband produced in Mrs. Goodwin an emotional state characteristic of those who have lost attachment figures. It expressed itself in the syndrome of separation anxiety: great restlessness, difficulty in concentration, difficulty in sleeping, anxiety, and tension. In addition there were feelings and behaviors found in other separation situations but of an intensity that may be more typical of permanent bereavements: intense sorrow, painful memory, hopeless pining for the lost figure.

Some of Mrs. Goodwin's distress was initiated by the loss itself, the departure from her life of the figure with whom her life had been shared. Some of it was a response to the fundamental disruption of the world she had constructed and which had become for her an unquestioned reality. Neither of these aspects of loss was fended off by Mrs. Goodwin's long foreknowledge that loss was to occur. Foreknowledge is important to recovery, but it does not greatly reduce the need to grieve.

> I was terribly depressed, terrible crying spells, very short with the children. I shouldn't say I hadn't any thought for the future—you always have thought for the future—but you just take each day as it comes. No plans, nothing to really look forward to. Very depressed, terribly much so. After about two months I came out of it a little, but I just felt alone, terribly alone and lonely.

> The first three months was really a very lonely, lost period.

This minimal improvement seems to have marked a change in the tide of her grief. From here on she began to look outward and to turn to others to assuage some of her loneliness.

> I wasn't going out, I wasn't doing anything—which wasn't good. Then in the fourth month I started to go back bowling. I had been asked to go out twice with my girl friends and their husbands. But I felt very much alone, not part of this group at all, and I didn't enjoy it.

> About five months after my husband died, the girl next door— who is also a widow; she's engaged to be married—called me up one evening. Her girl friend had died just before Jack died. She said, "I'd like you to come over for coffee." I said, "Well, all right. . . ." I went over and her girl friend's husband was visiting.

The widower later called Mrs. Goodwin's neighbor to ask the neighbor if Mrs. Goodwin would be willing to see more of him. The neighbor asked Mrs. Goodwin and, after some hesitancy, she said she would. Actually, Mrs. Goodwin seems to have felt an affinity to the widower from the start, perhaps because they were both bereaved. Soon, the two were going out regularly. Mrs. Goodwin's depression and loneliness subsided. She felt that the man she was now seeing had restored her confidence to the point where she began to feel that she was once again the person she had been. But was it the relationship that was responsible for Mrs. Goodwin's complete recovery? It contributed a great deal to her return to her old self, but Mrs. Goodwin had already moved toward a return to social activity. And, when the possibility of a new relationship appeared, she had the confidence and hopeful trust to invest in it. As we will argue in a later chapter, one of the indications that recovery is progressing well is a capacity to establish helpful and gratifying social ties, which then in turn contribute to further recovery. But those whose recovery is impeded are likely to have difficulty forming and maintaining the relationships they need.

## Mrs. Elliott: An Unexpected Loss

Let us now consider the experience of a widow who lost her husband suddenly, with no forewarning at all. Mrs. Elliott, the mother of four children, was just thirty when her husband, also thirty, was killed instantly in an automobile collision. This is how she was told:

> It happened on Sunday, about 11:30 in the morning. Some of his friends were going down the street, and they recognized his car in front of the service station. So they got out and they enquired at the service station. The people in the station told them that the driver was killed. Then they came over here to my house. They knew my husband was dead because they had been told at the service station, but they didn't want to get me upset. So they took me down to the hospital.
>
> I went to the accident floor and asked about it. The nurse told me, "A case about a half-hour ago, an accident on Wellington Street. We admitted just the passenger. The driver, the other man, is unidentified, over in the morgue." So all the way to the morgue I just prayed, "Lord, don't let him be driving."
>
> We went in and told them what we were looking for and that we wanted to identify him. But he was already identified. They had his name down, just like it was on the cards in his wallet. The man finally came up and took us down. You know, you have to go down, walk down the steps. And I knew he was dead. And if you know that, if you know somebody's dead, you just can't walk right in

there, this pantry like, and look right in there on him. . . . I couldn't be first. [His friend] didn't walk in; he just walked to the door and he turned around. . . . And then I had to get up the strength and courage to walk in there and look at him.

I walked in and felt his skin. It was just as warm as mine. He was lying there just like he's in bed some nights, with his eyes half opened. And I closed them, and I rubbed his face, and I called him for twenty minutes. And the man told me, "Lady, your husband didn't even go to the accident room. Your husband came right here, because he was dead when he left the scene."

Unanticipated death is extremely difficult to credit emotionally. Although Mrs. Elliott "knew" that her husband was dead before she actually saw his body in the morgue, she could not on seeing his body actually believe that this was death.

I didn't believe it. I stayed there for twenty minutes. I rubbed him, I rubbed his face, I patted him, I rubbed his head. I called him, but he didn't answer. And I knew if I called him he'd answer me because he's used to my voice. But he didn't answer me. They said he was dead, but his skin was just as warm as mine.

They had the cold window open and I stood there and I cried and cried. And I called him, I rubbed him, I closed his eyes and I patted his face, and he still wouldn't answer me. I rubbed his body and no answer. But I didn't see any breathing. I didn't check his pulse or anything like that because they had pronounced him dead. But I thought, well, maybe if I stay here and call him, maybe he'll answer me, because he didn't look like he was dead.

Unanticipated death is without context: it has no history, nothing leading up to it; there are no surrounding events, like worried relatives coming to hospital visits. This absence of context, this disjointedness, makes the death inexplicable, no matter how detailed the account of how it happened.

It's something you read about in the paper, you don't think anything of it. But once it strikes in your family like that—it's a mystery.

You know, if it had been in the hospital and he just died from sickness, then you'd say, "Well, at least he's out of his misery. He's not suffering." But accidental death—that is something else. I don't know. And with the children you've got to explain it. The two youngest, they're five and three, they still think their father's coming home. It's so hard to explain to them.

Three weeks after her husband had died, Mrs. Elliott still, on some level, expected his return. Again and again she remarked on her inability to believe that the accident had really happened:

I lay here at night and I'm listening for that key at the bottom door. I got his keys in my pocket, but *still* I lay here and listen for him. And it's been like that ever since he died. I listen for the key in that bottom door.

I went over and saw him and identified him and I still said, "Well, he'll be home." I know he's there, buried, but right now I don't believe it. I have it in my mind that he'll come home. It's a mystery how a grownup would say that. But I really have it in my mind that he'll come home around 5:00. Or he'll come and get his lunch around 11:30.

Sometimes I'm watching the news on television and I can just see him coming into the room. Like, I watch the news at noon. And if he was here eating lunch, I'd be sitting watching. And I can just see him coming through the room, saying, "Well, I'm going," because I'd leave him eating when I watched the news.

The inexplicability of the accident burdened Mrs. Elliott. It made no sense. She was repeatedly baffled as she tried to construct an "account," an explanation that would permit her to feel she understood how her loss had come about.

I wish somebody could just sit down and explain to me why a young man had to die. A lot of people have died, but I still want to know why it had to happen to him. With the children you say, well, God does things. But let little children know their father. I still can't

85

understand it, why he had to die. His being so young. I guess that doesn't have anything to do with it.

Sudden and, especially, accidental death, just because it is so difficult to explain, because it seems to have resulted from insufficient cause, is easily thought of as having been avoidable. Self-reproach seems natural: "If only I hadn't let him go out that morning. . . ." Mrs. Elliott refused self-reproach, but she did reproach her husband. Her husband had been killed in a small car he had just purchased. She had argued against the car: "The way I feel, if he had listened to me, and not got that car, or taken it back, like I begged him to, he wouldn't have died. That's how I feel."

Mrs. Elliott was not at home when the interviewer called eight weeks after Mr. Elliott's death. Two weeks later, ten weeks after Mr. Elliott's death, Mrs. Elliott was still having a bad time:

> I've been getting along, but some days are good and some days fair or bad. I haven't been getting any sleep at all. Last Saturday night I had such a bad night that Sunday I went over to the hospital to ask for something to get me to sleep. They gave me some pills. I don't want to get anything habit-forming, but I want something to quiet my nerves, where I could get some rest. I haven't got eight hours sleep since he died. I lay there, four or five o'clock in the morning. The doctor told me, when he gave me these pills, that he wouldn't guarantee that they would help me. He said it's a matter of time. This would have to wear off.

> I guess that's what makes me so upset and so cross all day. I can't take the children. I've been so upset. I've been so mean with the children. The doctor said it was my nerves.

Soon after her husband's death, Mrs. Elliott sought distraction by returning to work. Her two preschool children stayed with her sister while she was at work, and her two older children were looked after by her younger brother after their school day, until Mrs. Elliott's return. Mrs. Elliott, for the children's sake, regretted going to work, but felt that, emotionally, she had to have this escape from her home:

> I can't stand to stay here. I just don't want to be in the house. When I'm here alone at night, after the children go to bed, I have to sit here and look at the four walls. I can't stand it. Everybody asked, "Why do you want to go to work?" I'd rather be working than be here in the house. Be up until four and five o'clock and then stay here all day—it's no good.

Times when her husband would normally have been with her remained Mrs. Elliott's worst times.

> The hardest thing for me, I think, is at night. We have a neighbor works second shift and we hear his pickup truck every night. And my husband would always say something like, "When's he going to get his brakes fixed?" And every night I'm sitting here when he comes along, and that's when I really think about my husband, because he would always say something.

> When my husband was here I'd usually be in bed then, but now I don't go to bed. If I can't go to sleep, why go to bed? I wash my dishes, mop the bathroom, clean the house. That's the worst time, at night. And early in the morning, around six o'clock, when my husband and I would get up. And around noon, because my husband would come back and get lunch. Those three times in the day are very hard for me. Those are the worst times. But it's at night, when I heard the pickup truck—that's the very worst.

Mrs. Elliott was clearly impelled to turn toward her husband at such times, but this only served to aggravate her feelings of loss. She tried to cope with these by building up a fantasy relationship with her unseen husband, as if by conforming to his wishes to a greater extent than she ever had when he was alive she could compel him to protect or watch over her.

87

I think that if I do what he wanted he'll be pleased. If anything I do is what he planned to do here, if I carry out his plans, then I'll make him happy. And I try not to do things he didn't want me to do.

He would walk in the bathroom and find my clothes there, and he would start fussing. He would say, "Please don't leave your clothes in the bathroom." Always, he said that.

And now, when I do it, I think about it, and right then I'll take the clothes and put them in the hamper if they're dirty or else I'll take them and hang them up in the closet. That's one thing I know he didn't like me to do. Another thing is the refrigerator. We bought a new refrigerator. Sometimes I let three weeks pass and I wouldn't defrost it. And he liked for it to be defrosted every two weeks. And you know, since he's dead, I don't have too much time, but I thought about it this morning and said, "God, this refrigerator has got to be defrosted."

Mrs. Elliott experienced, as did other widows and widowers, various expressions of intense grief. Aside from her inability to accept emotionally that her husband had died—as demonstrated by her continued readiness for his presence at home, her acting in ways he would have approved, and the like— her distress seemed qualitatively like that of other widows and widowers. She spoke of appetite loss, loss of concentration, and tearfulness, but none of these seemed excessive at this stage of bereavement.

If I stayed home all day I might not eat anything at all. At work, on breaks, I eat snacks. But at home I don't want anything.

My strength is good. I don't get tired. But I'm so absent-minded, I can't remember what I'm supposed to do. I can be in the bathroom, have the water going in there, and something might be cooking in the kitchen, and I'll come out, sit down and then say, "Oh God, I left the water going in the bathroom," and run back and all the food will burn up. My brother said last night, "You specialize in burning." I take the food out of one pot, put it in another. That's how bad my mind is.

If I feel real poor, nights, I cry and get it out. Then I feel all right. I don't try to hold the tears in.

We saw Mrs. Elliott again thirteen months after her husband had died. Now it was clear that her recovery was not proceeding well.

I feel so tired. I feel as if, if I don't rest I might break down. And I don't want to break down. Sometimes I feel like I might not even make the day. I'll sit down and think about it, try to get dressed and go ahead on. I feel like, well, I won't sit here and try to die, I have got to live. And I just get up and build myself up. Sometimes in the morning I just lay in bed and I sleep and I wake up. And I don't even have any breakfast. I get up and I feel so tired I don't want anything to eat. But I go in and I push myself to fix something to eat, and I feel better. I try to do something. But I've had these days when even in the morning I feel so tired and so depressed, I feel like I won't make the day. But I just push myself. This can go on for two or three days or it's liable to be a whole week I'm so depressed and so tired. Sometimes my sister comes and she says, "You have to cook." And I say, "I didn't feel like it."

The restless energy that is so much a part of the early experiences of grief had been replaced by persisting fatigue. Some of this probably came from the sheer effort of holding down a job and at the same time caring, unassisted, for a home and family. But some seems to have reflected feelings of despair, and some may have resulted from her preoccupation with fending off memories of her loss that might subject her to intolerable pain. We can only guess at the sources, but the existence of unusual fatigue was unquestionable:

I'm very tired, because I'm working. I have so many places to go to, so many things to take care of. I feel as if, if I don't rest, I might break down. I feel like I'll take a week off and I'll feel better. I've meant to do it. I haven't been off for a while. I have things to be done— I have to cook and take care of the wash and take care of the kids —so I feel like it's for my own good to take off and rest. Sometimes I feel like I might not even make the day. I ask God to take it off

89

my mind and give me strength to go on and not just sit and throw myself away and try to die.

Unlike widows who were moving toward good recoveries, Mrs. Elliott cried about her husband's loss fairly often:

> I could be in the kitchen, I could be anywhere, and it comes on, I feel like crying. I don't want my children to know I'm crying. The oldest knows. He's seen me cry at night. But the younger ones, the only time they have ever seen me cry was when he died.

> Maybe I cry once a week, twice a week. It's according to the mood I'm in. If I feel down and out, then I might cry two times a day, but if I feel good, then I might go for a whole week and not cry. It's just the mood I'm in.

She continued to pine for her husband, and she still found the times when he would have been at home especially difficult: "I'm lonely at night. And Sundays—Sundays are the roughest day of the week because that's the time he was home."

The one area of improvement Mrs. Elliott reported was in her sleeping. She no longer lay awake until four or five in the morning. Her fantasies of his continued life were less evident by day, but her relationship with her dead husband continued in her dreams.

> I see him just like he was here. He'll be talking or something, like in the kitchen. And I'll wake up and it was all a dream, and I'm always disappointed. When it first started, it always felt like a big dream. At first I tried to make it be a big dream. But now I know he won't be back. I don't feel like it's a dream now.

> I tried to see him, but I can't. Or to hear him—like in the bathroom, you could hear him getting stuff out of the cabinet and getting a shave. I never hear that [now].

Mrs. Elliott had now accepted her husband's loss in the sense that she no longer harbored the belief that he was not really dead. And yet his death remained inexplicable to her:

At first it was like a dream. Now I know he won't be back. But always on my mind, I wonder how come he had to die so young. I know there are a lot of young people in the cemetery. There are teenagers that die. But it still always comes in my mind: why did he have to die and his brothers didn't?

Mrs. Elliott now, thirteen months after her husband's death, sometimes saw an older friend of one of her brothers, a man who was separated from his wife. The man appeared to be a reliable suitor. Mrs. Elliott had known him perhaps two months, saw him several times during the week and regularly on the weekend. But she felt herself not nearly ready to think about remarriage. Despite the new man, Mrs. Elliott was often lonely: "Sometimes I'm lonely, sometimes not. Some days are better than others. But nights, the nights are lonely. And Saturday nights, when I'm home, and some Sundays, I get lonely by myself. I do."

We saw Mrs. Elliott again two years later, three years after her husband's death. She told us that she was feeling better. But she remained lonely and driven to restless activity in attempting to ward off a "mental breakdown."

I'm working because of my loneliness. At night, you just sit and look at the four walls. Well, I don't sit. I don't sit and stare and think about it, because I feel, if I do that, I would probably have a nervous breakdown. After three years, you *should* get back to normal if you are *going* to get back to normal. Because if I had [kept the] feeling of being depressed, if I hadn't picked myself up, I would have probably been in a mental clinic or something. But I picked myself up, and started trying to bring myself back.

I kind of don't let anything worry me now. If I have something to do, I try to do it and get it off my mind, because I see so many people getting nervous breakdowns and things.

Mrs. Elliott nevertheless still had difficulty in accepting the fact of her loss. This was reflected in her agreement with the statement, "Even now I sometimes feel it's not real, that I'll wake up and it won't be true." She said, in response to this statement, "I do. I just feel like he . . . he may come home."

She continued to dream of her husband: "I dream sometimes twice a week of him. I see him and then I wake up and there's nobody. And I realize it was all a big dream."

The man she had been seeing at the time of our previous interview remained in her life. And yet, she said, she would not want to marry him: "I haven't even given it a thought, because I don't think I could go through it again."

Despite Mrs. Elliott's self-appraisal, hers does not seem to us a good outcome. She appeared much less capable of accepting attachment and its risk of loss than she had been before her husband's death. While she was no longer tense and anxious, she displayed an emotional flatness, an absence of engagement with work or friends or even the man she saw, that suggests less than full recovery. She continued to feel herself vulnerable to "nervous breakdown" if she should relax her guard. She was still lonely. And she still actively grieved for her husband's loss.[2]

## Comparison of These Reactions to Bereavement

Mrs. Goodwin and Mrs. Elliott are quite different women who had maintained quite different marriages. There is much in their accounts of their experiences that expresses these particularities. And yet there is much in Mrs. Goodwin's account that can be generalized to those who had adequate forewarning, and much in Mrs. Elliott's account that can be generalized to those who did not. Mrs. Goodwin was able to deal with her

[2]Another example of a severe form of this type of reaction, which led to alcoholism and admission to the hospital for psychiatric care, is given on pages 192–200.

husband's illness and impending death together with him; she was not required to confront his loss entirely alone. By her caring for her husband, by demonstrating her genuine devotion to him, Mrs. Goodwin was able to feel, justifiably, that she had not failed her husband or her marriage. When her husband's death came, it was understandable, and though the loss proved painful, more painful than she had expected it would be, she was not further burdened by an inability to accept that it was real. None of this was true for Mrs. Elliott. Mr. Elliott was taken from her suddenly, senselessly. Her need to care for him, to express her feelings of solicitude and devotion, could only be directed toward his dead body—and then were interrupted by an impatient morgue attendant. And because her husband's death had been so absolutely without forewarning, Mrs. Elliott could never know that similar misfortune was not waiting to strike her again in the next minute or second. It is significant, we feel, that while both Mrs. Goodwin and Mrs. Elliott established relationships with new men, Mrs. Goodwin could see in her relationship the possibility of a new and gratifying life, but Mrs. Elliott could see in hers only a new risk of disappointment and loss. Mrs. Goodwin could invest herself in the new relationship and resolve her loneliness; Mrs. Elliott remained emotionally guarded, and her loneliness was undiminished.

In conclusion, we would like to propose that there exists a constellation of symptoms which can justifiably be termed the "Unexpected Loss Syndrome." It would appear that this syndrome is likely to occur following major losses that are both unexpected and untimely. It is characterized by a reaction that includes difficulty in believing in the full reality of the loss, avoidance of confrontation with the loss, and feelings of self-reproach and despair. As time passes, the bereaved person remains socially withdrawn and develops a sense of the continued presence of the dead person, to whom he or she continues to feel bound. But this feeling does not protect the bereaved person from loneliness, anxiety, and depression.

These remain severe and hamper the person's ability to function socially and occupationally.

It appears to us that the marriage relationship engages the functioning of husbands and wives at the deepest cognitive and emotional levels. Sudden, unanticipated, and untimely loss of that relationship injures functioning so severely that uncomplicated recovery can no longer be expected.

The resurgence of attachment behavior that seems commonly to follow the discovery that a husband or wife is nearing the end of life appears to us to be of value later, for the survivor, as well as immediately for the couple. A number of respondents told us in one way or another, "We were never so close as we were in the last few weeks. I am so grateful we had that." Even though awareness of impending loss made for great pain, afterward the concluding period of closeness was treasured; there was recognition that it would have been worse if that final mutuality had not been possible.

We have already pointed out that to assert that forewarning of loss is of considerable value is not to assert that it reduces the magnitude of grief. Forewarning permits certain kinds of anticipatory preparation. There is learning to live with the prospect of loss, so that when loss in fact occurs, it is at least not unexpected. There is the making of plans for the future, to the extent that such plans are not felt as betrayals of the dying spouse. There are all the assumptions regarding the nature of one's reality that can be readied for examination and change. These kinds of anticipations are possible and useful. Later, when loss does occur, its occurrence will make sense, because it will be seen as the end result of an understood, if hated, process. But "anticipatory grief?" This, we think, occurs only rarely. And properly so: grief implies that there has been a loss, and it is important for the eventual recovery of those destined soon to be widows or widowers that they not later reproach themselves with having met loss halfway. To accept the spouse's loss while the spouse still lives is to become vulnerable to later self-accusation of having partially abandoned the spouse. Nor are husbands and wives ordinarily able to relinquish emotional investment in the spouse, whatever their understanding of the future. Attachment and love are not so tractable to the demands of expediency; they resist an attempt to withdraw them. Grief, we believe, begins with actual loss.

Grief is painful, whether there has been anticipation or not. But where there has been no anticipation, there is bewilderment as well as loss, inability to grasp the event, refusal to accept a world in which tragedy occurs so arbitrarily, an insistence on protest: "It makes no sense." Although unanticipated loss does not seem more painful than anticipated loss, it is more disabling and much more difficult to recover from.

There is one very important implication of these observations: if people can prepare themselves emotionally for a loss, then it follows that every opportunity should be taken to help them make such preparation. Means for achieving preparation might include giving appropriate warnings, confirming that these warnings have been understood, and ensuring that family members who are closest to the bereaved get every opportunity to come to terms themselves with the impending death. Those whose work is to care for the dying know only too well how often communication between doctors and patients breaks down at such times. Mrs. Goodwin described several instances of this. But communication can also fail between medical staff and the family. At the point at which her husband's death was imminent, it was only because Mrs. Goodwin showed unusual courage in facing up to the facts that she refused the nurse's facile reassurance that her husband was not about to die. Even so she allowed herself to be persuaded to go home instead of remaining at his bedside to the end, a decision that might have had serious consequences if she had not already been so well prepared for his death.

Because Mrs. Goodwin had nursed her husband so devotedly, she was assured that she had done everything possible to help him. By pushing herself close to her limit she absolved herself from any possible thought or accusation that she had contributed to his death. In a paradoxical fashion, the very absence of an efficient medical machine which would have taken over his care and deprived her of this opportunity may have aided her eventual recovery. There is a real danger that intensive care units and other inpatient facilities, to the extent that they take away from the family the opportunity to care for the dying individual, may create problems for the family in the future.

# Chapter 5

---

# *Conflicted Grief*

---

It must be that grief is more bearable in the absence of guilt. And I, who was always addicted to guilt, feel comfortably little of it now that he is gone. There is nothing that was not said between us. There are no If Onlys! There are few regrets. We knew and said that we gave each other joy; he knew that he was profoundly loved and respected by his wife and his children; he knew that his life had counted, that he had grown and never stopped growing; and that is perhaps more than most of us know before we die

[Lear 1979].

It might well be supposed that the intensity and duration of mourning would in part be dependent on the quality of the marriage that was lost. Our data support this assumption, but they do so in a fashion that may appear, at first, paradoxical. It seems not to have been the good marriages, the marriages in which there was contentment and mutual acceptance, where misunderstandings were infrequent, whose end was followed by unyielding grief. On the contrary, difficulties in recovery seemed more frequently to occur following the loss of marriages which were conflict-ridden, thoroughly troubled, in which one or the other spouse may well have contemplated separation and divorce.

## Assessment of Marital Conflict

We asked our respondents about the quality of their marriages in two different aspects. First, we asked in our lengthy interviews for detailed descriptions of how the spouses worked together in their marriages, the emotional tones of the marriages, and the ways in which the marriages were sustaining or distressing. Then, at the close of each of our interviews, we asked, among a set of fixed questions, "Would you say your marriage was very happy, pretty happy, or not too happy?" We also asked this same question of the still-married husbands and wives in our comparison study.

Table 5.1 displays the levels of marital happiness reported by both the widows and widowers in the bereavement sample and the husbands and wives in the comparison sample. There is no statistically significant difference between the two groups of responses. In both the bereaved sample and the comparison

### TABLE 5.1
#### Responses to Question Regarding Marital Happiness

|  | Bereaved Sample | | Married Comparison Sample | |
|---|---|---|---|---|
|  | Men $N=19$ | Women $N=48^a$ | Men $N=18^a$ | Women $N=49$ |
| Very Happy | 15 (79%) | 25 (52%) | 11 (65%) | 33 (69%) |
| Pretty Happy | 4 (21%) | 18 (38%) | 7 (41%) | 13 (27%) |
| Not Too Happy | 0 | 5 (10%) | 0 | 3 ( 3%) |

[a]One bereaved woman and one comparison man did not answer the question.

sample about two respondents in every three rated their marriages as very happy. The remainder, with the exception of five widows and three of the wives in the comparison group, rated their marriages as pretty happy.

The absence of difference between the marital rating of the two samples itself requires comment, for we might have expected that widows and widowers would more frequently idealize their lost marriages and so more frequently describe their marriages as having been entirely happy. Is idealization unaccountably absent from our sample? A close examination of our materials suggests that it is not: the very absence of difference between the bereaved group and the comparison group constitutes a demonstration of idealization among the bereaved, for their marriages, while some were extremely happy, included many of a degree of difficulty unmatched in the comparison sample.

To begin with, seven of the bereaved women—about 14 percent of the sample of widows—had been married to alcoholic men. Alcohol relatively often is implicated in early deaths, and this was true in our sample. Of the seven alcoholic men, two died of conditions directly produced by their alcoholism, including cirrhosis of the liver; two died of diabetic conditions exacerbated by alcohol, one of them in a coma brought on by his inability to match his insulin dosage to his intake of alcohol; one died in jail, possibly from injuries incurred in a street brawl; one died of a massive heart attack, of which there had been no forewarning; and the last died of cancer. Except for the last two—perhaps only the last one—alcoholism contributed to these deaths.

All seven of the marriages to alcoholic men were chaotic. In one, the man openly maintained an extramarital relationship. His wife said, bitterly, that during the last year of his life he was rarely home except for meals. As it happened, he died in the other woman's home. Other alcoholic husbands were also home only sporadically. The man whose death may have been the result of injuries incurred in a street brawl was described as having often disappeared from home, generally to join fellow winos who were, unlike him, homeless. And yet, among the seven widows of alcoholics, one said the marriage had not been too bad, although her husband had been alcoholic virtually their entire married life; another, whose husband's alcoholism had prevented him from ever holding a regular job, somehow managed to picture her marriage as a loving partnership; a third, one of the two whose husbands' combination of alcoholism and diabetes proved fatal, nevertheless described her marriage as having been happy and took satisfaction in having kept her husband alive much longer than his doctors had believed possible. The other widow whose husband died of diabetes complicated by alcoholism also found it possible to describe her marriage as having been happy, partly because her husband, despite his difficulties, had been able to provide her with much-needed emotional support. Only three of the seven widows of alcoholic men characterized their marriages as "not too happy"—the minimization of unhappiness itself an indication that idealization was at work within this group.

In addition, in those bereavements in which death came after a long terminal illness, the surviving spouses who rated their marriages as "pretty happy" or "very happy" had to discount months or years of attending and nursing husbands and wives who had become patients. Nor did illness, ordinarily, make husbands and wives more lovable. On the contrary, ill husbands and wives, frustrated by their suffering and their helplessness and despairing because of their condition, were often depressed and withdrawn. Sometimes they were angry at those on whom they had become, against their will, dependent. Some of the widows who had devoted their waking hours to nursing their husbands at home or who had neglected their children in order to keep their hospitalized husbands company reported having been nevertheless accused by their husbands of neglect. Widowers reported fewer such incidents, perhaps because their wives' expectations of attendance were lower, but many of them, too, found the last months or years of their marriages to have been wearing and distressing. All these experiences were set aside when widows and widowers described their marriages as having been happy.

Yet global assessments may be more easily idealized than memories of more nearly concrete events. Respondents in both samples were asked, "Which of the following have caused differences of opinion or have been a repeated problem during your marriage?" A list of eleven possible areas of marital disagreement was then read. Individuals in the bereaved sample significantly more often reported areas of disagreement or conflict than did those in the still-married group. (see table 5.2). Many

TABLE 5.2

*Bases for Marital Disagreement or Conflict*

|  | Bereaved Sample | | Married Comparison Sample | |
|---|---|---|---|---|
|  | *Men* N=19 | *Women* N=48 | *Men* N=17 | *Women* N=48 |
| Irritating Personal Habits | 5 (26%) | 24 (50%) | 7 (41%) | 17 (35%) |
| Being Tired | 4 (21%) | 15 (31%) | 5 (29%) | 17 (35%) |
| In-Laws | 8 (42%) | 16 (33%) | 3 (18%) | 5 (10%) |
| Disciplining Children | 4 (21%) | 15 (31%) | 2 (12%) | 10 (21%) |
| Being Away from Home Too Much | 7 (37%) | 10 (21%) | 2 (12%) | 7 (15%) |
| Time Spent with Friends | 3 (16%) | 11 (23%) | 1 (6%) | 8 (17%) |
| Your Husband's (Wife's) Job | 3 (16%) | 8 (17%) | 4 (24%) | 11 (23%) |
| Household Expenses | 3 (16%) | 9 (19%) | 2 (12%) | 3 (6%) |
| How to Spend Leisure Time | 4 (21%) | 6 (13%) | 3 (18%) | 9 (19%) |
| Not Showing Love | 2 (10%) | 6 (13%) | 2 (12%) | 3 (6%) |
| Religion | 2 (10%) | 2 (4%) | 2 (12%) | 4 (8%) |

of the widows and widowers who felt their marriages had been marred by conflict nevertheless believed that their relationships had been on the whole happy. As one widow put it, after noting that she and her husband had had many areas of disagreement, "It doesn't seem very important now."

The bereaved sample more often than the comparison sample reported disagreement in three areas in particular: relations with in-laws, discipline of the children, and time spent away from home—specifically, being away from home too much. In each of these areas there tended to be a discrepancy between what respondents felt to be the level of support they needed and the level actually provided by the spouse. The disputes over in-laws seemed often to turn on the in-laws' competing claims for their spouses' time and loyalty. Arguments about being away from home too much in some cases appeared to have resulted from spouses who had been too responsive to the competing claims of friends, in-laws, or work; in other cases the absence from the home seemed to have been a way of escaping a marriage filled with conflict. Some spouses had used alcohol to excess without actually becoming alcoholic. Gambling was also reported as a reason for a spouse having spent time away from home, and it, too, could express a wish to escape from an intolerable life situation, even while it made that situation more intolerable. In-law troubles might accompany troubled marriages; in our interviews, widows of men who had been alcoholic or had gambled or had in other ways been poor husbands sometimes blamed their in-laws for having supported their husbands' misbehavior.

Disputes over disciplining children seem to have been more frequent among the bereaved because the self-absorption of an ill father or mother made for rigid parental behavior. But beyond this, disciplining of children and children's treatment in general seemed often to be an area in which an otherwise tolerant spouse would draw the line. One widow who was regularly irritated by her husband's self-indulgence was nevertheless quiet so long as his "selfishness" was expressed only toward her, but she berated him when it was expressed toward the children. In another instance, a woman who was able to tolerate her husband's refusal to participate in the management of her home became angered at his failure to support her in managing the children. Indeed, each of the three areas in which the bereaved sample was significantly more likely to report having had marital disputes has to do with feelings of insufficient emotional support: that the spouse was not around enough, was not loyal enough, and was not helpful in dealing with the children.

Not all widows and widowers, however, reported areas of conflict. While some reported more areas of conflict than did any of our comparison husbands and wives, others reported no areas of conflict or only one. (Eight widows and widowers reported four or more areas of conflict, twenty-one reported exactly three, sixteen reported exactly two, while twenty-three widows or widowers reported either only one area of conflict or none at all.)

## Marital Conflict and the Reaction to Bereavement

We divided our widows and widowers into a Low Reported Conflict Group of twenty-three, who reported either no areas of conflict or only one, and a High Reported Conflict Group of forty-five, who reported two or more. Virtually all the marriages that were described in the interview materials as marked by contentment and amity fell in the first group. The second includes virtually all the marriages that were described in the interview materials as having been quarrelsome and contentious. In general, the number of areas of dispute seems to correspond reasonably well to the quality of the marriage as this might be inferred from our interviews with the widows or widowers.

## THE EARLY REACTION

Differences between these two groups in expression of grief at the time of the first interview were statistically significant ($p < .05$); a substantial proportion (twenty of forty-five) of the respondents who reported conflicts in their marriages were said by the interviewers to display little or no emotional distress, compared with only a few (four of twenty-three) of those reporting less conflict. Differences were even more highly significant six weeks after the bereavement; at that point, those who had reported extensive conflict in their marriages seemed to be much less affected by their loss than other widows and widowers. They were much less likely to report pervasive fearfulness and anxiety, much more likely to be socially active, and much more likely to feel comfortable among others (see table 5.3).

We can consider as an example a widow whose marriage had been quite troubled, although it was far from the most conflict-laden in the sample. When we talked with this widow six weeks after her husband's death, she seemed already to have begun functioning as an unattached person. Describing her marriage, she said that although she and her husband had been very close, they had had many fights. Her husband had been short-tempered and was often irritated by her gregariousness. They had argued, too, about their management of money. She had felt he was irresponsible; he had felt that she was too thrifty.

Both the widow and her husband had known that the husband was ill, following a heart attack he had suffered two years before his death. At one point, after an argument, he had said to her, "You'll be sorry when I'm gone." Repeatedly, when we talked with her, she recalled that comment.

Although depressed and grieving, this widow remained socially quite active. When we talked with her six weeks after her

TABLE 5.3

*Reported Conflict in Marriage and Aspects of Bereavement
Six to Eight Weeks after Loss*

|  | Nature of Marriage | |
|---|---|---|
|  | High Reported Conflict | Low Reported Conflict |
|  | N = 45 | N = 23 |
| Respondent has visited others. | 41 (91%) | 14 (61%) |
| Respondent agrees with statement, "I feel like a fifth wheel in groups." | 7 (16%) | 10 (43%) |
| Respondent agrees with statement, "I don't seem to laugh anymore." | 5 (11%) | 8 (83%) |
| Respondent agrees with statement, "I feel so scared." | 9 (20%) | 11 (48%) |
| Respondent "wants to get away from it all." | 2 ( 4%) | 6 (26%) |

husband's death, she described an evening at what seemed to
have been a dating bar—an outing most atypical within our
sample.

> I went out, not with a man, with my two girl friends, two weeks ago,
> to this place. It was just the three of us sitting at a table. And men
> came over from the bar to talk with us because we were by our-
> selves. But to me they all seemed like complete jerks. They were all
> married, to begin with. Their wives were on vacation or something,
> and they were out for the night. Well, they asked me to dance and
> I did. I didn't feel too badly about that. That was the first time I'd
> been out, and I enjoyed myself.

> I was talking to my girl friend last night. I said, "I bet you think I'm
> terrible, the way I carried on." She said, "I don't think you're terrible
> at all."

105

At another point this widow said:

> If I start feeling sorry for myself I usually get on the phone and call somebody. If I feel really low I can talk with my aunt. She's a character from way back. She's got a wonderful sense of humor. She'll talk for hours on the phone. She'll get me laughing.

Widows whose marriages were relatively low in conflict were, at six weeks, still immersed in grief. Mrs. Goodwin, described in the previous chapter, offers an example; so does Mrs. Burgess, who is considered later in this chapter. But the widow described here, like others whose marriages were high in conflict, seemed at six weeks to be recovering from her loss.


## Marital Conflict and Later Outcome


By the time of our third interview, thirteen months after bereavement, those whose marriages had been low in conflict were likely to have returned to effective functioning. Of the twenty-three widows and widowers whose marriages appeared virtually free of conflict, fourteen (61 percent) reported good outcomes. On the other hand, among the forty-five widows and widowers whose marriages appeared conflict-laden there were only thirteen (29 percent) who displayed good outcomes at that time (see table 5.4).

In the preceding chapter we argued that the extent to which a widow or widower was prepared for loss was a major factor in the course of recovery. When we consider only those who had little forewarning of their loss, the level of conflict in the marriage seems to have had little effect on the quality of recovery; there was about the same small proportion of good outcomes among those who had conflict-laden marriages as among

TABLE 5.4

Recovery from Bereavement, Thirteen Months after Loss,
According to Reported Conflict in Marriage

| | Nature of Marriage | |
| | High Reported Conflict | Low Reported Conflict |
| Appraisal of Outcome | N = 45 | N = 23 |
|---|---|---|
| Good | 13 (29%) | 14 (61%) |
| Intermediate | 13 (29%) | 5 (22%) |
| Bad | 19 (42%) | 4 (17%) |
| | P < .05 | |
| | Chi square test | |

those whose marriages were comparatively free of conflict (see table 5.5). In contrast, among those who had adequate forewarning of their loss, the level of conflict in the marriage seems to have been closely related to the quality of outcome. Those whose marriages had been relatively conflict-free generally seemed to return to effective functioning. Good outcomes were nearly the rule among them and bad outcomes quite absent. On the other hand, despite adequate forewarning, among those whose marriages were conflict-laden bad outcomes were relatively frequent. Indeed, considering just those with adequate forewarning, those whose marriages were extensively conflict-laden were about as likely to have bad outcomes as good outcomes (table 5.5).

Eight respondents in our full sample described marriages in which conflict was pervasive. Of the eleven areas of possible marital dispute, they said that four or more had been areas of conflict in their marriages. Thirteen months after their loss, this group of eight was remarkable for reports of tension, anxiety, and somatic symptomatology. Here is a list of the symptoms and medical treatments they reported:

TABLE 5.5

*Outcomes Among Respondents Differing in Reported Marital Conflicts and Extent of Preparation for Loss*

| Overall Outcome | Brief Forewarning Number of areas of Reported Conflict | | |
|---|---|---|---|
| | Three or more | Two | None or one |
| Good | 1 (10%) | 0 | 1 (17%) |
| Intermediate | 2 (20%) | 2 (28%) | 1 (17%) |
| Bad | 7 (70%) | 5 (82%) | 4 (67%) |
| | | | p not significant |
| | Long Forewarning | | |
| | Three or more | Two | None or one |
| Good | 7 (35%) | 5 (62%) | 13 (76%) |
| Intermediate | 7 (35%) | 2 (25%) | 4 (24%) |
| Bad | 6 (30%) | 1 (12%) | 0 |
| | | | $P < .01$ Chi square test |

*Individual A:* Complained of chest pain and urinary frequency. Neither condition was present before bereavement.

*Individual B:* Anemic, was taking injections of "liver"; complained of tension. Both anemia and tension were present before bereavement.

*Individual C:* Complained of a wide variety of symptoms, many associated with "nerves": feeling hot all over, damp hands, irregular menstruation, difficulty in sleeping, urinary frequency, headache, backache, chest pain, stomach-ache. Phobic in relation to shopping. Was taking tranquilizers, sedatives, alcohol; some indication of incipient alcoholism. Anxiety predated bereavement; other symptoms were much more severe at time of this interview.

*Individual D:* No physical symptoms. However, was taking tranquilizers. Had not taken tranquilizers before bereavement.

*Individual E:* Surgery for benign cysts in both breasts. Insomnia with nightmares. Suffered from headaches. Was taking tranquilizers, alcohol; some indication of incipient alcoholism. Headaches and insomnia had occurred before bereavement; became much more severe after.

*Individual F:* Tonsillectomy during first year of bereavement. Hysterectomy scheduled at time of follow-up (three years after bereavement). Eyes water, lump in throat, itching, loss of hair, dizziness and fainting, trembling and twitching, sweating, insomnia with nightmares, nervous tension. Was taking tranquilizers. Tension existed before bereavement; became much worse after.

*Individual G* (described later in chapter 8 as Mrs. Ryan): Had suffered a psychotic illness during the year following bereavement; under psychiatric treatment as an outpatient. Also suffered from insomnia with nightmares, hives, sick feelings, pains in the back. Symptoms began with bereavement.

*Individual H* (described later in this chapter as Mrs. Collins): Palpitations, sick feelings, difficulty swallowing, lump in throat. Suffered from congested or running nose. Pain in back, face, joints, and muscles; chills; insomnia. Some symptoms were present before bereavement; became much worse after. Other symptoms not present at all before bereavement.

We were able to obtain follow-up interviews with thirty-eight widows and widowers among those who had reported two or more areas of conflict and with twenty-one widows and widowers among those who reported at most one area of conflict. When we saw them in follow-up, two to four years after their bereavement, those who had had forewarning of their loss and whose marriages had been low in conflict seemed with few exceptions to have returned to their pre-bereaved levels of functioning. All were going out with friends or relatives. Only four appeared depressed, and only two were in less than good physical health (see table 5.6). To be sure, about half the group were more anxious than they had been when they were married, but in other respects the group seemed largely to have recovered.

This was not so with those whose marriages had been conflict-laden. Among this group about two out of five displayed

## TABLE 5.6

### Level of Reported Marital Conflict and Assessment at Follow-up Interview, Two to Four Years after Bereavement

| Assessment | High Reported Conflict<br>N = 38 | Low Reported Conflict<br>N = 21 |
|---|---|---|
| **Emotional** | | |
| Appears depressed | 17 (45%) | 4 ( 19%) |
| Exhibits some or great anxiety | 31 (82%) | 11 ( 52%) |
| Exhibits some or great feelings of guilt in relation to loss | 24 (63%) | 7 ( 33%) |
| Yearns for return of deceased spouse | 24 (63%) | 6 ( 29%) |
| **Physical** | | |
| Health is rated by coders as poor or fair | 15 (39%) | 2 ( 10%) |
| **Social** | | |
| Goes out with friends or relatives | 28 (74%) | 21 (100%) |
| Expresses concern regarding functioning in some role (as parent, worker, etc.) | 23 (61%) | 4 ( 19%) |

less than good social recovery and a similar proportion were in less than good physical health. Half the group continued to display guilt or anger, almost half were depressed, and about four out of five were anxious. More remarkable, almost two out of three had now begun to yearn for their husbands or wives!

How can we explain the frequency of failure to recover in the high marital conflict group, together with the surprising emergence of what might be seen as expressions of grief after an

110

earlier comparative absence of expressed grief? It seems to us that the most obvious inference is that a report of a conflict-laden marriage can be taken as an indication of a relationship marked by ambivalence. Marital conflict had produced anger and, perhaps, desire for escape, but coexisting with these feelings were continued attachment to the other and even, perhaps, affection. Anger interfered with grieving, and only with the passage of time did a persisting need for the lost spouse emerge in the form of sadness, anxiety, and yearning.

This superficial explanation for the association of ambivalence and the particular course of bereavement we have described will be developed in more depth later in this chapter.

## Conflicted Grieving

We found that ambivalent marriages often gave rise to relatively little distress during the first few weeks of bereavement, at which time the bereaved were likely to engage in social activities, but that they made for failures to recover marked eventually by severe grief and continued yearning for the dead spouse. Among our respondents, two thirds of those who were in our High Marital Conflict Group indicated continued yearning for the return of their spouses in the follow-up interview held two to four years after their loss.

This conflicted grief syndrome closely resembles delayed grief, a form of pathological reaction often found in psychiatric settings. In this syndrome, a relative absence of overt grief in the early post-bereavement period is followed by a state of generalized anxiety, self-doubt, and distress (see page 12). Delayed grief can be differentiated from the reactions to sudden or unexpected death described in the preceding chapter by the relative lack of "numbness" and "disbelief" in the early reaction. Unlike the suddenly bereaved, widows and widowers experiencing delayed grief found little difficulty in accepting the fact of loss. On the contrary, the death was sometimes experienced as a welcome end to a painful and protracted struggle. Furthermore, later grieving contained strains of guilt and remorse much less often seen in other conditions.

AN EXAMPLE OF CONFLICTED GRIEVING

Let us look at the experience of a widow whose marriage had been conflict-laden. Mrs. Collins was just thirty at the time of her husband's death; she was already the mother of six children, the oldest nine years old, the youngest nine months. She was described by the interviewer as a pleasant, attractive woman. This is how she described her marriage:

> Ours wasn't the best marriage in the world. I guess we had different ideas. We had a lot of differences. Drinking booze. We didn't have an ideal marriage. In all the time when we were married, we didn't really find any real closeness until he got sick. It was like, more or less, you go your way and I'll go mine. You know, we just stayed out of each other's way.
>
> A few times he'd lose all his money at the track. I didn't really complain. I really should have complained a little bit more. I wouldn't open my mouth. He'd come in about one and I'd say, "Do you have any money left?" And he'd say, "No." And I'd say, "Boy." I would never yell at him. I used to think, "Well, it's done. No sense in crying about it." I didn't think he was much of a father or husband. I didn't expect the impossible. I just felt there should have been more than just working, coming home, sleeping, and maybe drinking and playing cards. I wasn't happy with him. I had an empty life. And I don't believe he was happy. I think his life was empty. I think eventually I would have left him, and maybe he wouldn't have been able to take it. I don't know. Maybe things like that happen because, like I said, we had an empty life.

There were other problems. Mr. Collins seemed to prefer the companionship of his friends to his family. He worked hard,

112

but Mrs. Collins felt he was too ungiving to his children. At one point early in their marriage Mrs. Collins had left him.

I think it was about three years after I was married. I had three kids then. And I left him. My leaving him lasted Sunday night through Friday. I went down to my mother's, and Saturday morning my mother says, "The children want to go home. Why don't you go back?" She couldn't stand the kids. It was all right Monday through Friday because she worked all day, and when she'd come home I'd pretty well have the kids taken care of and ready for bed. But come Saturday, she says, "Why don't you go home and you and him try to make a go of it?" She almost threw me out of the door.

It was about seven years after this incident that Mr. Collins began experiencing pain in his right hip. The pain persisted despite the passage of weeks and when, finally, his right side began swelling, he saw a doctor who diagnosed cancer. There followed two years of hospital admissions interrupted by remissions until Mr. Collins's death.

Mrs. Collins felt that it was only in his final illness that her husband became approachable.

When he was sick, we got a closeness that was something that we didn't have before. Sometimes we'd sit for hours and hours, talk, sometimes we'd talk the whole night away. We'd stay up all night. We could tell each other anything and everything, and then we'd understand each other. In all the time when we were married, we didn't really find any closeness until he got sick. When he got sick, we got the kind of marriage I would have liked to have. We did things together—shopped, took the kids to the park. If only it had been that kind of marriage all the time.

Mrs. Collins's recovery from grieving appeared to be swift. In our second interview with her, held six weeks after her husband's death, Mrs. Collins said that she had been giving advice to a friend who had been widowed at almost the same time she had:

113

Two weeks after my husband died, my girl friend's husband died. I hear from her every night. She's a lot more—I'm not saying she's more bereaved than I am—but she finds it harder to accept than I do. She's just one of these people that's never been independent. I said, "It's too bad, but you've got to forget." She said, "I can't forget." But she doesn't know how to write checks and stuff like that. She never had to do it. I handled all the money in this family. Regardless of what it was, I handled it.

About a month after her husband's death, just before our second interview with her, Mrs. Collins went on a tour of Virginia's historical sites. The tour had been long scheduled, but it apparently had not even occurred to Mrs. Collins that she might withdraw from it because of her husband's death. She had been lonesome, but still, she felt, it had been a good experience.

I went on a tour to Virginia. Of course I got lonesome. I never went away without my husband before. We never had separate vacations or anything like that. And just this once I started to get a little depressed. The people that were with me asked, "What's the matter?" I said, "Nothing. I just don't feel good. I'm going to stay home tonight." And, of course, they went out. They just went along and everything was fine and I got over it. And when they came home we all sat up and talked and so they understood what it was, afterward. There were four to a room, and I was in with another widow and her little girl and her sister who was never married. It was a very nice hotel. And we had a wonderful time.

In this six weeks' interview Mrs. Collins described herself as having moments of depression, but apparently not much more. However, when we saw her thirteen months after her husband's death she seemed to be doing much less well than she had been earlier; it was more apparent that she was defending against grief. She said, for example: "I really keep busy, you know, even when I don't have to. I don't unwind. Like, I push myself too much, I think."

She was often irritable, tired, and restless, and she had begun to have bad days when she would feel very depressed. And now she found herself yearning for her husband's return.

> I guess about twice in this past year I really got in a real lonely, real down mood. I mean, so far down that you feel like you just can't get back up. I feel like, "Oh cripes, this is it, I just can't take any more." And I think about my husband, "Even with all your faults, I'll take you back."

This tendency to think of her husband and want him back surprised her. She tried to account for it on the basis of needing his help—"It's selfish, you know—me saying, 'Gee, I wish he were here to help me with this'."

She continued to think of her husband as watching over her. Her sense of linkage to him persisted. "Sometimes I think he's aware of things. But I don't really think he's alive. But, saying prayers at night, I more or less ask him to guide me and help me out."

Mrs. Collins's distress at her husband's loss was the more perplexing to her because it was associated with memories of an unhappy marriage. She knew she was not recovering from her bereavement, yet she could not justify her failure to recover by the marriage having been a happy one.

> My husband said, "Try to remember the good times, though there haven't been too many." There really weren't. But he said, "Try not to think of the bad in me." So I really don't. But I don't want to build up in my mind that he was wonderful. I don't want to think of everything as having been too good, because actually there was nothing really that good. And besides, I don't want to feel like I really lost something great.

> I get these moments of depression, and I really feel sorry for nobody in the world but me. There are times when I feel lonely. But that's something I felt all my life anyway, with my husband or without him. I guess you could say I really didn't have much of a marriage, anyway, really.

115

Mrs. Collins continued to think of her husband, often with anger at him for having abandoned her. The relationship that persisted in Mrs. Collins's feelings was as ambivalent as had been the actual marriage.

> Sometimes I get mad at him. Just for a split second I'll think, "Why did you have to go and die?" It just flashes through my mind, and then I don't think about it too much. You know, it just flashes through my mind. I get mad and I say, "If he was here, I'd slap him."

Mrs. Collins now described herself as severely lacking in confidence. In addition she reported suffering a variety of health problems—headaches, watering eyes, running nose, difficulty in swallowing, chest pain, nausea, indigestion, dizziness, nervousness, feeling hot all over, weakness, tiredness, and difficulty in getting to sleep. Although some of these symptoms had been present before her bereavement, they were now worse. Most of the symptoms are of the kind associated with chronic anxiety and tension.

When we talked with Mrs. Collins three years after her husband's death, she was, if anything, more depressed than she had been before. Instead of depression being an intermittent, momentary experience, it seemed now to have become chronic.

> Halfway down I feel like I wouldn't care if I died tomorrow. And then, deeper down, I feel like I do care. I can't explain it. Like sometimes I try to make the kids be enough for me, and sometimes I feel they're not.

> I'm moody. I mean, one day nothing bothers me, but there are some days when I feel like doing nothing. I'll still do things, but it will take all my energy, just doing little things.

> I sometimes get in a real lousy mood. I think almost everything goes into my mind, like where am I going to go from here? Or, where all this has happened, what's going to happen next? I don't like to feel that, because I don't like to think of the whys and wheres of things.

Mrs. Collins's ability to function autonomously was severely hampered by her conviction that, no matter what she did, it would turn out badly. Her absence of self-confidence was expressed most clearly in relation to driving. She said:

> I always wanted to have a car, especially for the kids, to take them places. And I really felt like I could do it. And then all of a sudden, I felt like I couldn't. I just feel like I can't, and I know that there is no sense in even trying to get a license if you don't have the confidence. I look at all the cars and I think, "What if I hit somebody? What if I crashed? You are not going to drive with six kids in a car. You'd probably smash up and everything, and Goodby Charlie." I feel insecure when I have that mood. Then I feel very unsure of myself, that I can't do anything. I mean, I'm not doing anything right, or anything.

Again and again Mrs. Collins's thoughts returned to her marriage. Its unhappiness and her husband's death seemed connected: "Sometimes I think maybe if we were more happily married this wouldn't have happened. I'm not saying it would have avoided the cancer. But maybe that's what I think."

Yet, despite her repudiation of the value of her marriage, Mrs. Collins continued to perceive her husband as being near at hand: "Well, like last night, when I went to bed, I don't know what it was, maybe it was the snow, but I kept seeing him coming through the courtyard. And he says, 'I'm coming down to pick you up.'"

Separation from her husband by death had not been accompanied by psychological separation, despite Mrs. Collins's wish, before her husband's illness, to achieve such a separation. The failure to recover here assumed a form we believe characteristic of the delayed grief that follows loss of an ambivalent marriage: a persisting sense of connection, but with the same mixed feelings that marked the marriage and, in addition, remorse.

Let us turn, for contrast, to an example of recovery from bereavement where the marriage had been conflict-free.

Mr. and Mrs. Burgess were both in their late twenties and had been married just three years when Mr. Burgess suddenly became seriously ill. Both were members of a religious group that was skeptical of medicine. In consequence Mr. Burgess postponed seeking medical attention. When he did, it became apparent that his kidneys had failed. Dialysis was unsuccessful. After steadily deteriorating, over a period of several weeks, Mr. Burgess died.

The marriage had not been without its quarrels, but they had been brief and soon resolved. It was, from Mrs. Burgess's account, a remarkably happy marriage. Here is what she said when we talked with her three weeks after her husband's death:

> I'll always be grateful for our marriage. I know that we had a lot happier marriage in three years than most people have in their whole life. We were happy the whole three years. Of course we had a few arguments, but we never had any real fights. We were just happy, always planning to do things together, to go on trips, and we were right in the middle of our new home, which was such a big dream of ours. We were very close and worked everything out together. And we discussed everything. I can't even think, now, of the little things we would disagree on.

Mrs. Burgess briefly questioned the religious beliefs that may have contributed to her husband's death, but then returned to her church for solace. The church taught that death was not a finality, but rather a transition. Nevertheless, when we talked with Mrs. Burgess six weeks after her husband's death, her thoughts and feelings were focused on her loss.

> Every once in a while I wish I could tell Dave something. I wish he was here to talk to. Not too long of a time goes by without thinking of him. I don't cry as much as I did at first. Mainly I cry when I hear songs on the radio. Dave's best friend drives me to work, and yester-

day I heard these songs and I started crying. So I noticed, today, he didn't turn the radio on.

Mrs. Burgess did what she could to keep busy. She had her work and her religion, and she was planning an outing with friends. But, unlike Mrs. Collins, she did not fill her life with hectic activities. Her grief was much more apparent. At six weeks after her loss she felt she was making progress, but she was deeply sorrowful.

I try to keep myself busy. I like to sew. And my religion helped me an awful lot. It's really helped me overcome grief to know—well, in our religion, life is eternal—to know that Dave is going on. And I'm so grateful for the time I had him. I can never lose the love that we had together. And I have to go on.

More than many other respondents, Mrs. Burgess was determined to return as soon as she could to her usual life. In good measure this was a teaching of her religious group; insofar as death is only a passing from one spiritual plane to another, it is seen as wrong to grieve too greatly. Mrs. Burgess tried to do things to take her mind off her loss. Nevertheless she had little energy for social engagement. At the six-weeks' point she said:

Other people can't help me overcome my grief. I have to do that myself. But they're helping in any way they can. Most people think I'm doing all right. I've been over my girl friend's for a weekend. And this weekend, Friday night, we're going to see a play. And Sunday we're going to the beach if it's a nice day. When we go out it takes my mind off my husband—until I see couples. And then I think about him.

I do find it hard to call people. Of the two of us, my husband and me, I think he was the more outgoing. But I'm not, myself.

When we returned for our third interview with Mrs. Burgess, thirteen months after her loss, we found her well along the road to recovery. She told us that she no longer carried the sense of enormous loss that had earlier burdened her. She said, "I feel grateful I had Dave, and I think of him as someone I'll always love. I think of him with gratitude that I had him as long as I did."

We saw Mrs. Burgess a fourth time three years after her husband's death. She was planning remarriage. Yet, even as she looked forward to her new marriage, she said of her first husband, "I just feel his love, and that will never die. It's with me all the time." Her recovery had been aided, we feel, by her memory of a marriage for which she could be grateful, for the confidence it had given her in her ability to give love to another, and in her own worthiness to be loved: "We had a very happy marriage. Very happy, and I'll always be grateful for it. Every time I think of him, I think of him with loving thoughts. I just hope my next marriage will be as happy as my first one was."

Neither Mrs. Burgess nor Mrs. Collins put her marriage entirely behind her. But whereas Mrs. Burgess could be sustained by memories of a happy marriage, Mrs. Collins could not surmount her memories of disappointment and anger. Mrs. Burgess's memories were a source of solace and strength, while those of Mrs. Collins contributed further to her distress and caused her to be wary of new commitments.

## The Syndrome of Conflicted Grief

To summarize the materials presented in this chapter, we have found that those widows and widowers who experienced a conflicted grief syndrome seemed at first not nearly so devastated by their loss as those whose marriages had been more conflict-free. They seemed less overwhelmed by grief and more capable of active social participation. But as time went on they seemed more frequently to be stuck in the grieving process, still unaccepting of their loss, self-reproachful and yearning for the return of the spouse.

Several possible explanations can be offered for the problematic nature of recovery from bereavement for a conflict-laden marriage, with some evidence for each. Freud, in *Mourning and Melancholia,* proposed that psychiatric depression ("melancholia") might be caused by the real or symbolic loss of a person who was ambivalently loved. His idea, as we noted earlier, was that in melancholia the lost figure has somehow been incorporated within the mourner. The mourner, once having done this, can persecute and punish the lost figure without risk of retaliation by punishing himself or herself. Why should the mourner fear retaliation from someone irrevocably lost? Only because the loss is not real within the mourner's unconscious. In the mourner's unconscious the lost person still exists, accessible to complaints, accusations, and demonstrations of the consequences for the mourner of having been abandoned.

On first consideration this ingenious theory seems to fit the evidence of our own and other studies. Ambivalence does seem to predispose to atypical grief. Furthermore, as is so evident in the comments of Mrs. Collins, that grief is frequently associated with persisting feelings of self-reproach. Finally, bereaved people, both those whose feelings are ambivalent and those whose feelings are not, sometimes do seem to identify themselves with the person who has died.

But there is something glib about the thesis. How can one person be said to incorporate and contain another? Are the self-reproaches of bereaved people really more appropriately directed against the dead? Our own data leave us in some doubt. When Mrs. Collins assailed herself for wanting her husband back, she was angry at her own failure to achieve autonomy, not any trait of her husband's she had taken into herself.

Still, there is another way of viewing incorporation that should be considered. Those to whom we have established attachments may not stop affecting us when we are no longer in touch with them. They may continue to engage us as partners in our interior dialogues, where they may persist as sustaining or as critical figures. Those in our internal community who are seen as loving to us may be easily accepted, easily made a part of our own thinking and feeling. But those who are seen as hostile, who seem to use the privileged position of membership in our internal world to criticize our motives and disparage our worth, require our constant defense. We may find ourselves continually confronted by them.

Freud pointed out the danger of "death wishes." In a marriage characterized by ambivalence, one partner may in desperation wish the other dead and out of the way. When this wish comes true, it is almost as if it were the wish that had brought about the death. The survivor feels like a murderer and may bitterly reproach himself or herself. He or she may feel without the right to happiness since any happiness could be seen as having been obtained at the cost of the other person's life. Continuing grief may also serve as a means of restitution. The reasoning here seems to be: "Since I did not love him enough when he was alive, I will make it up to him now by grieving for him forever."

Common sense suggests still other explanations for the phenomenon of pathological guilt after ambivalent marriage. To begin with, ambivalent marriages leave many causes for regret and self-reproach. As long as the marriage continues, there is hope that things might get better, but once a person is dead it is too late to say, "I'm sorry." The survivor mourns not only for the marriage that was, but also for the marriage that could have been, and was not.

There is some support in our materials for this view. We see the difference between Mrs. Burgess's feelings of gratitude for her husband's love and Mrs. Collins's feelings of regret for a disappointing relationship now forever beyond remedy. Mrs. Collins's distress stemmed not so much from having incorporated aspects of a husband toward whom she felt ambivalent—

as Freud's theory would have led us to anticipate—but rather from awareness that the relationship for which she grieved had never been what she wanted. Nor could she comfort herself with the memory of the closeness she and her husband had achieved during his final illness. Instead, that closeness, valuable as it was, made even more evident the emptiness of the marriage that had preceded it.

It is not unusual for those whose marriages were good to take solace in that fact. For example, one of the widows in our sample, a woman twenty-four years old, had lost her thirty-six-year-old husband three months after a brain tumor had been diagnosed. The marriage had been a good one, although her husband had earned rather little. At the thirteen-month point the widow said:

> I feel so bad and everything that he did die, but at least we were happy and we got along. I think I'd feel worse if we didn't get along, and it would bother me, and I'd be saying, well, I should have done this and I should have done that. But at least we did get along good, so that seems to make me feel much better. I don't know why, I just feel better.

INSECURE ATTACHMENT

With some hesitancy we propose as still another possible explanation for the association of poor outcome with conflict-laden marriages that, in the cases of some of our widows and widowers, pervasive problems in relationships with others underlie each. We do not mean to say that personality difficulties of husbands or wives are generally responsible for marital conflict. We are aware of too many instances of people who did badly in first marriages and are doing well in remarriages—and whose spouses are also doing well—for us to propose such a rule. Rather, we want to include as one among several possible explanations for the troubled course of grief after the ending of an ambivalent marriage an explanation that directs attention to the personalities of the individuals involved. In particular, we propose that some among those who form and remain in troubled marriages are individuals who, because of earlier experiences in their lives, have difficulty establishing more satisfactory attachments and, furthermore, that these same earlier experiences make them less capable than others of successfully recovering from loss.

Some of our respondents whose marriages had been conflict-laden did appear to have had difficulty in other adult relationships. One of the widows had been divorced by a previous husband on the grounds that one of the children of their marriage was not actually his. A widower whose marriage had been tumultuous had also been fired from two jobs for fighting. Conflict in marriage can be one expression of inability to trust others or of anger toward others.

Bowlby (1969) and Ainsworth and Wittig (1969) have proposed that a secure early relationship with parents provides a foundation for satisfying attachments in later life. Children who, for whatever reason, have not known the consistent presence of a caring and secure parent may be at some special risk of feeling inadequate and insecure as adults in all their close relationships.

Mrs. Collins can herself serve as an example of someone whose life was beset by insecure attachments. As a child, Mrs. Collins had never felt loved. Her father, who was in the army and so seldom home, died when she was in first grade. Her mother never showed much affection. Her mother married a second time, but Mrs. Collins did not enjoy a good relationship with her stepfather or her step-siblings. She grew up with little confidence in herself or trust in others. "I was always lonely," she told us.

Mrs. Collins felt that her insecurity led to an almost desperate need for reassurance: "When I have that mood, then I feel very unsure of myself or that I can't do nothing. Then I want somebody to tell me, 'You're great,' or something."

She described her quick commitment to her future husband,

when both were still very young, as having been driven by insecurity. She was not much more than eighteen when they met. They married within a year. "I think most of us look for love, especially when you don't get it. When you haven't had it, you kind of go overboard when you finally get it. And you think that you've got to grab it quick or else it's not going to last too long."

In her desperate need for affection she had chosen a partner who seems to have been incapable of giving her the security she craved. There was a child very soon and then another. Mrs. Collins discovered that her husband could not be called on for help, no matter how near she was to exhaustion:

> Like when my daughter became ill and needed to go to the hospital, I was so very, very tired. I couldn't even talk straight. I felt like everything was pressing down on me. I couldn't walk, I couldn't do anything. And when I brought her back from the hospital, I was making supper, and he said he was going to the track, and I said, "Oh, don't leave me now!" And I almost started to cry. And he said, "What's the matter?" And I said, "Oh, go ahead." And he goes....
>
> I honestly didn't believe he loved me or the kids; he didn't care about us one way or the other.

Perhaps Mr. Collins stayed away from his home because he did not think he could cope with the problems within it. But Mrs. Collins could find no better ally elsewhere. On the one occasion when she sought to return to her mother, her mother forced her back to her husband.

Mrs. Collins gave the appearance of being self-reliant. She had learned at an early age that she could count on no one but herself. But under the surface she felt terribly alone and yearned for the caring she had missed as a child. "I miss having someone to comfort me. Sometimes I feel like I'd like to be comforted like the kids do. Sometimes, I think that's foolish. I tell myself to grow up or something. But I think that's mostly what I miss."

Mrs. Collins's story suggests the stress that can be imposed on marriage by a hunger for caring attention, combined with disbelief in its existence. Such feelings, and the low self-esteem that accompany them, can make for acceptance of unpromising marriages and for hopeless misunderstanding as the marriage proceeds. "Just last night I was thinking about him and I was just thinking that I wish we were both more mature and grown-up, because I think as much as I was immature, I think he was."

When a troubled marriage ends, by death or by separation, such feelings make for difficulty in returning to effective functioning. After her husband's death, Mrs. Collins lacked the confidence in herself she would have needed even to consider making new ties:

> I feel so unsure of the future. Can I actually raise the children by myself and take care of them by myself? My sister says to me, she says, "I don't think you'd ever have trouble getting remarried if you wanted to," and I say, "Well, I have six children. It seems to me men don't really have the patience to cope with a bunch of kids." And I say to myself, "They would have to be some kind of nut." I think about what if I do get married again and what if I don't. Both of them scare me. . . .

> Nobody's going to help me, you know. And then I say, "Well, who could I ask?" And I don't really think about it. I just more or less accept it. I just want someone to like me for myself, and I probably don't want to give nothing to that someone.

In our final interview with Mrs. Collins there was some indication that she was about to make the same mistakes all over again. She told us that she had started going out with one of her husband's cousins, a man she had known for years. Like her husband this man was a gambler. She was skeptical of his ability to give her the security that she so badly needed, and yet she felt compelled to cling to him. It was as though she were compelled to repeat the same sequence of events she had undergone with her first husband. In a forlorn bid for happiness, she clung to another person who she expected would let her down and, in so doing, confirmed yet again her view of herself as unworthy of better. "If I'm happy I'm going to pay for it the next day, because it seems like if I'm really happy one minute, the next minute I'm crying."

MARRIAGE AS A LEARNING SITUATION

Finally, in our survey of possible causes of the association between conflict-laden marriages and failure to recover from bereavement, we must consider the effects on the widow or widower of years of unhappy marriage. Just as a well-functioning marriage can foster growth through the adult years, an unsatisfactory marriage can confirm and reinforce lack of trust in oneself and others. Those who have observed themselves tolerate years of unhappiness without being in any way able to improve their situations may, as a result, experience diminished self-esteem and self-confidence. This, in turn, might impede a return to effective functioning.

IN CONCLUSION

All the explanations we have offered for the association between marital conflict and accompanying ambivalence on the one hand and problems in recovery on the other can find support somewhere in our data. There are, to be sure, a few cases in which a marriage that seemed unsatisfactory was followed by what appeared to be relatively shallow grieving and this, in turn, was followed by what appeared to be a perfectly satisfactory recovery. These cases remind us that ambivalence and hostility are not one and the same thing. Ambivalence implies a mixture of love and hate: an attachment is present, however insecure it may be. There were a few widows and widowers in our sample whose attachment to their spouses had become so attenuated that they were hardly attached at all. Their feelings toward that person were not ambivalent; rather, they seemed to have withdrawn investment from the unsatisfactory marriage even as the marriage continued. By the time the husband or wife died, the marriage no longer meant what marriages usually do. One widow of an alcoholic man who was often away on binges had learned to be relatively indifferent to his absence. She also felt that the man had long before stopped functioning as her husband. To the extent that there was a difference in her life, his death made it easier, although she did note that she missed being able now and again to talk with him about their children. She felt little reason for remorse; she grieved only briefly and recovered quickly.

# Chapter 6

# *Chronic Grief*

Four days after the death of her husband, Prince Albert, Queen Victoria wrote:

> How am I alive after witnessing what I have done? Oh! I who prayed that we might die together and I never survive Him! I who felt in those blessed Arms clasped and held tight in the sacred Hours at night—when the world seemed only to be ourselves that nothing could part us! I felt so very secure. . . . I never dreamed of the physical possibility of such a calamity—such an awful catastrophe—for me—for All. [Elizabeth Longford 1964, p. 307]

Queen Victoria's grief has become famous. In 1887, twenty-five years after her husband's death, she wrote, in an open letter to her people:

> The enthusiastic reception I met with . . . on the occasion of my Jubilee, has touched me most deeply. It has shown that the labor and anxiety of fifty long years—twenty-two of which I spent in unclouded happiness, shared and cheered by my beloved husband, while an equal number were full of sorrow and trial, borne without his sheltering and wise help—has been appreciated. [*Daily Telegraph*, June 27, 1887]

Royal grief demanded royal mourning. There was something larger than life in the extraordinary lengths to which Victoria went to ensure that the memory of her husband was kept alive. She gave orders, which held good until the day of her death, that a photograph of the corpse of Albert lying on his deathbed, surmounted by an evergreen wreath, should be hung a foot above the unoccupied side of every bed in which she would sleep. She also ordered that a servant place nightly a clean nightshirt on her husband's side of the bed and a can of hot water in his basin. Nor was anything in the prince's rooms to be moved from its position on the night the prince died (Tisdall 1952). She had statues of the prince and memorials to him erected in all parts of England, still to be seen today. Sir Theodore Martin was commissioned to write a deferential biography.

But while Victora believed that her "great love" for Albert justified an equally "great grief," her subjects were unconvinced. Before long she had become convicted in the public mind of "morbid melancholy." She was persistently criticized for withdrawing from public life. Doubts were expressed for her sanity. It was many years before the British national consciousness integrated her enduring mourning with her other roles into an image of "the Widow of Windsor," and the criticism of her ended.

We, too, like Queen Victoria's subjects, would have characterized as unhealthy the course taken by her response to her bereavement. We would have seen something amiss in unremitting grief continuing year after year and in the unrelenting investment of energy and money in services and monuments to the memory of her dead spouse. Although the term "bad outcome" would rob Victoria of her royal dimension, clearly after her husband's death she remained, to a degree, damaged. Indeed, Queen Victoria can be taken as an exemplar of the most common form of poor outcome seen in psychiatric practice: chronic grief. Furthermore, the findings of the Harvard Bereavement Study might have caused us to anticipate that she would fail to recover from bereavement in this way.

## Yearning and Chronic Grief

We found that a number of indicators of emotional distress recorded at our first two interviews correlated significantly with outcome scores a year later. Some of these features suggested that the individual distrusted his or her ability to manage alone. These included overall anxiety and fear of nervous breakdown. Another such feature was simply the report of great problems in managing alone. Each of these predictors was associated with yearning for the deceased and preoccupation with thoughts about him or her. When these reactions occurred in conjunction with feelings of helplessness and indecisiveness, they sometimes persisted for several years. The syndrome of low self-confidence, yearning for the deceased, and feelings of helplessness thus provides an early indicator of a mourning process whose outcome is doubtful. When this syndrome, and especially the component of yearning for the deceased, does in fact continue for a long period of time—as was the case with Queen Victoria—the resulting condition can be characterized as chronic grief.

Our coders rated "yearning for the deceased" in their assessment of the very first interview, three weeks after bereavement. We subdivided the sample into a High Yearning Group, comprising those respondents who appeared to yearn "constantly," "frequently," or "whenever inactive," and a Low Yearning Group who yearned "never," "seldom," or "only when reminded of the loss." It is important to note that about two thirds of our respondents, forty-five in all, fell into the High Yearning Group and only about one third, twenty-three, into the Low Yearning Group; high yearning was by far the more frequent response. We found that high yearning correlated inversely ($r - 0.32$) with our outcome score at thirteen months after bereavement; high yearning correlated with poor outcome

131

(p < .01) and was still significantly associated with poor outcome at final follow-up two to four years later (p < .05).

This last finding may come as a surprise to those who see pathological grief as an inevitable consequence of the repression or avoidance of grief. After all, yearning can be regarded as intrinsic to grief, and if so we would expect that its absence rather than its presence should be a predictor of problems to come.

But our data tell a more complex story. Severe grief at the first interview was often, although not always, a sign that grief would still be severe at the third and fourth interviews. It is true that where the preceding marriage was ambivalent we tended to see delayed grief and subsequent problems in recovery. It is also the case that where the death came without forewarning we saw persisting shock and disbelief, together with an upsurge of anxiety, in a sort of impacted grief, again with subsequent problems in recovery. The second, however, is not incompatible with high yearning early in bereavement (as was displayed by Mrs. Elliott, described in chapter 4). Further, among those who were in neither the Brief Forewarning Group nor the High Marital Conflict Group, many displayed high yearning, and some of these widows and widowers also had subsequent problems in recovery.

### DEPENDENCY AND YEARNING

Severe grief, one component of which is intense yearning for the lost spouse, may serve well as an indicator of a grief process whose outcome is chronic grief, but it is only a link in the chain of causation. Something else must give rise to the yearning. It appears to us that the "something else" is most often the situation of having been highly dependent on the spouse.

We found a very strong association between the intensity of yearning at the first interview and our coders' assessments of the extent to which the respondent had been dependent on the dead person. Over four fifths of those rated as highly dependent were also rated high on yearning, whereas this was the case with only one of the eight rated as low in dependence (see table 6.1).

It appears to us that dependence on the lost spouse may lead to intractable grieving, of which high yearning a few weeks after bereavement is an early indication. We cannot be entirely confident of this because we must rely on retrospective information for our assessments of dependency, and it seems possible that those suffering from chronic grief may have concluded from this that they had been dependent whether they were in fact more dependent than average or not. Yet our case material convinces us that our former conclusion is correct. We give two examples in this chapter.

THE NATURE OF DEPENDENCY

Before considering these examples, let us stop to consider what might be meant by the term "dependency." "Dependency" is, in many ways, an unsatisfactory and ambiguous term. It can be taken to mean any situation in which one person relies on another to perform physical functions; thus an amputee can be described as "dependent" on his wife for functions that formerly he would have performed for himself. Or it can

TABLE 6.1
*Intensity of Yearning and Dependency*

|  | High Yearning N=45 | Low Yearning N=23 |
|---|---|---|
| Coders' Judgment of Relationship with Spouse |  |  |
| Highly dependent | 32 (84%) | 6 (16%) |
| Intermediate in dependency | 10 (50%) | 10 (50%) |
| Autonomous or otherwise not dependent | 1 (12%) | 7 (88%) |

be used to describe any situation in which one person seeks reassurance and comfort from another, as in the case of the frightened child who clings in a dependent way to the mother. Or, as in the case of Queen Victoria, it can be used to describe intolerance of separation from another person (this was the case even during Prince Albert's life).

We tend to think of "dependence" as being an attribute of a person. But in fact at least two persons and a situation are necessary—a person who is seen as "strong" or "able to cope," a person who is seen as "weak" or "not able to cope," and a situation in which coping is expected. Queen Victoria had been brought up to expect a very high standard of herself and others around her at a time when monarchs had a great deal more power and responsibility than they have today. She was helped to achieve this by her husband who had very similar ideals. But even before Albert's death the two of them were finding it very hard to maintain the standard that they had set for themselves.

To some extent their compulsive "goodness" was a reaction against what they saw as the licentiousness and neglect of duty of the monarchs who had preceded Victoria, and they attempted to set a standard that would be continued in their own children, several of whom were to become crowned heads of Europe. Victoria blamed Albert's last illness on her son, Prince Edward (later King Edward VII), whose behavior with a dancer had caused great distress to his parents. It was while returning from a visit to Edward in which Albert had remonstrated with the boy that the first symptoms of his illness came on.

In the circumstances it is hardly surprising that Victoria could no longer face her responsibilities when Albert died. The sheer magnitude of her task was such that she could not possibly undertake it. Nor could she give it up to her son, the one person entitled to succeed her. Instead she clung to the role of mourner which provided her with some sanction for withdrawing from public life, and it was many years before one of her prime

134

ministers (Disraeli) was able to redefine her role and coax her
to take a more active part again.

Clearly Victoria's "dependence" on Albert was at least in part
a consequence of the situation in which she found herself. In
another role she might have been anything but "dependent."
Similarly there are other people whose "dependence" reflects
the need of their partner to dominate the relationship rather
than their own need to be dominated. To make things yet more
complicated we sometimes find an interlocking of dominant
and dependent needs such that sometimes one and sometimes
the other partner is seen as competent to cope and look after the
other.

What we have in mind by the term "dependency" is the
inability to function adequately in the roles of ordinary life
without the presence, emotional support, or actual help of the
partner. Examples of dependency include a widow who had
been deeply depressed before her marriage, whose husband's
presence helped fend off depression, and a widower, very successful in his work, who had relied on his wife to manage
almost every detail of his life away from the office. (The story
of the widower is reported in the next chapter as an instance of
pathological grief in which brief forewarning was combined as
a risk factor with great dependency.)

INSECURE ATTACHMENT AND DEPENDENCY

Because none of our respondents was in a situation demanding unusually high levels of functioning, the sources of their
dependency might reasonably be sought within the histories of
the respondents themselves. Our data seem to us to provide
support for Bowlby's notion that emotional dependence is a
form of insecure attachment and that the tendency to form
insecure attachments is usually determined in childhood
(Bowlby 1969).

We know from the work of Mary Ainsworth and her colleagues that children form different kinds of attachments to

parents. Children who are securely attached to their parents turn to them for protection and reassurance when they suspect that they may be in danger—when, for example, a strange person is approaching them. At other times these children feel free to play and to explore. But other children, less trusting of their parents' continued accessibility or feeling the world to be at all times a threatening place, become anxious whenever they are separated from their parents. This causes them to cling all the more tightly to them. Their playing and exploring are then severely restricted by their need to have their parents close. The parent's freedom, of course, is also burdened by their exceptionally needful children (Ainsworth and Wittig 1969).

It is a likely supposition that the view of themselves and of others which individuals develop in interaction with their parents tends to be continued into the interactions and attachments of their adult lives. In our case, where we had sufficient material to make the judgment, it appeared that there was a connection between respondents' early experiences, their later marital relationships, and, often, the impact on them of bereavement. In the preceding chapter we described the case of Mrs. Collins, whose ambivalent attachment as a child to a rejecting parent, together with the loss by death of the other parent, was followed, years later, by a precipitous and unwise marital choice, a thoroughly unsatisfactory marriage, and, after bereavement, delayed grief and failure to recover. Of enormous importance in Mrs. Collins's history, we felt, was that her attachment relationships repeated the particular constellation of feelings established in her earliest attachments to her parents: she expected little, she felt herself greatly needful, and she swung between acting almost blindly out of need and disclaiming any need whatsoever. She was sure, after all, that no good could come from others anyway.

Some respondents who yearned intensely for the return of their spouses did not seem to have been dependent on their spouses for their own functioning. Other respondents who reported high yearning, however, seemed to have expressed in their marriages an unambivalent and quite constant reliance on the spouse for support in, for example, coping with the ordinary level of social risk involved in meeting new people.

Virtually all husbands and wives are attached to their spouses in the sense of relying on the spouse's presence to sustain their feelings of security. One component of grief, shared by virtually all our respondents, was the anxiety that is a consequence of losing the spouse's presence as a security-fostering attachment figure. (Of course, grief involves much more than this, just as love involves much more than attachment feelings.) It is the husbands and wives who were attached in the special sense of becoming extremely anxious when without the spouse's presence, even to the point of being reluctant to leave their homes by themselves, that we think of as emotionally dependent.

These respondents, we believe, had learned in their childhoods to see their worlds as dangerous and potentially hostile and to see themselves as barely capable of ensuring the continued protection of caring parents. They had learned that they could rely on those pledged to them only if they were eternally vigilant to forestall separation. They tended to react to all forms of separation by intense anger and distress, together with a fearful holding on to the attachment figure. An outlook of this sort may be fostered by parents who are themselves overanxious and who also encourage the fearfulness of their children by disparaging their children's efforts at mastery and by emphasizing the dangers of the world.

As table 6.1 indicates, those among the bereaved who yearned intensely for the return of the lost spouse were also usually characterized by the coders as having been dependent on the spouse. These were respondents who seemed to need their spouses' support to maintain their own functioning. Some had relied on their spouses to deal with essential areas of their lives in which they felt themselves to be incompetent; others had relied on their spouses to provide them with feelings of security. Some respondents, however, displayed high levels of yearning but did not indicate unusual need for their spouses' contributions for support. Rather they had had marriages of unusual closeness and sharing, and they now greatly missed their partners' companionship. Each of these kinds of marital relationships was associated with intense yearning for the spouse's return, but their implications for recovery seemed different. It seemed especially the marriage associated with yearning *and* dependency that gave rise to chronic grief.

The respondent who provides our first example, Mrs. Webley, had parents who seemed to have fostered anxious attachment in her. Her parents supervised her closely right up to the time of her marriage and made her feel that if she relied on herself she would surely go astray. She said, "Before I was married, my mother and father told me what was right and what was wrong." Naturally enough, Mrs. Webley chose as a spouse a man who could play the role her parents had played. As Mrs. Webley put it, "After I was married it was him; he told me what to wear and what not to wear and where to go."

### MRS. WEBLEY: AN EXAMPLE OF A DEPENDENT RELATIONSHIP

Mrs. Webley was a woman in her early thirties, the mother of a nine-year-old daughter. She described herself, in our first interview with her, as both indecisive and painfully shy. She had been married for twelve years to a man whom she had known to be a diabetic at the time they married. Indeed, she had been attracted to him partly because of his need for the kind of help she felt able to provide:

> I've always wanted to be a nurse. My mother was a practical nurse. I'm drawn to sick people, and the sick come to see me. Like, if any of the kids around here get hurt, they yell for me. I was closer to my husband because he was sick. He always needed me. And I was usually there when he needed me.

138

Her husband's need for Mrs. Webley's support helped to balance her own dependence on him. She may have felt freer to rely on him—more able to trust him—because she so clearly was relied on in turn. Despite her husband's illness, he had been the source of emotional strength in Mrs. Webley's marriage. When she had been without her husband's reassuring presence, Mrs. Webley had felt fearful, almost paralyzed:

> I depended on him for telling me what to do and doing things for me, because I'm afraid of people. I never liked to go shopping, because there were too many people around. He always did the shopping. I was always afraid of people, all my life. That's why, I think, I quit school, because in the last two years of school, in discussion and debates, I used to get up in front of people and I couldn't talk.

Mr. Webley's death was not entirely unexpected. His diabetic condition had gotten more and more difficult to control over the years. But it was only when he was hospitalized, two months before his death, that it became evident that he would not live long. Mrs. Webley's actual preparation for her husband's death was relatively brief.

In the weeks after her husband's death, Mrs. Webley found it difficult to manage even the routine chores of life. She dreaded going shopping. When she did shop she became acutely anxious because she felt that people in the supermarket were aware of her, watching her. But being alone was almost equally painful; then she became so tense and anxious she could hardly bear it: "I feel like I'm ready to scream. Especially if I'm alone. Like, sometimes at night—I'm sitting here—I just feel like I'm ready to scream."

To keep herself functioning, Mrs. Webley hit on the device of summoning her husband's memory. The feeling that he was nearby, accessible to her, was deeply reassuring. Even when she did not consult him directly, she could ask herself what he would have wanted her to do. She said, six weeks after her husband's death:

> If I'm going to do something, I'll stop and think, would he do it? Would he want me to do it this way? Or would he want me to do it somehow else? Like, last night, there was a dress that I thought of for my daughter. And I said, "Well, I'm a little short. Maybe he wouldn't want me to get it for her, since we are a little bit short of money."

Mrs. Webley's yearning for her husband's return was intense. She encouraged her daughter to join her in the feeling that her husband had not disappeared from their lives: "I try to teach my daughter that the brightest star up in Heaven, that's your daddy watching you. And if you find a brighter star, *that's* your daddy watching you."

When we saw Mrs. Webley at the end of the first year of her bereavement, she appeared depressed and apathetic. She had started work to keep her mind occupied, but while it was of some help, it was not enough.

> I don't feel like working any more. I go in because I force myself to go in, but I just don't feel like working. I force myself because I have to, I have to work. But I just don't feel like doing it any more. I just sit around and watch television, that's all—which I've never done before. It's like you're lost. You're in a lost world, and there's nobody to do anything for.

Despite the passage of the year, her husband was constantly in Mrs. Webley's thoughts. In the days immediately after her husband's death, she had been unable to believe that he had really died. Now she accepted that the death had really occurred, but her sense of loss seemed insurmountable.

> I have got myself knowing now that he's gone, that there's no one going to bring him back to me. But I do miss him terribly. I'm still

involved with him too much. I can't explain it. I keep saying, "Why did you have to go? Why can't you be here to help me? Which way am I supposed to go?"

After a year of being on her own, Mrs. Webley was struggling to find an independent base. She now regretted having relied so heavily on her husband's direction. She saw herself beginning to make small changes—for example, permitting her daughter to wear slacks:

> I think I will always depend on his decisions, the decisions he made before. But a lot of them I try not to do like he did, like slacks for my daughter. I know darn well that he would never like her to have them, but I'm letting her have them.

At this thirteen-months' point, Mrs. Webley's reliance on her husband's memory continued, as did her yearning for his return. In her conversation with us, a momentary appreciation for the gratifications of being able to do what she wanted was immediately followed by a description of her continued subservience—now, to be sure, a bit reluctant—to what she believed to be her husband's wishes. While she displayed some movement toward recovery, in truth it was limited.

> This way, here, I can come and go. It's freedom. But anything that comes up that I have to do about the house, I'll always think if he would want it that way, would he give me the okay to go ahead? I think back to see how he thinks. Some of the decisions I'll overrule. Still, a lot of decisions I'll say, "Well, he wouldn't want me to do it, so I won't do it." Some days I'll get mad and I'll do it anyhow. I know the decisions are wrong, but I'm trying to learn how to do it myself.

We saw Mrs. Webley again three years after her husband's death, two years after the interview in which she made the comments quoted above. Much had happened in her life. She had begun seeing another man, had become pregnant by him, and had given birth to a second daughter. She hoped the man she was seeing would marry her, but said that he had so far refused. Nevertheless, because of this new relationship, Mrs. Webley was no longer lonely. She still at times thought of her husband, but she no longer did so constantly, nor did she still feel that his values and principles directed her life.

Because Mrs. Webley needed someone to provide her with support and direction, she foundered badly after her husband's death. Her recovery was contingent not on the passage of time, during which the processes of healing might occur, but rather on the entrance into her life of someone who would play the role her husband had played. The man with whom she became involved, although less satisfactory as a source of support than her husband had been, seemed to provide enough reassurance to make it possible for her to function. With his presence in her life, Mrs. Webley seemed largely to have recovered from her loss.

# Correlates of Intense Early Yearning in the Reaction to Bereavement

We have noted that while yearning for the lost partner is a quite typical expression of grief in the first few weeks, reported by about two thirds of our respondents, intense yearning associated with a history of dependency in the marriage is an early indicator of what may become chronic grief. It is of value to consider further the concomitants of this intense early yearning.

## THE EARLY REACTION

Feelings of insecurity were reflected in the immediate reactions to loss among about half of the High Yearning Group.

Striking is the perplexity expressed in the question, "What will I do now?"—a question said by more than half the high yearners to match their feelings (and by only three of the twenty-three low yearners). Three fifths of the high yearners reported inability to concentrate (this was reported by only one of the low yearners). Doubts of their own mental health were expressed by about one in four of the high yearners through agreement with the statement, "I'm worried I might have a nervous breakdown," (none of the low yearners agreed with this statement). Similarly, about a third of the high yearners (compared with only one of the low yearners) agreed that sometimes they wished "someone would just take over." (See table 6.2).

TABLE 6.2

*Concomitants of Intense Yearning for Spouse's Return Three Weeks after Loss*

| | Intensity of Yearning | |
| | High Yearning | Low Yearning |
| Statement | N=43 | N=23 |
|---|---|---|
| What will I do now? | 24 (56%) | 3 (13%) |
| I can't concentrate. | 26 (60%) | 1 ( 4%) |
| I'm worried I might have a nervous breakdown. | 10 (23%) | 0 |
| Sometimes I wish someone would just take over. | 13 (30%) | 1 ( 4%) |
| I feel empty. | 36 (84%) | 13 (57%) |
| I'm so lonely. | 33 (77%) | 10 (43%) |
| I don't care how I look. | 8 (19%) | 0 |
| Why did this happen to him/her? | 27 (63%) | 7 (30%) |
| My husband/wife knows and sees everything I do. | 19 (44%) | 5 (32%) |
| It's not real. | 16 (37%) | 3 (13%) |

Both high and low yearners commonly expressed feelings of emptiness and loneliness, but these feelings were expressed by all but a few among the high yearners and by only about half the low yearners. All eight of the respondents who agreed, "I don't care how I look," were among high yearners. It may be that no longer caring about how one looks expresses a sense of alienation from others.

Like the Brief Forewarning Group described in chapter 4, some of the high yearners also had difficulty in accepting the reality of the loss. About a third of the high yearners agreed with the statement, "It's not real," whereas this was agreed to by only three of the twenty-three low yearners. The high yearners were twice as likely to state that the dead person still saw everything that they did (44 percent and 22 percent). This last assertion seems to express, if not actually a need to turn toward the dead person as a source of support, at least a sense of being under that person's surveillance. It is what we would expect in a group of people who have relied heavily on the partner to sustain their own functioning.

THE LATER REACTION

In subsequent weeks most of the features which distinguished the High Yearning Group at the first interview began to diminish, and the differences from other groups became less striking. By the six-to-eight week interview, while there remained differences in yearning, other differences had faded. However, at the thirteenth-month interview, yearning was still pronounced among most of those who had been high yearners at the first interview, and two thirds reported that they still thought of the dead person a lot, every day, always, or most of the time (see table 6.3). (This was reported by under a quarter of the low yearners.) The high yearners were much more likely to be lonely and much more likely to become tearful during the interview. In short, they were much more likely to display continuing—indeed, chronic—grief.

TABLE 6.3

*Concomitants of Early Intense Yearning for Spouse's Return Thirteen Months after Loss*

|  | High Yearning N=45 | Low Yearning N=23 |
|---|---|---|
| Cried at the interview. | 16 (36%) | 3 (13%) |
| Preoccupation with memories: respondent thinks of deceased "a lot, every day, always, or most of the time." | 29 (64%) | 5 (22%) |
| Loneliness reported by respondent often or always. | 20 (44%) | 4 (17%) |

Extremely striking in this group are the findings from our follow-up interview, held two to four years after the bereavement (see table 6.4). At this time, of the eighteen who had displayed low yearning in the first interview, about two thirds were rated by our coders as doing "better than average." Only three in this group gave strong evidence of depression, anxiety or disturbance of affect. In contrast, among those in the high yearning sample only a third were rated as doing better than average, and slightly more than half gave evidence of depression, anxiety, or disturbance of affect two to four years after bereavement.

Here we feel is our strongest evidence both for the frequency with which chronic grief occurs and for regarding intense yearning as an early harbinger of chronic grief. Taking our follow-up sample as a whole, about a third gave evidence of some aspect of the persistence of grieving two to four years after the loss. Those giving such evidence were disproportionately among those who had early been high yearners.

TABLE 6.4

*Concomitants of Early Intense Yearning and Aspects of Outcome Two to Four Years after Loss*

| | High Yearning<br>N = 41 | Low Yearning<br>N = 18 |
|---|---|---|
| Respondent expresses: | | |
| Agreement with "Deep down I wouldn't care if I died tomorrow." | 22 (54%) | 3 (17%) |
| Moderate to severe anxiety at interview. | 23 (56%) | 3 (17%) |
| Moderate to severe overall disturbance of affect in current life. | 22 (54%) | 3 (17%) |
| Coder thinks respondent is doing better than average. | 14 (34%) | 12 (67%) |

Again we might note the importance of dependency in differentiating those high yearners who are at high risk of chronic grief from those who are much less at risk. To emphasize this we present two cases, one of a widower in whom high yearning was an expression, in part, of dependency and one of a widow in whom high yearning expressed, in contrast, only feelings of distress at the loss of a much loved spouse.

MR. NORTON: AN OVERRELIANT HUSBAND

Mr. Norton was in his late thirties at the time of his wife's death. He was the father of two boys, aged eleven and nine. He worked as a department head for a government bureau, a demanding job that frequently required late hours. During his marriage he had relied on his wife to keep his life in order. It was not until his wife had died, of cancer, that he realized just how much he had relied on her to care for his home and children and to do errands and pay bills, all of which he had now to learn to do:

> I didn't know how dependent I was on my wife. You start doing all these things that you haven't done and you find out how stupid you are. I never realized how much I depended on her until—well, until I had to do the cooking and the washing myself.

> My wife handled all the money. I guess she had a schedule when she paid the gas, the telephone, and the electric, and all that. I never questioned her. I just gave her my money, and she took care of it.

But more than relying on his wife to manage money and care for his home and children, Mr. Norton had relied on her to maintain his links to others. He was a cool, rather distant man. His wife had been the sociable one:

> The main thing that I remember about her is that she was an extremely outgoing and friendly kind of person. After living in the town eight years, practically everybody in the town knew her. She was in a great many activities. She had a fantastic capacity for—I don't know—acquiring friends, shall we say? She probably had more friends in this town after eight years than most people have who have been living here all their lives.

Mr. Norton could not bring himself to say how very important his wife had been to him emotionally. He did say that they liked being together and preferred activities they could share, like skiing and church socials and going out with old friends. A year after his wife's death he would say, "The nicest thing that could happen would be if I could find another woman like my wife. But I think that's wishful thinking."

Mr. Norton's wife had been the one who arranged for time to be spent with friends. It was she who kept up contact with both her family and his. Although two of Mr. Norton's sisters lived nearby, he did not see them often after his wife's death. Indeed, he saw hardly any adults other than colleagues at work, none of whom he was really friendly with.

There was just one adult Mr. Norton did see: his cousin, at his home. During his wife's illness the daughter of his aunt occasionally helped Mr. Norton care for his children. About a month after his wife's death Mr. Norton arranged for his cousin to come daily to his home to look after the children on their arrival from school and to prepare the evening meal.

Mr. Norton tried dating. He spent an evening with a woman whom he had known for many years through his work. The evening, he said, was one of physical intimacy and emotional distance. A second evening left him as lonely as had the first. He did not make another date.

A year after his wife's death, Mr. Norton was both socially isolated and deeply depressed. He felt his life was empty. He was willing, he said, to give up, to die. Without his wife, it seemed to us, he preferred withdrawal to the anxieties of starting anew.

We saw Mr. Norton a year later, two years after his wife's death. In the interval his cousin, five years younger than he, seemed to have moved into the role once played by his wife. Now, in addition to caring for the children and keeping the house in order, she watched television with Mr. Norton, just as his wife had, and on occasion went out with him to dinner and a movie. They were considering marriage, although they were hesitant because one of Mr. Norton's children was cool to the cousin.

Despite having found someone new to share his life, Mr. Norton was still, two years after his loss, depressed. His cousin, even though she provided him with a great deal, could not entirely replace his wife as a companion nor as effectively maintain Mr. Norton's relationships with friends and family—nor could she, apparently, do nearly as well as his wife had in making him feel securely cared for. And so Mr. Norton had continued to feel lonely and despairing. Asked about his attitude toward life, Mr. Norton said: "My general attitude toward life hasn't changed at all. I thought it stunk before, and I still think life stinks."

MRS. BRUNNER: AN AUTONOMOUS WIFE

For contrast, let us look at an instance of a widow who, although unquestionably attached to her husband, was not dependent on him. Mrs. Brunner was forty-five years old at the time her husband died. She and her husband had been married for twenty-one years. They had one child, a boy, born just five years before Mr. Brunner's death. Mrs. Brunner described her marriage as having been extremely close. She said, in our second interview with her:

I think we were a little bit closer than most married couples are. My husband was the type of man who never went away from home. He was always home. And he always stayed home. He never went out. The only time that he ever went out without me was to his lodge meeting once a month and to his union meeting once a month. Otherwise he was home. He loved his home and he loved his child.

At this time, two months after her husband's death, Mrs. Brunner was often distressed and often overcome with feelings of loss.

I think I miss him most when it gets to five o'clock, when he normally would come home from work. And I miss him on weekends because we were always together. And around ten-thirty to eleven we would always have tea together and talk before we went to bed.

I miss his companionship. I miss him around the house and drives together on Sundays. If we had anything to do in the house, we always did it together.

Although Mrs. Brunner missed her husband greatly, she had not been dependent on him. She had insisted on being involved in the management of finances in her home. Unlike many other widows, she knew how her household income should be dealt

149

with. Even more important, she had complete confidence in her ability to manage on her own. She contrasted her situation with that of another young widow:

> This friend of mine that lost her husband, she doesn't even know anything of what he had for insurance or whether the home is taken care of or anything. She hasn't got the first idea where to look for anything because he always took care of everything. She didn't know where to find the papers or anything. I, of course, knew where everything was and knew everything I had to do. I've always managed the home, and I've always taken care of bills and everything. And I think that has helped me a whole lot.

Mrs. Brunner's parents lived in London. She had no family of her own in this country. Although she had many friends, was active in her church and worked part-time in a jewelry store near her home, her husband had been the only person with whom she talked easily. He had been, she said, her closest friend.

About the time of their son's third birthday, Mr. Brunner had begun to display perplexing symptoms: occasional dizziness, loss of equilibrium so that he would bump into doors, lapses of memory. He was referred to a psychiatrist who recommended a neurological examination. This showed nothing, but Mr. Brunner was not satisfied and checked himself into a hospital. A series of tests led to a tentative diagnosis: diffused brain tumor, resulting in fluid pressure on the brain. The condition could be relieved, he was told, but not cured. It would be fatal.

For almost two years after this diagnosis, Mr. Brunner was in and out of the hospital. He would become disoriented, suffer excruciatingly painful headaches, enter the hospital, be treated, return home. After a time he would again experience disorientation and pain and have to re-enter the hospital. Mrs. Brunner remained unfailingly caring and solicitious, while still meeting her responsibilities to her son and her job. Asked how she had been able to keep herself going, she said:

I'm the kind of person that I feel that each person has their own life to live. I never did want to be dependent on anyone else. We were brought up to stand on our own two feet. It was always understood when we left my parents' house that, if sickness came or anything, they would be willing to help us, but otherwise, that was it. We had to stand on our own two feet. My mother felt that that was the only way to do it. She said, "Never have a leaning post, because when the leaning post falls you fall with it." So we never did. And I think that's probably why I was able to face up to a lot of the problems I had the past two years.

Finally there was a last hospitalization. Mrs. Brunner was still maintaining her routine when she was called by her husband's doctor and told her husband was dying:

I was ready to go to work on Friday morning when the doctor called and told me that my husband was very low and he didn't think he had very much longer. And I asked him at that time, "Has he already passed away?" And he said, "No, but he is very close to it." And he advised me to come. So I took my little boy to a neighbor's and I called my minister, and he told me not to drive the car, that he would come and he would take me to the hospital. So he took me to the hospital, and when I got there he had already passed away.

When we talked with Mrs. Brunner, three weeks after her husband's death, although she was grief-stricken, she was able to say "loss and grief happen in every life and we have to face them." Eight weeks after her husband's death she felt her life to be under control, an assessment with which our interviewer agreed. Asked whether she feared a nervous breakdown, Mrs. Brunner said, "That's the last thing on my mind," and she remained well able to cope throughout the first year of bereavement.

Mrs. Brunner had difficult times, of course. But she dealt with them in her characteristic way: she neither tried to repress painful memories nor did she restrict her activities in order to avoid them.

I miss our going out together. We all three [herself, husband, and son] used to go places on Sunday. We'd go out to dinner. I take Freddy [son] places and I miss him [husband] but I still take Freddy. It's hard to go in many of the restaurants that we used to go to together, but I feel that I should take Freddy to the same places the same way that I always did. I find it hard going to church and not having him with us, but I still make myself go because I feel that Freddy needs that training.

We returned to see Mrs. Brunner three years after her husband's death. We then learned that a year and a half after her husband's death she had begun to see a bachelor neighbor, a fellow member of her church, and not long before our call they had married. Mrs. Brunner said that she still, sometimes, thought of her first husband and still, sometimes, missed him. But she was no longer lonely. Her life, she felt, was good.

Mrs. Brunner exemplifies a potential for autonomy coexisting with genuine attachment. Her husband was cherished by her; his loss precipitated her into sincere grief; and yet she was able to continue to meet her daily responsibilities and, without undue anxiety, began to reorganize her life so that she might at some time in the future once again find it gratifying.

## In Conclusion

We have argued in this chapter that among the majority of widows and widowers exhibiting intense yearning early in the bereavement is a smaller group whose yearning expresses not only a sense of continued connection to their spouses but also a sense of inability to manage alone. These are the widows and widowers who were dependent on their spouses during marriage. And these are the widows and widowers whose grieving is likely to resist resolution. We regard it as a disorder of attachment, a condition in which the biologically determined ties that link two people together and normally ensure mutual security and effectiveness have become distorted to the point where security and effectiveness are impaired.

We have suggested how this may come about, but we have not explained why it sometimes continues for an inordinate length of time. In this connection we can postulate four factors:

1. The person whose fear of unfamiliar and potentially dangerous situations and people leads to withdrawal from social contact with others may be creating a situation which is self-perpetuating. Without the support and reassurance of others, the chronic griever lacks the security that would foster and lead to re-engagement with others.
2. By continuing to turn toward the fantasy of a continued relationship with the dead partner, the bereaved are able to maintain an illusion of security. To recover, it is necessary to give up this fantasy. The widowed Queen Victoria's ministers soon discovered that on all matters of policy, Prince Albert's word was law. Had he survived, the Prince would, no doubt, have changed his mind about many things, but once he was dead his words became sacred. Any attempt to question them became a threat to the Queen's security and was treated as such.
3. The lack of confidence either in one's own power to survive or in the outside world as a safe place to venture may make the security of an obsolescent world preferable to the anxiety of reality. It is easy to see why many elderly people for whom the future may hold very little prefer to remain invested in the past.
4. The observable expression of grief is socially sanctioned, and the mourner is treated with gentleness and tolerance by family and friends. Those who tend to see themselves as helpless may find it tempting to continue in the role of mourner in the hope that the sympathy and support of others will continue.

If we are correct, the essential determinant of chronic grief is insecurity. It is insecurity that fosters emotional dependency and, later, a refusal to budge from a position of chronic mourning. Whatever would allay this insecurity would help individuals confront the pain and anxiety of moving toward recovery. The presence of supportive friends and relatives should be useful; so, too, should a therapeutic alliance with a committed, knowledgeable professional caregiver.

# Chapter 7

---

# *The Recovery Process*

We have shown that good outcomes are less likely if the death occurs with no forewarning, the marital relationship has been conflicted and so ambivalent, or the relationship has been characterized by excessive dependence on the spouse. In discussing these conditions, we suggested reasons each might lead to a poor outcome or interfere with a good one. We now develop a more general statement of the nature of the recovery process to provide a context for our earlier discussion.

## The Tasks of Grieving

The nature of the recovery process was aptly characterized by more than one widow or widower who said, "You don't get over it; you get used to it." Those who recover from bereavement do not return to being the same people they had been before their marriages or before their spouses' deaths. Nor do they forget the past and start a new life. Rather, they recognize that change has taken place, accept it, examine how their basic assumptions about themselves and their world must be changed and go on from there. Each of these steps requires courage, effort, and time. Three distinct tasks in recovery are: first, that the loss be accepted intellectually; second, that the loss be ac-

155

cepted emotionally; and third, that the individual's model of self and outer world change to match the new reality.[1] Let us consider each of these in turn.

INTELLECTUAL RECOGNITION AND EXPLANATION OF LOSS

For widows and widowers to engage in their activities without additional anxiety, they must continue to feel that the world makes sense. For this to happen, the loss they have sustained has to have a rationale: they must be able to understand it. The death that comes as a bolt from the blue is disabling partly because it makes no sense. Widows and widowers who lost spouses with no forewarning at all often complained that it seemed to them impossible that someone could be so much a part of their lives at one moment and in the next have vanished.

Making sense of loss requires developing an "account," an explanation of how it happened. The account, if it is to be useful, must be felt to be true and must answer whatever questions the widow or widower might have. It must include identification of a cause that led to an inevitable process, the outcome of which was the husband's or wife's death.

One widow's account went something like this: "There was so much anger in him, I can't help but think it had something to do with the cancer. And then, when the cancer began, it just kept on going." A widower's account might be paraphrased as: "She had this kidney trouble, but we never expected that it would make childbirth dangerous. But then it turned out that having the child was just too much for her."

This is not to say that an adequate account is sufficient for recovery; only that it is necessary. Without an account that settles the question of "Why?" widows and widowers

[1]Worden (1982) has formulated a similar classification of the tasks of grieving: first, to accept the reality of the loss; second, to experience the pain of grief; third, to adjust to an environment in which the deceased is missing; and fourth, to withdraw emotional energy and reinvest it in another relationship.

can never relax their vigilance against the threat of new loss.

EMOTIONAL ACCEPTANCE

Emotional acceptance can be said to have taken place when the widow or widower no longer feels the need to avoid reminders of loss for fear of being flooded by grief, pain, or remorse. For this state to be reached, there must be repeated confrontation with every element of the loss until the intensity of distress is diminished to the point where it becomes tolerable and the pleasure of recollection begins to outweigh the pain. The process is difficult, time-consuming, and painful. It seems that emotional acceptance can be achieved only as a consequence of fine-grained, almost filigree work with memory. It requires what appears to an observer to be a kind of obsessive review in which the widow or widower goes over and over the same thoughts and memories. If the process is going well, they are not quite the same thoughts and memories; there is movement—perhaps slow—from one emphasis to another, from one focus to another. Only if the process is stuck, as in chronic grief, will the review become truly obsessive, a continuing rehearsal of the same thoughts and memories.

In a recovery process that is going well, the review may be spread over the first four months or so. By the end of this time, the widow or widower will have experienced the memories and thoughts most closely associated with the loss. This is not to say that the widow or widower now becomes impervious to new pangs of grief. Indeed, it may never happen, even in a good recovery, that the widow or widower achieves an invulnerability to distress on being reminded again of how much was lost. What is achieved by the work of review is, rather, that the widow or widower no longer suffers a continuous, oppressive awareness of loss and pain and no longer needs to avoid thinking of the spouse's death in order to function without distraction.

RECOVERY FROM BEREAVEMENT

Early in the grief process a measure of distancing or denial is entirely compatible with recovery. In the first days and weeks, many widows and widowers feel they must have relief from the intense pain produced by their loss, and they obtain this relief by directing their attention away from the loss. This is a defensive maneuver we call "distancing." It is tenuous, difficult to maintain, and easy to interrupt, yet many find it necessary if they are not to be exhausted by pain. An instance of distancing is the widow who throws herself into cleaning the house, not only because she has a great deal of restless energy but because she must do something to take her mind away from her bereavement. (This may be an example of the "displacement activities" found in many other species at times of frustration and conflict.)

"Denial" is the term preferred by psychotherapists for a type of distancing produced by a refusal to acknowledge reality. "It can't be true" embodies the essence of this defense. But although there are many who attempt to deny the implications of bereavement, there are few who successfully deny the fact of death; denial is easily undermined.

When widows and widowers are engaged in distancing and denying, mention of loss can "remind" them of it and send them into tears. In truth, they have not forgotten; they have only directed their attention away so as to gain some respite. With the passage of a few weeks or months, the feeling of being raw is likely to diminish, the pain to be less intense, and distancing and denying to be less needed.

Denial of loss and grieving, continued beyond the first months of bereavement, may be incompatible with recovery because of its requirement that continued attention be given to maintaining a belief system contrary to reality. Going on as though nothing has changed is a hopeless task. It requires refusing to give validity not just to the empty place at the dinner table but also to the aching heart.

We have noted that emotional acceptance of loss is rarely

158

complete. Few among the bereaved ever arrive at a time when they are no longer susceptible to a flash of memory or a sudden association that subjects them again to intense pain, to an urge to cry aloud, or to a need to search for and cling to the person who has gone. Continued vulnerability to these pangs of grief is compatible with recovery so long as defending against vulnerability does not absorb attention, reduce capacity for gratification, or interfere with functioning.

The repeated review by which emotional acceptance is obtained can be painful to friends and relatives, as well as to the widows and widowers themselves. Friends and relatives may urge that the review be terminated long before the widow or widower has adequately come to terms with the past. What this can mean is that after a time—often, a rather brief time—the widow or widower is left alone with the work of review. This is unfortunate but should not be surprising. It takes sensitivity and, perhaps, experience to distinguish between the normal process of recovery, in which there is slow but steady movement in review, and chronic grief, in which obsessive review is unbudging. And it takes great tolerance for another's pain to be accepting of either.

A NEW IDENTITY

The bereaved woman who insists that she is "Jack's wife and not Jack's widow," while expressing an admirable loyalty to her marriage, displays as well a commitment to an obsolete identity. Maintaining an identity at odds with reality requires endless mental alertness. It requires maintaining one identity even while acting in another. For instance, a widow may apply for Social Security but continue to buy food that her husband would have enjoyed. It means, too, being inattentive to possibilities for new satisfaction that would be entirely appropriate to a widow or widower but inappropriate to the married—such as considering a geographical move or seeking a new attachment.

What we mean by an "identity" here is simply a reasonably consistent set of assumptions about one's own self. It is on the basis of such sets of constructs that we make choices and plans. They should, therefore, correspond reasonably well to our actual wishes, potentials, and situations.

At least three separate and conflicting identities are available to the newly bereaved individual. First is an identity based on the assumption that the marriage continues. The widow or widower may refer to the spouse in the present tense as though the death had not occurred and may continue to consider the spouse's wishes and needs in household management or personal planning. Second is an identity based on the assumption that the spouse no longer exists and there is no further obligation to the spouse. Third is an identity based on the assumption that the spouse has been transported to another sphere but can still be affected, at least to some degree, by the bereaved individual's thoughts and behavior. This last identity is the one adopted by the "mourner"; it is expressed by the widow who dresses in black and withdraws from social life. Whereas grief is an emotionally-based reaction to loss, mourning can be a duty to the dead. (It can also be a duty to other members of the family and to society at large.)

In the early stages of bereavement the bereaved find themselves shifting uncomfortably from one identity to another. Whenever we become aware of a discrepancy between the world that is and the world we had assumed to exist, we experience a sense of bewilderment or discomfort. For the new widow, writing the word "widow" on a form, setting aside a bright dress, or responding appropriately to the question "How is your husband?" points up a conflict of identities. Only as time passes and the work of relearning the world is carried out is the new widow or widower likely to lose this sense of fragmented identity and to feel relatively comfortable with one predominant identity.

To a marked degree religious and cultural beliefs about death define what it is that the bereaved have to accept. In Western societies obligations to the spirits of the dead are few. It is not necessary, for example, that the widow or widower feel inauthentic unless dressed in black. It *is* necessary, however, that there be recognition that loss has occurred and acceptance of being currently without a partner. These are inescapable realities that must be integrated into the widow's or widower's current identity.

Movement toward a new identity is consistent with intervals in which the widow or widower feels and may even act as if the partner were still present. Widows especially, but sometimes widowers as well, are strengthened by being able to "talk with" their dead spouses. They are not hallucinating when they do this. They know the spouses are not there, but they find it comforting and sustaining to be able to talk through a problem, perhaps when doing the dishes, with the feeling that the spouse is there to listen.

In this respect, as others, it does not seem desirable to be so committed to a particular program of recovery that helpful practices are avoided. Some widows and widowers may find value in restricting the time they give to sad and painful reminiscence, while others may not. Some widows and widowers may want for a time to retain their married selves, while others may want to move toward new identities more quickly. So long as the widow or widower continues to move toward recovery, the path chosen is not important.

## The Roles Played by Others

One of the reasons bereavement is so devastating in its effects is that it undermines feelings of security. A central figure in life has been lost and the widow or widower left alone. But friends and relatives can serve as new guarantors of security. It is for this reason, we think, that it is so important for widows and widowers to have people rally around in the early days of bereavement. Just the presence of people who can be trusted, quite apart from whatever they might provide, helps the bereaved to keep anxiety in check.

Nevertheless, we did not find the number of ties to friends and family at the time of bereavement, nor the frequency with which friends or family were seen during a widow's or widower's marriage, nor even the apparent strength of these social ties at the time of bereavement to be predictive of the quality of recovery thirteen months later. Vachon et al. (1980) also found that the presence of supportive relationships, while valuable at the time of bereavement, has no significant association with later recovery.

We did find, as is noted above, that widows and widowers were grateful for the presence of others during their times of deep grief. But what seemed to matter most in fostering recovery was not so much how many people were initially available to a widow or widower as whether their support was utilized as time went on.

The continued presence of supportive figures was itself an indicator of how well the widows and widowers were managing their bereavement. Mrs. Brunner (described in chapter 6) had no family of her own in this country, but after her loss she maintained relationships of great value to her with her husband's family, with friends, with coworkers, and with fellow members of her church. In contrast, Mr. Norton (also described in chapter 6) had parents, an aunt, and sisters all within easy driving distance, as well as an extensive circle of married friends, but quite early in his bereavement he withdrew from them all. Mrs. Brunner did well; Mr. Norton did not. The way they dealt with those family and friends initially available to them both indicated how well they were doing in moving toward recovery and influenced their further movement.

The constellation of an individual's social ties is not an unchanging characteristic of that individual. Rather, the nature and quality of an individual's social ties are constantly being established and re-established. Those respondents who had relied on their husbands or wives to maintain their social ties seemed especially likely, after bereavement, to become isolated. But some others, as one expression of continuing anger or deep grief, permitted themselves to become isolated. Thus, the number of social ties before bereavement did not predict well what their nature would be after bereavement.

A secondary reason for the absence of correspondence between the initial quality of social ties and eventual recovery is that there were some widows and widowers who seemed able to maintain active social contacts without being supported by them. They put a good face on things, no matter how they felt. Mrs. Stevenson, whom we describe later in this chapter, provides an example.

Some of the widows and widowers who did well found it valuable to modify their relationships with relatives and old friends and to develop new relationships reflecting their new identities. They found it useful to have at least some relationships with people who shared important elements of their new identities so that they could validate them. Especially in the early stages of bereavement, although not so early that movement toward a new identity would itself be found to be painful, relationships with people in the same boat—other widows or widowers—could provide the understanding and matching experience necessary to fend off feelings of isolation. No widow or widower developed a social world limited to other widows or widowers, nor wanted to; but, as the instance of Mrs. Goodwin (described in chapter 4) may suggest, there was great value in having some relationships of this kind.

Many of the widows and widowers whose recoveries seemed best had moved toward remarriage, and those among them who actually did remarry were, apparently, the most content with their lives. But, with the exception of two widowers who seemed to have remarried partly out of desperation, the willingness to consider remarriage required first a major revision of the assumptive world of the bereaved. Thus, movement toward remarriage, like the maintenance of ties to friends and kin, was both a consequence of recovery and a cause of further recovery. The approach to a good recovery, in this sample of young widows and widowers, tended to lead to renewed capacity for social engagement and, after some time, readiness for a new marital or other intimate relationship.

## Predictors of Poor Recovery as Impediments to Recovery

The reason brief forewarning, marital ambivalence, and dependence are associated with poor outcome is, we believe, that they interfere with the tasks of grieving. Although each of the factors leading to poor recovery undoubtedly interferes at many points in the recovery process, there may be some rough correspondence of factor and the particular aspect of the recovery process that is interfered with. It may be that brief forewarning makes for difficulties in intellectual recognition and explanation just because the death seems so unconnected to anything that went before. Marital ambivalence may create problems in emotional acceptance for many reasons, including the complexity of feelings, the intensity of guilt and remorse, and the difficulty of acknowledging and accepting feelings and behaviors that the widow or widower would now want to disown. Finally, it may be that dependence interferes with the development of a new, autonomous identity, in part because the bereaved continue to assume that security can be found only in continued linkage to the dead partner, in part because they have so little confidence in themselves or hope for the future.

The predictive elements we have identified are not, however, the only possible impediments to recovery. A tendency to doubt one's own capacities and to be without hope for the future, quite apart from dependence on the spouse, may well impair recovery. So can a deathbed commission from a dying spouse that amounts to a prohibition of recovery.

We have only a single instance among our cases of a dying husband directing his wife not to grieve for him. Despite it being only a single instance, it is most instructive in connection with the importance of moving through the recovery processes we have outlined. The widow, Mrs. Stevenson, was in her early forties, the mother of three children ranging in age from four to twelve at the time of her husband's death. Her husband died of pneumonia following surgery for removal of a tumor from his lung. Both he and Mrs. Stevenson had known for about three months that he would require surgery and that there would be a risk associated with it. Nevertheless, it was only a few weeks before Mr. Stevenson's death that surgery was performed and the Stevensons were told that the tumor was malignant and that Mr. Stevenson could not expect to live much longer.

The abruptness of this news meant that Mr. Stevenson's death, while forewarned, had about it elements of suddenness. For this reason, Mrs. Stevenson might have been expected to have difficulties in recovery. On the other hand, the marriage had been a good one, so that Mrs. Stevenson had no reason for remorse or guilt, nor had she been unusually dependent on her husband during the marriage.

Mr. Stevenson had insisted to his wife, even before he was told that he would die, that should anything happen to him, his wife should avoid any "public display of grief." Mrs. Stevenson said:

He would say to me, "If anything ever happens to me, I don't want you to go to pieces. You got to have class. I don't want you scraming and hollering." He would talk to me and he'd tell me that if anything happened to him, to keep a cool head. He wanted me to go on as if nothing had happened. He didn't want me to make any scenes. He just wanted me to go on living, as though nothing happened.

Deathbed commissions to a spouse have enormous force, and after Mr. Stevenson's death, Mrs. Stevenson did her very best to follow his wishes; "I behaved as he wanted me to. I did what he asked me to do. I didn't even cry at the funeral. I'd think about him and say to myself, 'Well, if he were here, I know he would want it this way.'"

Mrs. Stevenson returned to work only a month after her husband's death. Briefly, she wore dark clothes at work. She felt she had to, for her own sake. Then, in accordance with her husband's wishes, she returned to her normal wardrobe. Six weeks after her husband's death, she said: "I went back to work. I did wear mourning, but I'm going to get away from it now. There's no sense in it. And he didn't want me to."

When we last saw Mrs. Stevenson, in our thirteen-month interview (we were unable to obtain a follow-up interview with her), although she was somewhat withdrawn with us she told us that she had remained socially active, that she still kept up with her many friends, and that she had continued to meet community responsibilities she had undertaken during her marriage. But she seemed without hope or direction in her life. She said: "I don't know what the future will bring and, well, I won't say that I'll never get over it, but I think that I'll just love him."

Mr. Stevenson's commission to his wife appeared to have been effective, not only in that it fostered her continued social engagement, but also in that it made more difficult her recovery and her relinquishing of commitment to him. Because Mrs. Stevenson could not reveal evidence of her loss, nor accept the time out our society normally provides those who have suffered loss, she was hindered in the development of a new social identity. Because she had to pretend to cheerfulness when with others, she was able to engage in the work of grieving only when alone. And because she was prohibited from expressing her grief to others, she could not enter into relationships in which the grief could be acknowledged and so validated. No wonder, then, that at the thirteen-month point she had neither hope nor energy for new satisfactions in life.

## The Recovery Process and Recovery

Our assertion that recovery requires intellectual recognition, emotional acceptance, and a new identity appropriate to the changed life situation is based only partly on our reading of our data. It is also based on our understanding of what has to be achieved in order for recovery to occur. We think that those who had good outcomes were characterized not only by adequate functioning in their social roles, and freedom from physical and emotional symptoms that could be traced to the bereavement, but also by emotional investment in their present lives and by hope regarding their futures. Furthermore, we think these good outcomes display a return to a genuine capacity for experiencing gratification. In short, people with good outcomes were going on with their lives. And it is hard to imagine how "going on with their lives" could be possible without accomplishing the tasks we have identified as essential to recovery.

We have already noted that there are any number of different ways in which widows and widowers go about the tasks of grieving. Nevertheless, it appears to us that where recovery is going well, these tasks have been largely accomplished by the

167

end of the first year of bereavement. Certainly, there is by that time an acceptable account of the loss and the work of review has been largely, if not entirely, accomplished. The new identity may still be somewhat fragmented, and it may actually take two or even three additional years before it is firmly established. But by the end of the first year of bereavement, it is possible to recognize whether recovery is occurring or not.

# Chapter 8

---

# *Consequences of Failure to Recover: Case Studies*

---

When I wake in the morning, when it is
still dark . . . with the tears streaming down
my face, and Colm [son] sleeping so well
and reminiscently against me, and think of
Dylan, and pine, as keenly as a sick cow
for its calf, just removed, for the feel of
him; and go on daftly waiting for him to
come back when I know he cannot; but it's
not a bit of good for reason to tell me that;
it cannot stop the wanting so badly,
reasonable or not; and where can I put it,
what can I do with it?

CAITLIN THOMAS
*Leftover Life to Kill*

In this chapter we shall examine four instances of failure to
recover from grief. In each, the loss was unanticipated and the
early reaction to bereavement resembled that described in
chapter 4. In the first instance, this was complicated by fear of
depression, leading to avoidance of grieving as a defense against

169

depression. In the second, recovery was complicated by over-reliance on alcohol as a means of dealing with grief; in the third, by emotional withdrawal as a means of self-protection; and in the fourth, by depression and apathy.

Our first concern is to show how central is the role of unresolved grief to subsequent psychological difficulties. Each of the respondents described in this chapter, with the possible exception of Mrs. Ryan, our first case, might have been expected to do at least fairly well if he or she had not been bereaved. Mr. Neilson, our second case, and Mrs. Delaney, our third, would probably have maintained their adjustments to life. Dr. Siegel, our fourth, would very likely have had a brilliant career. Our second concern is to suggest how various the consequences of unresolved grief can be, and how, in each instance, it was an already existing vulnerability that complicated the course of grief.

It is important to keep in mind that the losses sustained by our respondents were enormous in magnitude, complex in their implications, and, in that the deaths were all untimely, atypical. It is an inherent paradox in our attempts to grasp the dynamics of human behavior that "pathology" can be a reasonable response to an unreasonable situation. In this chapter we are concerned to show how what might be characterized as psychological difficulty or even psychiatric illness can be an understandable consequence of loss. It is important to us that attempts—our own and those of others—to analyze the problems of people defined as patients do not leave them feeling categorized but not understood. The first requirement of a caregiver is to care.

# The Psychiatric Significance of the Three Grief Syndromes

The patterns of reaction recognized in traditional psychiatric diagnosis have not, so far, proven very useful in increasing our understanding of the special problems of grief. The studies described in chapter 1 indicate some alternative syndromes that better characterize pathological grief than do traditional categories. In addition to various nonspecific conditions that reflect pre-existing neurotic traits, these include chronic grief, delayed grief, and inhibited grief (see page 15), as well as mixed pictures in which more complex reactions occur.

Of course, like most psychiatric diagnostic categories, these categories of pathological grief are descriptive rather than etiological diagnoses. They imply a pattern of reaction rather than a particular cause. In this respect they resemble conditions of unknown or multiple etiology, such as epilepsy and asthma, rather than conditions whose causes are known and unitary, such as measles and tuberculosis.

In attempting to reconcile the particular symptoms of pathological grief with the three grief syndromes described in this volume we must realize that the latter have the advantage of combining etiological and descriptive features. Thus, the *Unexpected Loss Syndrome* links unexpected loss with reactions of disbelief, avoidance, and anxiety leading eventually to states of anxious withdrawal; the *Conflicted Grief Syndrome* links conflicted attachments to minimal early grieving but later pining and anxiety; and the *Dependent Grief Syndrome* links clinging or over-reliant attachments to reactions of immediate pining and chronic grief.

These syndromes, expressive of different forms of failure to recover, can become serious enough to warrant psychiatric intervention. Indeed, there is reason to believe that most people who develop psychiatric illnesses soon after an experience of bereavement suffer from one of these syndromes or from a mixture of two or three.

We re-examined the records of interviews with twenty-seven psychiatric patients whose illnesses had come on during the terminal illness or within six months of the death of a family member.[1] Among these twenty-seven people, four had illnesses which bore no resemblance to the grief syndromes described here, and in at least one of these the illness seemed quite unrelated to the bereavement. In another four cases the information obtained at interview does not allow a reliable assessment to be made.

All of the remaining nineteen people showed the grief syndromes described here. Four had suffered unexpected bereavements, and three of these were quite typical of the pattern described in chapter 4. Seven had had dependent relationships, six of which had led to reactions typical of the type described in chapter 6. (In three of these, dependency during the marriage appeared inverted; that is to say, it appeared that the deceased person was more reliant on the survivor than vice versa. It seems to us now that the surviving spouse required for his or her own functioning the security of having another's dependence.) Three had reactions following conflict-filled marriages that were like those described in chapter 5. Finally, there were five patients who had mixed reactions in which unexpectedness, ambivalence, and dependency coexisted in various ways.

Delayed grief reactions were most likely to be associated with unanticipated and conflicted bereavements (as we found in our Boston sample). Chronic grief was most often associated with dependent bereavements, again just as was the case in the Harvard study.

To sum up, all but four of the twenty-seven patients displayed syndromes we had found to be associated with failure

---

[1]These were the psychiatric patients previously studied by Parkes (1965).

to recover from grief. This seemed to us strong evidence that psychiatric patients whose entrance into treatment occurs shortly after a bereavement are very likely to be suffering from pathological grief.

Is the difference between pathological failures to recover and those that do not require psychiatric attention simply one of degree, or is there some qualitative difference that determines why one person copes with unresolved bereavement without seeking psychiatric help while another comes to be regarded as mentally ill and to seek professional help? If we accept the fact that it is the patients who define themselves as sick by seeking medical advice, rather than doctors who define sickness, then the essential characteristic of pathological grief would seem to be the patients' awareness that their existing methods of coping are insufficient to meet their needs. Viewed in this way, the presence or absence of a supportive family may determine whether or not people see themselves as sick. We are forced to the conclusion that there is a social element in diagnosis which may initiate and influence the entire diagnostic system.

The most common presenting symptom in psychiatric settings is "depression." This can best be defined as an all-pervading feeling of unhappiness associated with helplessness and hopelessness. Of course, unhappiness is very common in the early stages of bereavement, and it seems that it is only when unhappiness is associated with an unusual degree of helplessness or hopelessness that a person can be said to be "depressed" in the psychiatric sense. But helplessness and hopelessness are relative terms. People feel more or less helpless in relation to the life tasks that they see before them, and they feel more or less hopeless in relation to their prospects of eventually achieving a "life worth living." Again we come back to a recognition of the fact that it is not only the specific characteristics of individuals, their capacity for optimism and their resilience, that decide whether or not they will develop pathological grief, but also the particular circumstances of their lives that may or may not give just cause for hope.

Psychiatrists have repeatedly emphasized the importance of self-esteem as a key factor in deciding whether or not a person will cope with stressful situations unaided or will require psychiatric help. We would add to this *other-esteem:* having the esteem of others who can be relied upon to provide protection and help when it is needed. As long as a person has a reasonable degree of self-esteem and other-esteem, he or she has little grounds for feeling helpless or hopeless in the face of loss.

With these comments in mind, we turn now to an examination of failure to recover in the Harvard study.

## Mrs. Ryan: Ambivalence, a Hypomanic Reaction, and Disorganization

Mrs. Ryan, an attractive and articulate woman, was thirty-nine at the time of her husband's death. Her husband had managed a paint supply warehouse after having failed in a small business of his own. His income, although higher than average, was barely adequate for the Ryans' family of six children.

The marriage had been an unhappy one, at least in part because of Mrs. Ryan's dependence: "He was mad at me a lot because I was never an independent person when I was married to him."

Mrs. Ryan's description of her marriage suggested that her dependence provoked her husband's anger and her husband's anger, in turn, caused her to cling all the harder, until her husband began to withdraw from her.

At one point, when Mr. Ryan was dividing his time between his business and his friends and giving very little attention to his wife, Mrs. Ryan had proposed a separation. Eventually, however, the Ryans reached a *modus vivendi*. But though the Ryans became somewhat happier, they still argued a great deal.

A lot of people thought he didn't like me because we argued so much. But I think it was on account of the fact that I was the closest one to him, and he had to take his tensions out on someone, and I was the only one that he could take them out on. He couldn't take them out on his mother or his children without causing hatred. So he took them out on me.

After the birth of her sixth child, Mrs. Ryan suffered from what was diagnosed as a post-partum depression. This is what she said about it:

This was after my sixth child. I had a lot of problems at the time which I couldn't talk about. My husband was wrapped up in his business, and he wasn't coming home, and I had five small children at the time and a baby. And it was the last year of my mother's life, and I could sense that. And I was worried about my mother, because I was the only one around—the rest of the family was working.

The anticipated loss of her mother at a time when her husband was clearly unable or unwilling to support her, together with the demands of a large family, were too much for Mrs. Ryan.

I was losing weight, and my mother advised me to go back to the hospital and get a physical check-up. And I went in and the doctors found nothing wrong with me physically, so they figured it was a post-partum depression. I know today that that wasn't true. Now I know that if I could have talked about my problems with a doctor I would never have suffered a breakdown. But I couldn't talk to anyone. So they said it must be a post-partum depression and advised my husband, and he contacted this hospital and I was in the hospital for about a month.

While in the hospital, Mrs. Ryan was treated with electroshock. The temporary loss of memory for recent events that commonly follows shock was interpreted by her as an indication that the shock had done damage. This whole episode left her with a great fear of becoming depressed again.

After Mrs. Ryan's discharge from the hospital things improved at home. A hospital psychiatrist told her husband that Mrs. Ryan's primary problem was that she was isolated in her home. Having heard this, Mrs. Ryan's husband began regularly to take her places. She said:

> My husband was a man's man. He never took me out. If I went out, I went out with my sister or my girl friends. He was just devoted to his friends. And then the doctor told him, after I had the breakdown, "The biggest problem with your wife is that she doesn't get out." And I did enjoy going out with him, for dinner and everything. I always enjoyed his company. In fact, I was very happy. We weren't madly in love or anything, but we had a very nice way of living. I took care of the kids and the problems at home, and he brought the money in. And we did go out and enjoy ourselves.

It was not long after this change in Mrs. Ryan's marriage that her husband developed what at first seemed to be a stomach flu and then was diagnosed as hepatitis. He was hospitalized and after a few weeks, his condition still unimproved, he had an exploratory operation.

> The doctor called me at twelve-thirty. I was reading my prayer book at the time. I had come to the prayer of victory when the telephone rang. So I said, "Oh, this must be a good sign." And the doctor told me that it was very bad news, that he had an inoperable tumor on the pancreas. And that they did what they could; they fixed up the ducts to the intestines, and he would lose his yellow. And I remembered that his father had a tumor on the pancreas and he died from it when he was fifty-eight. So I said to the doctor, "How long does he have to live?" And the doctor said, "About two months."
>
> Of course, that was the end of my conversation with the doctor because I was terribly upset. And then he called back that night and he said, "I was talking to the chemotherapist, and possibly we can

help your husband through drugs." "Well," I said, "that's like a rainbow after a thunderstorm." There was a chance, a hope.

At the same time that her husband was in the hospital, one of Mrs. Ryan's children was diagnosed as having rheumatic heart disease. That child was then admitted to the hospital. The pressures on Mrs. Ryan were considerable. She began to show symptoms of anxiety. But she seems, at first, to have kept her fears to herself.

After my child was admitted to the hospital I stopped in at some friends. They were having a party. And a friend of my husband's drove me home. And I was talking to him. I said, "I feel as if all these devils are trying to get at me." I hadn't told anybody that I had had my son admitted for rheumatic fever. All these problems I was keeping to myself. The only problem they knew about was my husband. And I must have had that feeling within me that something was real wrong. And then the next day I went to church, and I had to leave church because my head was aching. I had this nervous tension. Well, from July to September I couldn't go out of the house. The only time I went out was to the hospital. I just couldn't talk to people about all the problems, and it was making me very nervous. And I knew I had to rest here in the house, take care of myself, and just go visit the ones in the hospital and try to keep myself composed.

I didn't know what it was. My head was aching. My arm was going on me. Even my legs started developing a little limp. I went to the doctors and they gave me different medicines. But it never really cured me.

Eventually, Mrs. Ryan discovered that she could use alcohol as a tranquilizer and as a means of unlocking pent-up feelings. She explained this in her own way:

The end of August I was telling my girl friend about all my personal problems and the tension. And she has been recovering from nervous tension for a year. She was on all types of tranquilizers. She

177

said, "Why don't you try a glass of beer?" Well, I had never drunk beer before. And I started to take a glass of beer, and it was wonderful the way it relaxed me. See, my stomach was manufacturing gas, and the beer would have me burp right away. And it would release the tension in my head. And it would relax me more so that I could talk to people.

But her drinking became another source of conflict with her husband:

This was another thing my husband didn't like. He had never seen me drink before. And when he came from the hospital I had gotten into the habit of having a glass or two of beer a night to relax myself and so that I'd sleep well. He had never seen me do that before. And he was worried that I might turn into an alcoholic.

But when I used to visit him in the hospital and I told him I was sick, that I didn't feel good, he wouldn't give me any sympathy. He would get mad. He would say, "We can't have two sick parents." So I couldn't go to him looking for sympathy. I had to help myself. And the beer did help me. Then, when he got home, he was so mad about me drinking a glass of beer. And the glass of beer does not ever get me intoxicated, it just relaxes me a little bit.

Just as her husband had formerly dealt with Mrs. Ryan's problems by distancing himself from her, now she attempted to deal with his illness by distancing herself from him.

When he first came home, it was October, and I was looking forward to the parties at the club. And I was planning a costume for a Halloween party. And he was mad at me. He said, "That's all you can think of, is a silly Halloween costume. You have no sympathy for me." But there was nothing that I could do for him. I could give him personal attention, like clean clothes, and all that. But I couldn't go in and sit down and talk to him every day and say, "I know you are going to die," and be morbid. It would be a terrible way to live. I had to keep up my morale, his morale, and the children's morale. He used to get aggravated because he thought I had no sympathy for him. I did, but I couldn't let my mind dwell on it, because otherwise, I knew, I'd get so sick that I would possibly end up with a mental breakdown and would do no one any good. So I kept myself active that way.

Mrs. Ryan avoided depression by keeping her mind fully occupied with activities. Even when resting, she determinedly directed her mind away from her husband and his condition.

I was preparing for this party and then, after that, I had to go out and shop for Christmas, and after Christmas, there was always something to keep me active all the time. And I had a little game I played with myself that when I lay down to rest I never thought of him. Even to this day, I don't want to think of him. I think of something that will give me pleasure, like if I went to a party and had a good time. I think of that, but I won't think of him. Because if I think of him even to this day I feel very sick. It's just an awful feeling. It's, well, it's sort of like a depressed feeling.

He was a big, strong man, 175 pounds, and I saw him go down to 120. And I saw different things happen to him, like he loved his children so much, yet he knew he couldn't live to see them grow up. And I had to see his heartbreak at that. And the heartbreak about me—he hated to leave me. In fact, he used to get mad at me and say, "Well, I wish you three husbands." You know, all this sort of thing. And, "Oh, you'll have a good time when I'm dead and buried." He'd joke like that. And I know it was just his way of talking.

Then she added, revealingly, "we never talked seriously, anyway."

The exploratory operation had taken place in April. Not long after the following New Year's Day, Mr. Ryan developed a fever and had difficulty in breathing. He asked his mother and sister, who lived nearby, to come see him before he went to the hospital. Then he went to the hospital in an ambulance. Mrs. Ryan, recalling that time, said:

The doctors were always amazed at me because I'd go in there and they never saw me cry or anything. I'd go in there every night. It was a regular habit of mine. From six to eight o'clock I'd go in and visit him—with somebody else, of course, because I never went by myself. And I'd always try to be cheerful. After the first shock of the operation, I really couldn't discuss too many things with the doctor as I had nervous tension. If I started to discuss it, my head would start pounding. And this afternoon he had been in a terrible depressed state. And there was a big blush that started creeping up from his stomach, up to his neck. So that night, after the doctor went to see him, I said to the doctor, "What's wrong with my husband?" And he said, "You know what's wrong with him?" And I said, "Yes." I said that he had an inoperable tumor and that he had two months to live. And then I said, "What's wrong with him now?" And he said, "Well, I think he's starting to go downhill right now." And I said, "Do you think it's his heart?" Because he had a pain in his arm. And he said, "Well, if it was his heart or anything, we would do nothing for this man, because he has a very bad tumor, which is going to kill him anyway." As if there was no hope at all. And I got quite upset. I started crying, the first time anybody had ever seen me cry. That a doctor could be so callous as to say that he wouldn't do anything for a person.

Mr. Ryan did not in fact die that night. He had a bad time, and looked as though he were failing, but he rallied. Then, a few nights later, when Mrs. Ryan was at home, Mr. Ryan did die.

I had an awful lonely feeling for two weeks before he died. And before he died, oh it was terrible on me. It was as if the inside of me was being torn apart, and I had the feeling that things weren't right. Well he died Wednesday morning, about four or five. But Monday night I was getting very uneasy. And Tuesday I had the blues, I was crying because—I think it was just some kind of premonition, that I knew something was going on. And my mother-in-law called me at two in the afternoon. She said, "Come right in, he's very bad." And I went in, but he was the same as he had been the night before, so I wasn't too alarmed. But he was heavily medicated. And the doctors had had him anointed again, and had him X-rayed and thought he was bleeding internally. And he said that his condition was very poor. I stayed there from two until ten. But where there was no change in him, I figured I have a large family to take care of, and my own health which I was trying to protect because all the family depended on me. So I went home, because I had a terrible pain in my back. And I had asked God that if he died I'd like to be with him. I left at ten. My mother-in-law left at one-thirty and my brother happened to be at the hospital that day and he stayed there all day. I kept telling him to go home, and he wouldn't. He drove me home, and he drove my mother-in-law home, and then he went back to the hospital. At about three-thirty in the morning my husband said to him, even though he was heavily medicated, "I'm dying, Kevin. Do you mind waiting?" I said to my brother, "You should have called me then." But he didn't. He called my sister upstairs about four-thirty in the morning and said that my husband had died. So I felt bad. It's something that I expected, naturally. But I said that I wanted to go in there.

I just got up and I went in. He looked the same. The nurse had just put on fresh bedclothes. And she had his hands folded like they would be in a casket and his legs crossed. And I felt as though I was able to give him my personal good-by because his body was still warm. Even though he wasn't breathing, I felt as though he was still there.

Like many of the widows and widowers who had had ambivalent relationships with their spouses, Mrs. Ryan's grief, three weeks after her husband's death, seemed muted. She was cheerful, and she did not seem to be yearning for her husband's return.

I think the funeral went off perfectly. They said it was one of the biggest funerals that ever came out of that church. Somebody got up to the count of sixty cars. And I think it went off perfectly.

I walked up the aisle and no tears came to my eyes until near the end of the aisle the tears started. I was very proud of myself because I don't like to display my emotions.

And then I got in the car with my children and they didn't cry like I thought they would. And we went along, and I didn't look back to see who was following. We got to the cemetery, and I was very happy that it had snowed because I think if I was ever buried in the winter time, I think a cemetery in the winter with no snow on the ground is a very cold, cold place to leave a person. And I said to my children, "I'm glad it snowed because it is pretty here. You know, it's nice and white. There's no footmarks or dirty snow at all. It's a very pretty place."

After the funeral, everybody was around, and I stood there with my children, and the priest was going to walk off, and the funeral director said, "Aren't you going to say a few words of comfort to the mother and the widow?" My mother-in-law and myself. And, I don't know what I said to the priest, but I said something like, "Oh, you don't have to bother." I talked to him later and I said, "You didn't have to console me, Father, because I wasn't crying, because he was a man very well prepared to die." And there was no one that knew it better than me. So what was there to be sad about?

About three o'clock I was sitting at the table and my brother-in-law had kept telling me to sit down. And I had been busy waiting on people and so forth, and I sat down. And, all of a sudden, the tears started coming down my eyes. And my brother-in-law said, "Oh, this is wonderful, Joanie, I've been waiting to see you cry." Because he never saw me cry. But I said, "I've been crying since May 1. I don't have to cry now."

I remember when my father died three years ago, I used to wake up in the morning crying. Before I was fully awake, I was crying. But I was so prepared for my husband's death that I don't have this feeling. When I think of him, I cry. But I am not in constant mourning. My father's death was a sudden death so I did my mourning after, where my husband's death was something that I was prepared for.

Five weeks later, two months after her husband's death, Mrs. Ryan hardly seemed to be grieving at all. Yet, as she talked about her activities during the interval since our last meeting with her, it became evident that she was avoiding feelings of sadness. She said:

At first, naturally, I thought of him quite a bit. And I had to fight to get him out of my mind. But now I don't think of him that often so I don't have the big fight with myself. And when I do, I just close my eyes and just try to block him away.

Other people's sympathy, because it reminded Mrs. Ryan of her loss, was terrifying for her. She said:

> The first night I went out after my husband died, this woman came up to me and said, "Oh, how's your husband? I heard he was very bad." And the tears started rolling down her face. And right away I wanted to cry. I wanted to run home and hide. That's what I wanted to avoid all the time—sympathy. If anybody gave me sympathy, I just wanted to run the other way.

Within a month of her husband's death Mrs. Ryan had begun immersing herself in social activity. As has been noted, she and her husband had been members of a social club. Now she began attending alone. When nothing was happening at the social club, she would visit a cocktail lounge near her home.

> My sister and I stopped at a cocktail lounge near here and I had a couple of bottles of beer. And I met a newspaper reporter there that I had met with my husband, although he didn't remember my husband. And I was in a gay mood. So I said, "I'm going to Hollywood next week, and I'm going to stay at the Beverly Hilton." And he said, "Oh, you can't afford it." He didn't know I was a widow. And he said, "Well, you'll be outclassed out there. The women are beautiful." And I kidded him back. I said, "Oh, yes, I'm definitely going to Hollywood next week." And I was amusing everybody at the bar by the way I was talking. Of course, the bartender knew about my circumstances, and he was going along with me and everything. But the reporter, I could have given him the punch line any time, that I was a widow, but I didn't, not until the end. And then I just told him. And he looked at me.

Most of Mrs. Ryan's social activity seemed to be sited at the club. One party she attended lasted all night.

> I came home about five-thirty or six in the morning, and then I had to sleep and rest Saturday, and then I had to go to my son's basketball game that night. And they won. And this friend of my husband's, he was there, and he was so thrilled, and of course we went

to the club again to celebrate the victory, and so I was out two nights in a row.

Mrs. Ryan's tirelessness and hyperactivity seem to have been a manic defense against grief. While we cannot be sure about the causes of Mrs. Ryan's reaction to her husband's death, we suspect that her experience with depression had terrified her and that she was now trying in every way she could to avoid sinking into grief. Her defensive measures, however, prevented her from engaging in the painful process of relearning that is grief and so achieving emotional acceptance of her loss. She had constantly to keep herself from thinking and feeling.

Mrs. Ryan was excited by the possibility that men might be interested in her. Insofar as her anticipations were unrealistic—and later events suggested that they were—they, too, were symptomatic of a flight from depression. Referring to the dance that took place at the social club that evening, she said:

> The men were good. At first my friend's friend—he's a married man but he never takes his wife out socially—he danced with me. And then, as I had a few more drinks, I got more sociable with other men and I danced with others. They were all very good to me. And the man I ended up with, he's a single guy. He'd be a nice prospect for me. [laughs] I had never talked to him before I said, "Hello." But when I have a drink in me, I get very talkative. And he treated me not like Ronnie's widow; he treated me like a single girl. And I think he's a little bit interested in me. So we'll see what develops in the future.

The interviewer was struck by Mrs. Ryan's flow of speech and her general animation. Mrs. Ryan followed her story of the dance and the man who might be interested in her with the comment: "As far as romance in life, I have to keep romantic thoughts in my head to keep myself happy. If I don't have any romantic thoughts in my head, I think I'd be lost. So I have a few right now. I don't know whether they'll develop."

To this the interviewer responded, "You seem to be kind of

exhilarated about it." And Mrs. Ryan then said, "I have the feeling that there is a destiny cut out for me. I don't know what it is, but I have that feeling. I've had that feeling since my husband's illness, that all these things shouldn't be happening to me but they are."

Briefly, Mrs. Ryan now returned to the theme of God and devils that she had voiced in our first interview with her.

> Why should I lose my husband? I don't know. At first I thought devils were involved. I thought devils were involved in my life. But God is supposed to be good, and He's not supposed to be mean to people. Of course, I felt guilty at times about different things. I shouldn't have done this and I shouldn't have done that. At the beginning I felt as though all the devils in the world were after me, because too many things were happening at once; my husband got ill, my son got ill, my sister was hospitalized, and then my head starts going off. I was worried about myself. And this is why I felt devils were involved.

At this point Mrs. Ryan told us that there were several reasons why she might have feelings of guilt about her husband's death. She had already told us of their joking that he would develop cancer by his early forties. Now she told us that when she had been so neglected by her husband, before her admission to the hospital, she had spent some time with another man; although all they had done was talk, she felt guilty and intensely uncomfortable about it.

Our interviewer asked Mrs. Ryan whether she did not herself think it odd that she hadn't experienced the sadness that normally was associated with loss. Mrs. Ryan said:

> I didn't experience it at all. I mean, I was going and going and going, since my husband got sick, and people were amazed, the way I kept myself going. I visited him every night. I was with him as much as he'd allow me to be. And people called me up to keep my spirits up, but they'd always be amazed that my spirits *were* up. And then, when he died, naturally I was all tensed up, but I kept myself going

the following week. Then I got the hives, and I got knocked completely for a loop, and I slept for a week. I really didn't do anything. But before, when my husband was ill, I wouldn't sit around and feel sorry for myself. I'd go out and talk to somebody. I'd go visit my girl friends. I'd go some place. A lot of people objected to me going out and leaving him alone, but I always just went out for an hour because I knew that I needed it.

There were, to be sure, breaks in Mrs. Ryan's defense. At times she herself recognized the true nature of her fantasies. She said:

My husband's friend came in last Saturday night, and he was talking to me, and I was telling him about how I'm going to be walking down the aisle and I'm going to have my children as bridesmaids, and the minute he left, I was tired. So I went to bed and I just cried my heart out. I cried because, maybe, I felt sorry for myself. I don't know. But I know it's all talk, it's all big talk with me.

Mrs. Ryan's sister was worried about her apparent absence of grief.

My sister brought a magazine that had an article on widows so I could read the article. It said that lots of times depression will hit you a year or two years later. And my sister said, "I'm afraid that's what's going to happen to you."

Mrs. Ryan herself had some sense that things were going wrong, that her gaiety was forced. She also had some awareness of her fear of depression. She said:

I went to this party Sunday and I was talking, just to keep things going. And I was talking to my girl friend the next day and I said, "You know, I'm getting real worried about myself and the way I talk." When I'm out socially, I make jokes about myself being a widow. Most widows will sit back demurely, but I force myself on people. I say I'm just putting on a big act, but how much of it is an act? That's what worries me. I mean, is there some psychological reason buried within me that I'm acting like this?

The only thing I'm afraid of is if I get depressed. I don't want to get depressed. I want to keep myself going. And in order, I think, for a woman of my age to keep herself going, I think she needs masculine attention. I mean, I don't want to be a sad sack for more than twenty years. I want to still be young. And I'm afraid unless I find somebody . . . because if I don't find a person, I'm going to start feeling very sorry for myself, because the years are going to be creeping up on me and I'm not going to be getting any younger.

Mrs. Ryan sometimes used thoughts of someone new entering her life to reassure herself that her loss had not been irreparable. Thus she fended off the sadness that was so frightening to her.

When we saw Mrs. Ryan again, thirteen months after her husband's death, it was clear that her life had gone very badly since our contact eleven months earlier. She talked ruefully about the period immediately following her husband's death when we had last seen her. At first, she said, things were all right:

I was having a ball going out drinking. And I was really very happy right after my husband died. I did very well. I had gone to a party at the club and I came home with the club president. That was the first time I had ever been in the arms of another man through my whole married life. And I was very happy that night.

But reaction to Mrs. Ryan's behavior came quickly from friends. She began to feel herself ostracized.

That time at the club was the last time I was really very happy because a lot of strange things happened afterward. My friends, that I had been so devoted to, well, they sort of cooled off, and I couldn't understand what the reason was. One of them kept saying to me, "You should join a widows' and widowers' club. You don't want to go to the club." And I couldn't figure out the reason. It seemed as though they didn't want me in their company any more.

Mrs. Ryan felt that her girl friends had turned against her because of her success in attracting men. She knew that they believed she was having affairs, but she was not, she said. And yet there were times when she had gone out and gotten drunk and the next day had had no memory of what had happened. Once she had awakened in a man's apartment without knowing how she had gotten there.

Mrs. Ryan's impulsivity took still another form: real estate ventures. The death of her husband had left her with a good deal of insurance money. She found a house she believed to be just right for her and put down a deposit on it. But then she felt the house was too near the club from which she now felt excluded, and so she changed her mind about buying it. Then, having refused the house (and lost her earnest money in the process), she became convinced that the house had been meant for her and that she had somehow frustrated God's plan for her.

Nine or ten months after her husband's death, Mrs. Ryan found herself in a state of depression, despite the attempts she had made to ward it off. She said:

> I was very despondent and I tried to keep going and I went into an awful state of my nervous system. I wouldn't go out. My nervous system, which had been hit during my husband's illness, started hitting a very low tone. I started, like, drying out. I hit a very, very low emotional tone, like exhaustion. I could hardly talk. I just wanted to sleep all the time. I knew I wasn't doing things right. I wasn't sending the kids to school. I didn't care about anything. One night, about one-thirty in the morning, I called the priest and I said, "You'll have to do something about me. I'm not taking care of my kids. I really don't know what I'm doing." So he contacted my family and they came down. And I said that I thought that I would have to go to the hospital. I said, "I've really flipped my lid. I've just lost track of everything."

> They got me to the hospital, and I thought I'd have to stay in there for a couple of weeks. But the psychiatrist said, "She'll go home, and she'll take care of her children, and we'll help her out."

The psychiatrist, according to Mrs. Ryan, told her that in reaction to her husband's death she had developed two personalities, one a "free" personality, the other a continuation of her married self. Indeed, this may be as good a way as any of describing the development of two distinct identities, each with its own assumptive world: one a new identity based on the assumption that she was no longer attached to her husband, the other a continuation of her identity as a wife. Mrs. Ryan saw herself as trying, with the psychiatrist's help, to establish a single identity developed from these two conflicting selves.

At the time of this third interview, a month after the anniversary of her husband's death, she had not yet permitted herself to experience grief; she was still terrified of depression, despite the break in her defenses that had brought her to request hospital admission. On the anniversary of her husband's death, she had a momentary feeling of despondency, but almost immediately thereafter she found herself feeling nothing at all. At the time of the interview, she said, "I just feel very dead now. I don't have any feeling at all."

We saw Mrs. Ryan again for a last interview about thirteen months after the third interview, a little more than two years after her husband's death. Her life seemed to have moved still further along the direction that was evident in the third interview: a preference for "deadness" rather than the sadness or depression that might be its alternative; withdrawal from friends; dependence on the hospital psychiatrist.

At the time of this fourth interview, friends had virtually disappeared from Mrs. Ryan's life. In their place, Mrs. Ryan saw her relatives. It might be surmised that the friends, identifying her as unstable, withdrew from her, whereas relatives, arriving at the same assessment, made themselves even more available. In addition to her family and the hospital psychiatrist, Mrs. Ryan had begun to participate actively in an outpatient group organized by the hospital clinic. In this fourth interview she talked almost as much about events in the group as she had talked in the first interview about events in the social club to which she and her husband belonged. She made no reference at all to the social club.

Mrs. Ryan continued to act on impulse and, again, some of this took place in the area of real estate. She had bought a house and moved herself and her children into it. But she and her oldest child, a boy approaching fifteen, had quarreled continually. The boy, she said, had become aggressive. She was afraid of him. She didn't like living with him in the same house. One day she went to a real estate agent and asked that her house be sold as quickly as possible. In two days, she said, she had moved into a rented apartment in her former neighborhood. She did not make a place in this new apartment for her oldest son.

Asked how she felt about what was happening in her life at the moment, Mrs. Ryan said how perplexed she was that things had gone so badly since her husband's death.

> I have to figure how all this screwiness has happened to me, because I always knew what I was doing. I was always a very competent person. I was always a good mother. That's why I came back to my old neighborhood. This is where I was a good mother. All my married life I always did God's will, never my own will. Like I married my husband, I had children—I went along with God's will. And even when my husband died, I figured it was the will of God. And I don't go out and hurt people. But I'm hurting myself. And by hurting myself, I'm hurting the children.

Quite clearly, the defense against depression employed by Mrs. Ryan had been severely disorganizing. She had devoted so much time and attention to keeping engaged with new experiences that little was left for realistic self-assessment and almost none for realistic planning. In addition, the deviant character of premature, driven sociability had alienated others and so made for eventual isolation.

If she had not been so frightened of becoming depressed, Mrs. Ryan might have been able to grieve sooner than she did.

And she might indeed have become depressed sooner, for as we have seen, her reserves of help and hope were not substantial. There is reason to believe that her dependency might have precipitated her into chronic grief. But it may be that depression is not necessarily so much to be feared if it evokes the support that is needed. Once Mrs. Ryan allowed herself to "break down," her family rallied round and a psychiatrist helped her to focus on the real loss for which she needed to grieve. He may not have achieved very much—her defenses were too fixed for that—but she did, at least, recover sufficiently well to resume responsibility for the care of her family.

Whether another course of electroshock or the prescription of antidepressant drugs would have been any more effective is doubtful. Our own clinical experience suggests that physical methods of treatment are rarely effective in cases of this kind. At the same time it would probably be wrong to conclude that other treatments, such as psychotherapy, have nothing to offer simply because of the limited success achieved in this case.

It is worth noting that one drug was considered by Mrs. Ryan to have been helpful—alcohol. Alcohol is, as we have seen, the most popular drug on the market. Mrs. Ryan recommended it as a night sedative, a tranquilizer, and an abreactant or "tongue loosener." If we add to this the undoubted social supports that can be found in many of the establishments in which it is consumed, it is easy to understand why 25 percent of the widows and widowers in our study reported that their consumption of alcohol had increased during the first year of their bereavement.

Like other drugs, however, alcohol does have side effects, and more than many drugs, it is habit forming and may encourage hypomanic avoidance of grief. These properties need to be taken into account if we are to evaluate its place in the lives of the bereaved. Also it is freely available without prescription, so that control of the dosage is entirely in the hands of the widow or widower, its use limited only by that person's good sense and

191

financial means. The problems inherent in its use by bereaved people are well illustrated by the case of Mr. Neilson.

## Mr. Neilson: Alcoholism and Social Withdrawal as Consequences of Failure to Recover

Mr. Neilson was forty-two and had been married for sixteen years when his wife went to the hospital to have their sixth child. At four-thirty in the morning he got a call from the doctor which he described in our first interview:

> He said, "She's not doing too well." So I went over at four-thirty in the morning. And then he came downstairs and he said, "Well, she seems to be doing well," he said. "We've stopped the bleeding." And he said, "You can either go home or you can stay around for a while. . . ."
>
> They called me the second time at six-thirty. And I went over to the hospital. And the nursing sister came in, and she spoke to me for a few minutes, and I knew there and then that she was dead. They were still working on her, but I knew she was dead, although she didn't say it. About ten minutes after, the doctors came in, three of them, and they told me to sit down and talked to me for a while and told me what happened. The doctors told me that they tried their best. They said it might not happen again for another ten or fifteen years. It was a rare case, a case which will happen but they can't do a thing about it.
>
> I was in a state of shock. When I went home people started asking me, and I couldn't remember what they told me, the doctors, I was so shocked. They had worked on her all night until after she had the baby. Eight doctors worked on her practically all night plus the nurse, the nursing sister. The baby was born about two-thirty in the morning. And she died about six-thirty in the morning.
>
> The nursing sister came in, and she sat down and talked to me for about ten or fifteen minutes, and she said, "Do you want to see

192

her?" I said, "No." I wouldn't go. I wouldn't do it. I was just stunned.
I wasn't even crying. I wasn't doing anything. The nursing sister
said, "Look, you can't sit here like this. It's not going to help you
one bit." She said, "I think you should see her." So I agreed. And
I went in and saw her, and she was just like she was asleep, just the
way I always remembered her. No pain, no nothing, in her face. I
broke up a little bit there.

I was glad I went to see her. If I hadn't, I would have felt it to this
day, I think. That took a little bit of the shock off. Then I started
thinking, what's going to happen? How am I going to handle it? And
when I left the hospital and I came home, I felt like putting my fist
through the refrigerator or putting my fist through the window.
When I came home that morning, I was still a little shocked.

I was mad. I said, "What the hell? Why me? What's the sense of
this? Is there a reason? What's the reason behind it? There's no good
reason." You start thinking: "Is there a God?" You start wondering.
You're mad. I don't know. I was going around. I couldn't sit down.
I couldn't talk sensible. Or, in my own mind, I didn't think I could.
But the people that came in said, "You're handling it very well."

A great many arrangements were made quickly after the
death. Mr. Neilson had to call his wife's family and tell them
what had happened. He arranged for his wife's body to be
flown to the family's home. He purchased plane tickets for
himself and the six children. Two days after his wife's death he
and his children were 500 miles away, at the home of his wife's
sister: "I'd say I never really slept, the way a person should
ordinarily sleep. And eating; I wasn't eating. I never ate right.
I mean, I'd just nibble at something, and sometimes I'd just
throw it right up as soon as I'd get it down."

He stayed with his wife's family for one day after the funeral.
While there he arranged for the baby to be looked after by his
wife's sister. That done, he collected his other children and
returned home. "I wasn't good by any means. But I figured, it's
over, now I've got to just pick up the pieces and start back. So
I stayed home for two or three days, and then I got back to
work. It kind of helped to get back to work."

Mr. Neilson's younger unmarried sister had lived with him and his wife before his wife's death. Now his sister took over responsibility for the older children. "It helped to know that the kids were safe, that they were going to do their homework the way she always helped them with it. My sister knew her plan and what she wanted to do. And that took a lot of weight off me."

Mr. Neilson said that he had been pretty good with the kids in the few weeks since his wife's death. He hadn't been impatient or irritable as he might sometimes have been earlier. But, when the interviewer suggested that despite his remaining even-tempered he might feel the loss of his wife as a kind of emptiness, he agreed:

> Yes, I get that feeling. Not during the day, when the kids are around, but when I come home from work in the night, like if I don't get home until twelve-thirty, I feel empty. I feel, coming home, I feel kind of a funny, funny feeling that I'm going into an empty house. Even though the house is still full of kids, it's just not the same. Even if she was in bed, well, she'd always say good night, or she'd be half-awake. I'll tell you right now, I get an empty feeling in the night, I really do, kind of a sad feeling inside.

Mr. Neilson had a difficult time accepting that his wife's death was really no one's fault. He knew, intellectually, that he should not blame himself. And yet there was the question— why did they have to have still another child? Asked by the interviewer whether he thought that it might be his fault that his wife died, he said:

> No, not now, because I thought that, too—I did think that way. I didn't think it was my fault she died, but I said, "Well, why did we have to have this sixth child? We have five." That went through my mind afterward. But we wanted this one. We wanted this baby. We never tried to avoid children. Before she got pregnant, about a year ago, she was talking to me. She said, "It's going to be funny with no baby around the house," because we were so used to having a

baby all the time. And so we had another baby. It was nobody's fault. I don't blame myself for that, or her, or anything else. I think it was just an act of God.

Mr. Neilson described how hard he had found it at first to accept his wife's loss. His initial response was one of disbelief: "At first, I wouldn't accept this thing; I refused it. I said it shouldn't happen to me, and all this. Why me? Why a good person like her when she never hurt anybody and she had so many friends?"

Later, when he could accept the fact of his wife's physical absence, Mr. Neilson had a sense of her continuing presence in spirit, watching over the family. He said, at the three-week point:

> I know she's not here. That's it, she's not here. That's all there is to it. I never get it in my mind that I'm going to look around and she's going to be in the kitchen; but the way I think, I think she knows just what's going to happen, that she's watching over us, she's watching us all the time. I think she is.

Mr. Neilson was at first extremely lonely; he could not concentrate and found himself restlessly searching for a goal. In the three-weeks interview he said:

> Nights when I come home, I'm lonely. I'm lonely, yes, I'm lonely all the time. I'm going to be that way for a while. I can't concentrate. I'm restless, also. There's a lot of things I haven't been doing around the house. I just couldn't get to them because of the effects of this. I'm not myself. I'm a little restless. I fidget around and I should be doing this or doing that but I haven't got the goal, I haven't got the push to do it. Yes, I can go to work. Even at my work, I think my work has been affected by it.

Five weeks later he thought there had been some improvement. The nights were still bad, but not as bad as they had been. He had had episodes of dizziness and of trembling. He was worried about what would happen to the kids if something were to happen to him. But for the most part, he felt he was doing better.

Mr. Neilson had always been a beer drinker. Now he seemed to be drinking more than he had before his wife's death. This was in part because he no longer had to be concerned about his wife's disapproval, but also because stopping off for a beer on the way home postponed his entrance into the now-empty house.

I never, ever got drunk or stayed out, none of that, but, well, after shopping, if I had a couple of glasses of beer she'd say, "What do you need a couple of glasses for?" But she was never furious. But last week, when I was coming home I stopped one night and had a couple of glasses of beer, and I didn't even enjoy it. I mean, it was nothing to me, I could have even gone home, but I just couldn't face the idea of going home to the empty house. If I thought the kids weren't well handled, I wouldn't touch it. But I know there's somebody here seeing nothing happens to them.

Having a glass of beer, I guess it's something just to break the monotony. Like today, without the kids all morning, they were over my sister's all night, I just felt that—I did a couple of washes—and when she was around I'd do it gladly, I'd always do it—but now I don't feel like doing it.

In the third interview, however, one year after Mr. Neilson's wife had died, it was clear that he had not moved very far toward recovery: "I read an article one time about something like this, and they said that after a year or so you start to forget, but I still haven't.

Asked how often he thought of his wife, he said: "She's still on my mind all the time."

Constantly; I'd say constantly. Like if the kids are talking, like one wants a new pair of shoes, I'd think the way she'd do it, see through her eyes, "If they don't need them, don't get them," or things like that.

196

Whenever I do anything, it's the same idea, she comes to my mind and I say how would she do it? And I'll do it just the way I think she would do it. I just try to follow a pattern that she set.

I can visualize her right now. I visualize her in the kitchen cooking or sitting down reading a book in the night. She used to be quite a reader. Things like that. It's not quite as clear a picture as it was, I'll have to admit that.

I've felt a little depressed at times. A few times I was quite discouraged over different things. I do a lot of thinking. I stopped reading. I stopped everything that I used to do. I used to read a lot, and I used to watch television—no, I never bothered with that too much—but I've lost a lot of interest in things, such as following sports. Well, I watch football and all that goes with it. But I just don't have the same old interest in it.

Mr. Neilson's withdrawal of interest in activities extended to housekeeping chores. Before his wife's death he had been most conscientious about maintaining the house:

It irks me a little bit because I should be doing things around the house—small things, like a light that's out in the hall that needs to be fixed, which I could fix, and the doorknob, or something to that effect. But I ignore them because I've come to a point where I just don't bother with them where I should. A year and a half ago I would have been doing those things like nothing. Get up in the morning and just do them.

Mr. Neilson said that he had withdrawn socially. He once belonged to a church group but now found himself uninterested in it. Nor had he been interested in sociability: "I was invited a lot of places New Year's, around the neighborhood, just next door or the next door over. I wasn't a bit interested. I didn't go."

It will be clear from this account that Mr. Neilson's reaction to his wife's death corresponds to the syndrome of unexpected bereavement described in chapter 4. After an initial reaction of

**197**

shock and numbness, with associated anxiety and tension, he was finding, a year later, that his life was dominated by her absence and that he had withdrawn from social activities.

In Mr. Neilson's case, however, there was now an added complication:

> One of the superintendents in the office called me in and said, "You're not drinking too much, are you?" I said, "No." I said, "I don't miss time or come in drunk, or anything like that. But it's part of my life now to get out in the morning just to talk to somebody." And, I said, "It's so lonesome now." And all he told me was, "Just be careful. Just watch it. Don't get into trouble." So I said, "All right."

> I've been drinking beer since I was twenty years old, and it's part of my life, and it's something that you just can't change overnight. Lately, it's been a little too much. Too much time out of the house, when I should be in, when I've got a house where I should be looking after it. But it's just the idea that I got to get out. I got to. I get a closed-in feeling.

We talked to Mr. Neilson again three years after the death of his wife. He seemed to have moved no further toward recovery than he had at the end of the first year of his bereavement. The problems he had then with depression, with drinking, with inability to become interested in on-going activities remained. Indeed, Mr. Neilson felt that things had been getting worse. He was tired, irritable, lonely, and depressed: "I'll tell you the honest truth: I've let things go that I know I can do. I've let things go. I haven't got the—what would you call it?—the push? Well, I haven't got the push to do it."

Mr. Neilson had already had the first demonstration that he had become alcoholic. The summer following the first anniversary of his wife's death he had taken the children to their summer home. For two days he went without beer or whiskey. He developed delirium tremens and was hospitalized.

Mr. Neilson continued to think of his wife, as he said, "almost constantly," but there had been some change.

I haven't got her out of my mind yet. [But] I don't shed tears anymore, let's put it that way. I used to, but that's gone, anyway. I've come to the conclusion she's not here. She's not coming back, so that's all there is to it.

I can look at her picture now. It doesn't faze me to do it, not like it would have maybe a year ago. I just think, when I look, "Look what the kids lost."

But I guess you never get over it. You never forget. Let's put it this way: if there was a remarriage or something, well you'd get over it, but you never forget. And you will never be yourself again. It takes a lot out of you. I'm not quite the same person I was. Time and age does that, plus the hurt.

I try to live her kind of life and try to get the kids to live her kind of life, which was a perfect life. I mean, she was a wonderful woman. That's the way I look at it and I try to get my kids to look. I used to remind them. I'd say, "Look what a good mama she was, she was always looking after you and everything." But now I've stopped that.

Mr. Neilson continued to be lonely and despairing, and he continued to drink as almost the only way of dealing with his feelings. "I get discouraged sometimes. Then I have a few drinks. It's the same as it's been. Lonely."

Because we had followed Mr. Neilson from the time of his wife's death we could recognize that his alcoholism and withdrawal from friends (other than tavern friends) and from his responsibilities as the head of a family and as an employee were reactions to the totally unforewarned death of his wife. But on top of this the use of alcohol had now become a problem in its own right. As we have seen, alcohol, as a treatment for grief, sometimes does relieve some of the misery by deadening the pain and by dulling awareness of the loss. It fosters

199

distancing and denying. It also facilitates sleep, and in some instances it makes talking about the loss a bit easier. All these effects of alcohol encourage the sufferer to rely on the drug, to increase its dosage, and to escape more and more into a twilight world of intoxication. The consequences of this escalation need no spelling out. For Mr. Neilson they included delirium tremens, a serious condition, and evident failures in social roles.

Mrs. Ryan also used alcohol to excess. But it would be wrong to blame either's problems on "the demon drink." In each case, the misuse of alcohol was itself a symptom of disabling grief.

## Mrs. Delaney: Intensification of Tendencies Toward Emotional Isolation as a Result of Loss

In general, our materials support the idea that those who have the capacity to form secure attachments not only have more satisfactory marriages but also deal better with bereavement, all else being equal. This is not invariably the case. One of our respondents was a twenty-one-year-old widow whose parents had separated when she was very small, leaving her to be brought up by a long succession of foster parents. At one point, describing how she typically related to others, she noted that she was hard on people as a precaution. She had learned to keep her distance from all others, for fear of being hurt anew. Her marriage, as she described it, had been extremely cool. She said that during the marriage she and her husband had led quite separate social lives. After her husband's death—in an industrial accident—she felt little need to grieve. The loss of her marriage was not devastating, and her recovery from bereavement was judged good.

This widow was, however, quite exceptional. There were others among our respondents who had learned from unhappy childhoods to be cautious in forming attachments, but their caution did not prevent their marriages from becoming anchors to their emotional lives. Bereavement then confirmed them in their tendency to distrust and made them even more given to distancing themselves from others.

This seems to have been the effect of bereavement on the third respondent we discuss in this chapter, Mrs. Delaney. Like the preceding two cases, Mrs. Delaney's loss was without forewarning. She was in her early forties, the mother of two children, thirteen and nine years old, when her husband died suddenly, one day after he had been hospitalized with a coronary occlusion.

Mrs. Delaney had had a most unhappy childhood. Her parents had divorced when she was about two. Her mother then remarried, after which three more children were born. Mrs. Delaney said that she and her older sister were never accepted by her mother and stepfather. When she was five, she and her sister were handed over to her grandmother to be raised. Mrs. Delaney felt she had been rejected by her father when he left her home and by her mother and stepfather when they gave her to her grandmother to raise. She said:

My mother always lived near us. But it's who you're with, it's the one that takes care of you and does everything for you, that you have feeling for. On Mother's Day we always used to buy my grandmother everything. We thanked my grandmother; we never thanked my mother for anything. We even told my mother; we said, "We never lived with you. You're more like an aunt, you're not like a mother to us."

Mrs. Delaney married soon after high school. Although her husband, as she described him, was a responsible family man, his closest relationships were with his friends.

201

He was the type that he had friends, he didn't have them for a year or two, he had them for years and years and years. The only time he was really contented was when he was out with the fellas. He liked to play cards.

If he went fishing, he went with the fellas. He had a lot of friends. That was an outlet for him. And they used to go to the track or something like that, and play cards. The only enjoyment he had was out with the fellas.

Mrs. Delaney, for her part, was content with the arrangement in which her husband had his own life and she had hers. She was not terribly sociable, she said, but when she did go out, she, like her husband, went alone. When her husband invited her to accompany him to a baseball game or a card game, she declined.

He loved baseball. And when he went to a baseball game, he took the kids and their friends—he took them all to the baseball games. And I hated baseball. I'd stay home and watch television or anything. They wanted me to go, but I never went to baseball games. I can't stand baseball games. And I couldn't stand cards.

It seems likely that the distance maintained in Mrs. Delaney's marriage was in part a product of Mrs. Delaney's having learned early in life that close relationships were not to be trusted. Both Mr. and Mrs. Delaney invested themselves in their children. They both cared about their home. Mrs. Delaney was as good a wife and mother as she could be, Mr. Delaney as good a husband and father; that they were not close to each other seems not to have been an issue for them.

Mrs. Delaney felt that her husband had made most of the important decisions without consulting her. She was at times resentful, but ultimately she accepted his authority.

He was a wonderful father, but he wasn't as good a husband as he was a father. He dominated the children, and they did as he wanted and everything. But he tried to dominate me like he did the kids. Like, we had wanted a summer cottage, and we almost had the papers signed and everything. And at the last minute, he decided he didn't want it. And I was upset about that because, after all the bank president went through to get us the mortgage, he just said he didn't want it, and that was all there was to it. It was too bad for that man to go through all that work, but he didn't want it, and that's how it was.

On first talking with Mrs. Delaney, we might have predicted a poor outcome to her bereavement. Her husband had died without forewarning, and in addition, there was some contentiousness in the marriage and some dependency on Mrs. Delaney's part. On the other hand, Mrs. Delaney's early losses had clearly led her to maintain a "safe" distance from those to whom she was attached as a defensive strategy.

When we saw Mrs. Delaney thirteen months after her husband's death, her recovery presented a mixed picture. At first her children had been troublesome—because, Mrs. Delaney thought, her husband had been the parent responsible for discipline—but things had recently improved. Social Security and her husband's pension plan together provided enough money for the family. Mrs. Delaney had obtained a job as a housekeeper at a nearby college, worked hard on the job, and for the most part was happy with it. All this would seem to the good. On the other side, although Mrs. Delaney tried to keep herself from thinking about her husband's death—itself an indication of failure to recover—she still grieved and still cried occasionally. Like other widows with little forewarning, she could not explain to herself why her loss had happened: she was bitter that a husband so good, so devoted to his family, should have been taken, when men who were dissolute and utterly irresponsible continued to live. She was not able to redefine her identity: she still felt herself to be a married woman, with a married woman's obligations, even though her husband was dead.

Mrs. Delaney felt she had a special reason for bitterness because of her other losses. She felt that she already had had more than her share of sorrow. Her grieving, too, was deeper because this loss elicited responses to her earlier losses. The interviewer wrote, after the thirteen-month interview with Mrs. Delaney:

> Last time Mrs. Delaney grieved for her husband and her children. This time she grieved for herself, rejected by both mother and father, dominated and controlled by a husband who is no longer here to manage her life. She has defended in every way against this recognition of her feelings, but they were so close to the surface that the least little prick drew blood.

Now, as before, Mrs. Delaney avoided establishing new relationships. She was fairly close to one of her husband's sisters. But, as she said:

> I'm not the type, I don't think, to get very close to anybody. I really don't think I was ever very close to anyone. I don't think so. I mean, I had friends that I knew for years, and I have them now. Like Barbara, I've known her since we were fifteen years old. But I really don't think I'm close to her. I mean, she's not a person that I could talk to. I don't think I'm really very close to anybody.

> [At work] I don't get attached to anyone. I mean, I'm friendly to them, but I couldn't see myself going visiting them. I feel that you're friendly there, [but] I wouldn't have anything to do with them on the outside. I don't have anything to do with anybody. I don't know. Maybe I am cold.

Mrs. Delaney's one date during the year took place when her children were away at camp—two weeks during which she felt truly bereft. She went out with a man on the janitorial staff of the college at which she worked.

> I only went out once in the whole year. It was a fellow from the college, who works in maintenance. He has never been married. And he owns a lot of land. I mean, he's wealthy that way. But he's as tight as anything. He has it, but he'll never spend it. And he took me out one night during the summer. The children went to camp,

and I was lost for that two weeks when they were away. So I went out with him. Well, maybe it was me, because he was so nice and he tried to please me and everything, in every way. But I couldn't get home quick enough. I felt, "What if I ever met anybody that I knew?" It's an awful feeling. Even though my husband is dead, I felt guilty for being out. And that's the one time I ever went out. I said, "I have to go home." And he said, "What's the matter? You should forget about the past." And I said, "I can't do that. The way I feel, I'm still married, even though he's dead." It's an awful feeling. He's asked me out since, and I've said, "No. I couldn't go out with you. When I was out last time, I couldn't get home quick enough."

Mrs. Delaney's inability to relinquish her married identity may be in part an expression of Mrs. Delaney's dependency during her marriage. But there was also in it a restatement of her defensive strategy of keeping herself invulnerable to new loss by forming no new relationships.

Mrs. Delaney was uncertain about whether her bereavement had made her even more reluctant to form relationships with others than she had been earlier. Her aunt, however, assured her that it had.

I think I'm a colder person. I'm not that friendly. I can't be bothered with things that I could before. Like people going down the street say, "How are you?" I don't care how they are, and I don't bother asking. I suppose it's an awful way. I'm not that friendly. When I'm going any place I can't be bothered standing talking to anyone. I want to get where I'm going.

I think that's me, though. I don't really think my husband dying had anything to do with it. I don't think I'm a very affectionate person. I don't get attached to people. When I was a kid I wasn't wanted. Maybe that's why I feel this way, that I don't get attached to people. But my aunt says I was better before than I am now. So I don't know. I think I may be colder now than I was before.

We were unable to obtain a follow-up interview with Mrs. Delaney, but the pattern of her life seemed already established: her life would revolve around her children; her part-time job would provide her with a sense of something useful and interesting outside her home; and she would remain distant and guarded toward the possibility of any new intimate tie.

## Dr. Siegel: Chronic Grief and Impaired Functioning

Dr. Siegel was thirty years old, and had been married for six years, when his wife died suddenly of a heart attack while at work. Dr. Siegel had completed a Ph.D. in applied mathematics and was doing further graduate work in computer science, a new field for him, at the time of his wife's death. Neither Dr. Siegel nor his wife had known that his wife had anything wrong with her. In our first interview with Dr. Siegel he described for us how he learned of his wife's death:

I was in my office when I was summoned by a telephone call from the place my wife worked. She worked here at the university. It wasn't my wife calling, it was somebody else. So I put my overcoat on, and I ran the four blocks to where she worked. When I entered the place I saw some policemen there. I didn't realize anything. A girl asked me to enter a room, to take off my overcoat, to stay there. She said, "Wait here," and she went away. I was waiting, not nervous at all. I didn't have the least idea. Then the same employee returned, and I asked, "What happened?" And she said, "The doctor is with your wife." And I asked her, "Did she faint?" And she said, "Yes." And I asked, "Has she recovered?" And she said, "Not yet."

I was a little worried, but not very much worried, because that would be a natural thing, that you faint and don't react immediately. I never thought about death. So when I was talking with the girl I heard the voice of the doctor saying, "Where is Dr. Siegel?" And he came to the room and said, "I have a very serious thing to tell you." He said that my wife would be unable to work, that she was sick.

I thought it would be temporary. Finally he said, "Your wife is dead."

I couldn't believe it. I couldn't believe that this very same morning she took me to my office and she went to work. I don't remember very clearly what happened then, except that I felt that all my life was meaningless.

Dr. Siegel and his wife had one child, a boy aged three and a half. His wife's parents had been visiting them for a couple of weeks, staying in their apartment and looking after their son while they were at work. Dr. Siegel's father-in-law had been told that he, too, should come to the office where Mrs. Siegel worked. Dr. Siegel said to us: "About fifteen minutes after they told me, my father-in-law came. They had called him too. When he came in I was shouting and screaming, hitting out. I said, 'Walter! Walter! Betty is dead!' "

Dr. Siegel was unable to sleep the night after his wife's death. A friend stayed with him and let him talk.

I went home about five or six with my father-in-law. I think we cried. Somebody brought some tranquilizers, but they had no effect whatsoever. I couldn't sleep all the night. We have very close friends, a couple here at the university. He teaches Classics. His wife stayed up all night with me. And I talked to her. I had to talk, to say what my wife meant for me. I couldn't talk with my father-in-law because he was suffering as much as I was. And my wife's friend stayed all night without sleeping, listening to me almost without saying anything. I was talking and talking about Betty, about what am I going to do without my wife? I slept a little bit but not very much.

That night, pills I had didn't help me. I drank a lot of alcohol. I was drunk and crying. But I couldn't sleep.

Dr. Siegel had been dependent on his wife as well as attached to her. He had felt that his wife was the only person in his life with whom he was emotionally close; in addition, he had relied on her to manage virtually all the practical affairs in their shared lives.

Betty was almost my life. My parents were immigrants, and I felt that my mother, because of her economic situation, neglected to give love to me when I was a child. I felt that my wife was the first time that I had love.

We were tremendously happy. Many people feel that only when they lose something do they realize its value. This didn't happen to me because I knew, when she was living, the value of my wife. I felt that my wife was the best thing that could ever happen to me. I wanted to have a marriage and to be a good scientist and to have a good family and that was all.

When our checks came back from the bank, I would draw only one. All the other checks were drawn by my wife. She controlled everything. She managed the house. We have a child, a very, very lovely child. He's three and a half. And my wife was always in charge of his education, even though I had a very close relationship with my child.

The day after his wife's death, in conformity with Jewish religious requirements (although neither Dr. Siegel nor his wife had been believers), Dr. Siegel's wife was buried. When we talked with Dr. Siegel three weeks later, he said that his memories of that day were sharply etched, despite his fatigue. And yet, as is characteristic with unforewarned deaths, even three weeks later he could hardly believe what had happened. On the Thursday morning his wife had taken him to his office; on Friday afternoon he was part of a funeral assemblage at her burial.

There was the issue of what Dr. Siegel was to tell his son. Psychologists who have worked with small children generally suggest telling the children the truth, although telling it in such a way that the children can assimilate it rather than be overwhelmed by it. Dr. Siegel chose another tack. He told his son that the boy's mother had gone on a plane trip. The boy's grandparents had recently arrived by plane, and the boy had been on planes himself. He understood that planes transported people to otherwise unreachable places. Dr. Siegel also told the boy that it was unlikely that the boy's mother would return soon. Later, Dr. Siegel felt, he would tell the boy the truth.

Dr. Siegel and his wife's parents agreed that, temporarily, the parents would take care of Dr. Siegel's son. They thought the arrangement might last a few weeks, perhaps at the most a month or two, during which time Dr. Siegel would prepare himself to care for his son as a single parent.

In our second interview with Dr. Siegel, held about a month after the first, six weeks after his wife's death, Dr. Siegel described reactions that included not only expressions of grief quite compatible with normal recovery but also some that suggested problems to come. Dr. Siegel said he continued to feel his wife's loss almost as a physical pain: "It's a sadness, something that you have in your chest. I cannot describe that feeling. It is like a heavy stone in my body that I carry, a pain inside of my chest. The first two or three weeks, the pain was heavier, more painful. But it still continues although not in the same degree."

Dr. Siegel said that he thought of his wife almost all of the time:

> Almost everything reminds me of her. For instance, today somebody said he was going to see the movie *Jules and Jim,* a French movie. I saw that movie with my wife. Yesterday I was talking about French writers, and I remembered that my wife was very familiar with French writers. I remembered then that when we had our first date I took her to see a movie about Emile Zola. So I associate almost everything with my wife.

Strongly suggestive of a recovery process tending toward chronic grief was Dr. Siegel's continued intense yearning for his wife's return. "I wish I could see my wife again. I think I imagine that. I think I dream of that. I can't remember what I dream but that's the consciousness of the dream that I have when I wake up."

Also suggestive of a recovery process going badly was Dr.

209

Siegel's continued reliance on a drug—again, alcohol—for relief from distress. "I used to drink alcohol casually. But since the death of my wife I have found a kind of relief there. It helps me let go of my feelings of the absence of my wife."

Dr. Siegel had embarked on his current course of study with his wife's encouragement. His wife, even more than he, had felt that there was greater promise for him in the field of computer science than there had been in the branch of applied mathematics in which he had previously specialized. He, on the other hand, had been uncertain about making what amounted to a shift in field. Just before our second interview with him he had taken a final examination in his new field and had passed with a very high grade. He had been helped in this achievement by the feeling that taking the examination was a project he shared with his wife and that his wife was with him during it.

> I was afraid I was going to fail. But I was surprised that through the four hours' examination I didn't feel tired. Four hours of concentration and nothing disturbed me. I didn't feel I was looking for anything. I felt that my wife was with me in the examination because it was my wife who suggested that I should take up this subject. And I felt that if she suggested it, that I was going to do it right.

The examination over, however, the realization that his wife was not in fact with him became more nearly real. "Joy in life was something I was accustomed to sharing with my wife. Now it hurts me to think of her. I compare what is going on now with me with what was before and I feel the difference. The memory hurts me."

Asked whether there had been a change for the better or worse in his grieving, Dr. Siegel replied that there had been no change at all. The pain associated with the memory of his loss may, perhaps, have diminished. But he was as sorrowful, as inconsolable, as he had been earlier. Indeed, Dr. Siegel's despondency had been increasing. Now he reported combating suicidal impulses.

I didn't think about suicide for the first fifteen days, or the first thirty days, but since then I have had thoughts of suicide. But I have too much responsibility: I can't afford to commit suicide. But when I start to feel the loneliness of the night and have to think of the pain the day produces, I feel all alone and then nothing is enjoyable.

Adding to Dr. Siegel's distress was a feeling of having somehow contributed to his wife's death. Dr. Siegel and his wife had engaged in intercourse the night before her death, and now Dr. Siegel worried that the exertion and the excitement might have somehow affected her. Then, too, his wife had been tired in the weeks just before her death, and Dr. Siegel blamed himself for not having been more concerned about this. Despite an autopsy report that described a congenital heart defect as the cause of his wife's death, and despite the flimsiness of the accusations he made against himself, Dr. Siegel could not rid himself of a feeling of guilt.

Along with this feeling of guilt, he felt bitterness at the injustice of his wife's death. As is characteristic of a loss without forewarning, it made no sense. It was wrong. It could not be explained, and it could not be justified.

Another indicator of a recovery process going badly was that Dr. Siegel was becoming more and more isolated. So long as his wife's parents were with him, he failed to notice that he was withdrawing from friends. But in the weeks following their departure he came to recognize that he was more isolated than he had previously been.

My friends don't try to get in touch with me. I think they are concerned about themselves. They can't dedicate time to me. I went to dinner one night at the home of the friends who stayed with me that first night. I felt that she and her husband felt embarrassed. They have changed in respect to me. But some other friends, very good friends, invited me to a party, and I said, "No," because the party would have meant so much to my wife. And that night I would be very, very upset. I would feel the lack of my wife tremendously.

211

We returned to talk to Dr. Siegel just a year after his wife's death. We moved up the date of the interview from the thirteen-month point our schedule called for because Dr. Siegel was planning to leave the city.

We found that Dr. Siegel had progressed little in the ten months since we had last seen him. If anything, his yearning for his wife's return was clearer and stronger than it had been. He said:

> I was very close to my wife. Since she hasn't been with me I haven't any sense of time. I remain completely empty. I remember perfectly everything we did together, when we came here to this city, what she needed, how she did things. Her presence is very much in my mind.

> Yesterday I was at the cemetery and, without much control of myself, I said, "When are you coming back? If you could only come back." I didn't have much control of myself, of my logical self.

Dr. Siegel had not been able to reorganize his life so that he could care for his son (now four-and-a-half years old). Instead, his son had remained with Dr. Siegel's parents-in-law through the entire year. For the month just after our second interview with him, six weeks after his wife's death, Dr. Siegel had joined his son at his parents-in-law's home. When he returned he found it almost impossible to establish a satisfactory living situation for himself.

> When I came back here I was alone, and I needed to find an apartment and to cook for myself and to take care of the apartment. It was the first time that I was completely alone. And I think that was the first time that I suffered very much. I was having an awful time. I still can't manage to remain in my apartment alone very long. I feel suffocated because of the memory of my wife. When I would think of my wife, of the good times that we had had, I couldn't bear it. The happy memories were all painful.

212

Dr. Siegel had lost much of the energy he had formerly brought to his work. His work, like everything else in his life, seemed essentially without meaning.

> I haven't anything to fight for. Even though I finished my year with very high marks, I think the highest that I had in my entire life, I did it partly because I wanted to go to the cemetery and say to my wife, "Look, here is my best. I owe that to you, because you were expecting it from me." And I did it. But I don't care in the least for my profession or for my career. Most of the things I did in my life were just to show her, because she could enjoy what I was doing. Now that there is no more Betty that can enjoy my work, I don't care. I'm not upset if something goes wrong. I'm doing quite a good job, but I didn't used to try to do a good job, I used to try to do my best. Now I don't. I just try to meet my responsibilities. I have a colleague who is a very competent professional, very capable, very competitive, and he wants to be very successful. I don't care in the least about that. Before I would have wanted to be first. Now I don't care. My wife's death changed that.

A year after his wife's death, Dr. Siegel clearly had failed to recover.

> I still haven't found a way to enjoy life. Many of my friends say that you can find pleasure in your work, but I don't feel like working. I used to read a lot, but I don't read anymore because I don't have the peace of mind. I'm restless. I start to read a novel and it makes no sense. I try to keep a sense of humor when I am with people, but when I am alone I become depressed.

> I think for the first time I don't worry about my death. Before, I was scared about death. Now, I don't care. Sometimes I wish that I could pass away. I don't feel any pain in thinking I could die. Sometimes I feel as though I could lie down right now. Why do I have to continue?

We saw Dr. Siegel for a final interview four years and three months after his wife's death. In the three years since our third interview, Dr. Siegel's life had not gone well. His graduate and

213

postgraduate career had been brilliant. But now his work was only adequate, not nearly what had been expected of him.

> I have not been under extreme pressure or been doing extremely demanding work. So my work has not been entirely satisfactory for me. I really feel that I don't have the peace of mind. Before my wife died, I was a very devoted and hard worker. I think that explains why I did so well in my courses. And after she died, until I finished my examinations, I still worked pretty hard. But since then I don't think I have done anything which I can say is a substantial contribution to anything.

His son had continued to live with his parents-in-law. Dr. Siegel visited when he could. He was hoping he could bring his son to live with him in the near future, but he worried that he might not prove a capable parent. The self-doubt that had contributed to his dependence on his wife may have been exacerbated by her loss.

Just as had been the case at the time of the third interview, Dr. Siegel's dominant mood was one of sadness, restlessness, and loneliness. And, just as had been a pattern with him then, he sought out company as a source of distraction.

> At night I really feel very much alone. Very seldom have I been able to settle down and stay by myself. Usually I have some sort of social engagement: dinner, cocktails, dates. When it comes Saturday, that's when I feel much more alone. Saturdays and Sundays, most of the time, I come back into the office. I don't do very much. I come back into the office and go for lunch, go for a walk, something like that. I'm not really able to do anything. I'm very restless. In the evening I try to be with company. That's the way in which I try to hide my loneliness.

Dr. Siegel said he did not now think of his wife very often. He was depressed almost constantly, but it was as though his sadness and sense of loss had become separated from the image of his wife. Grieving had become a part of his personality.

Chronic grief often has as one of its aspects a reduced capacity to fulfill responsibilities. It is unfortunate that the widow or widower who suffers from this condition is likely to be seen not as impaired by chronic grief but only as despondent, since this view of the condition discourages effort to obtain psychiatric help.

## In Conclusion

The four people described here survived bereavement but with lives that were grayer and colder than they might have been. Their symptoms were different: Mrs. Ryan's sometimes hypomanic and occasionally depressed behavior; Mr. Neilson's alcoholism; Mrs. Delaney's greater coldness of personality and distance from others; and Dr. Siegel's depression and apathy. But all had lives that became more constricted and much, much sadder.

One conclusion we would offer is that failure to recover from bereavement may take the form of constriction and sadness associated with a wide variety of other conditions. We believe that only if the underlying grief is resolved will there be genuine recovery. We also believe that in this area as in others, prevention is better than cure. There are ways, we believe, to fend off failures to recover. It is to this concern that we next turn.

# Chapter 9

## The Prediction of Outcome

### Who Should Be Helped?

In the preceding chapters we have attempted to show how particular circumstances can give rise to particular types of grief. Here we address a different question. Given that some people will come through the stress of bereavement relatively unscathed while others will be thrown into lasting difficulties or even develop psychiatric illness, how can we identify at the time of bereavement those people who are at special risk? If we can answer this question we shall have satisfied the first condition for the development of a viable program of preventive psychiatry. The second condition to be met is the development of effective methods of intervention, methods that will reduce the risk of a damaging bereavement.

It might be argued that since all bereaved people are to some degree "at risk," we should provide all of them with help. But this assumes that the help available is relatively unlimited and that, even for those who have no need of help, bereavement support can never do harm. In actual fact neither of these circumstances is likely to obtain. There will probably never be enough properly selected and trained bereavement counselors to help all bereaved people, and even if there were, there is reason to fear that attempts to counsel people who do not need counseling could do more harm than good.

People who have been referred for help sometimes find themselves stigmatized as "sick" and regarded as unreliable. Some begin to think of themselves in this way, and anxiety about their own mental health may further undermine their confidence and ability to cope. Although bereavement counseling services do not carry so pronounced a stigma as psychiatric services, there is a real danger that people who turn to such services will experience a subtle undermining of their self-confidence. In the end, only scientific evaluation can tell us whether the costs of bereavement counseling outweigh the benefits. The evidence available at this time seems to indicate that bereavement services that focus their counseling on bereaved people at special risk do succeed in their aim of reducing risk, but unselective services may be without overall beneficial effects (Parkes 1981a).

SELF-REFERRAL

Many bereavement services rely on self-referral. They assume that people who need help will ask for it while those who do not ask for help do not need it. This assumption, which underlies many social and clinical services, implies that people who need the service are aware of their need for help, that they are able and willing to seek such help, that they trust the people who are offering the service and can afford any expenses involved in obtaining it. Sadly, there are many bereaved people who do not satisfy all these criteria. In fact, some of the very factors that, in our study, predicted poor outcome after bereavement—feelings of anger, guilt, despair, and hopeless yearning for the dead spouse's return—are likely to reduce the probability that bereaved people who need help will make the effort to ask for it. Further, they may belong to a social group that lacks knowledge of or trust in the purveyors of help; they may be too poor, too immobile, or too depressed to seek help;

or they may not believe themselves entitled to the time and attention of others. Here, as elsewhere, those most in need of a service may be least well equipped to obtain it. We think that an awareness of risk factors would enable bereavement services to be more wisely used.

Some services rely on referral by doctors or other professionals who are assumed to be able to assess risk, and it is true that there are a number of professionals around at times of bereavement who may be in a position to do so. Usually this kind of risk assessment takes the form of an educated guess. After taking a careful case history, the adviser uses a combination of knowledge and intuition to decide whether or not to press the bereaved individual to seek help.

We tried something like this in our study. We asked our coders to predict the eventual outcome of recovery on the basis of what they could learn from the tapes of the first two interviews. (This is different from the coders' *rating* of outcome, which was based on the third interview, thirteen months after the death of the spouse. That rating was one of the bases for the actual outcome score.) The instructions to the coders required that they consider a number of factors that might indicate either "effective" or "ineffective" regulatory behavior—which in our view was likely to mean effective or ineffective movement toward recovery—before assigning respondents to one of five categories of predicted outcome.

### INSTRUCTIONS FOR CODERS' PREDICTION OF OUTCOME

*Polar Consellations of Reactions to Loss*
These are reference points for assigning a predictive rating to bereaved individuals. Read carefully before making predictions.
1. *Hypothesized "Effective" Regulatory Behavior:* Survivor attempts to understand the medical cause of death, participates in the funeral arrangements, allows himself or herself to cry and express his or her need for emotional and practical support and assistance from others, spends time thinking of deceased and reviewing the past either alone or with others, recognizes and accepts anger about

being abandoned, begins to confront realistic problems and consider alternative solutions.

2. *Hypothesized "Ineffective" Regulatory Behavior:* Survivor fantasizes that the deceased is simply away, goes through the motions of the funeral with a need to control all expression of sadness; whenever memories occur they are suppressed; survivor keeps constantly busy to take his or her mind off the past, relies on alcohol or television to dull the pain, refuses to admit feelings of anger, and is hypercritical of others.

### CODER PREDICTION OF OUTCOME

1. Individual will fall at the positive end of a continuum of adaptive outcome.

   The indices that will cause an individual to be assigned this rating are: indication of a lessening of the symptoms of crying, anxiety, protest between the third and eighth week; recognition of feelings of anger; free expression of feelings to others; ability to use others for support and assistance; behavior that approximates the polar type of effective behavior.

2. Individual is likely to experience a mixed outcome, but one that will fall more at the positive end of the continuum than the negative.

   The indices that will lead to this rating are: the constellation of regulatory behaviors is mixed, but either there are more kinds of behavior conforming to rating 1 or there are certain crucial indicators, such as admission of anger, that tip the balance in favor of a more positive outcome.

3. Outcome is indeterminate in its directionality.

   The constellation of regulatory behaviors is equivocal because of the balance of indices.

4. Individual is likely to experience a mixed outcome, but one that falls more at the negative end of the continuum than the positive.

   Reasoning is the same for rating 2, but the balance of indicators is in favor of a more negative outcome.

**219**

5. Individual will fall at the negative end of a continuum of adaptive outcome.

This rating will be given to those who most clearly approximate the polar type of ineffective behavior, with the following as alternative indices: acquisition of symptoms similar to those of the deceased; pronounced ascription of self-blame; excessive concern for others who are grieving in lieu of actually grieving oneself; reactions approaching panic produced by reminders of the death; overactivity without a sense of loss or with absence of all affect; aimless wandering; sudden appearance of psychosomatic symptomatology.

Table 9.1 shows how the score derived from this assessment correlated with twelve measures of outcome. All of them were

TABLE 9.1

*Correlation of Coders' Predictions of Outcome with Twelve Outcome Measures*

|  | r. |
|---|---|
| Anxiety/Depression | 0.49[a] |
| Socializing | 0.47[a] |
| Resilience | 0.46[a] |
| "Combination Score" | 0.43[a,d] |
| Acceptance | 0.42[a] |
| Guilt/Anger | 0.41[a] |
| Level of Functioning | 0.39[a] |
| Health Questionnaire Outcome | 0.36[b] |
| Valuation of Self | 0.31[b] |
| Attitude toward the Future | 0.24[c] |
| Movement | 0.22 |
| Physical Health | 0.21 |

[a]$p = .001$, when $r = .38$
[b]$p = .01$, when $r = .30$
[c]$p = .05$, when $r = .23$
[d]the outcome measure referred to in chapters 2–8.
(Fisher and Yates [1963].)

predicted successfully, all but two at statistically significant levels.

OTHER PREDICTIVE FACTORS

Clearly, an educated guess based on the criteria used by our coders could be a valid method of assessing the risk of bereavement. We attempted to improve on the coders' predictions by adding to them our short list of eighteen predictive variables. We then conducted a multivariate analysis to identify the combination of variables that gave the best prediction of outcome. Appendix 4 lists the variables that emerged.

The first and most important predictive variable was the Coders' Prediction of Outcome, but predictive power was greater when the seven other assessments were added.

Appendix 5 presents an Index of Bereavement Risk based largely, although not entirely, on the analysis of appendix 4.

## Further Evaluation of Index of Bereavement Risk

Subsequently we have had opportunity to test the predictive value of the Index of Bereavement Risk in London, England. Here one of us (C.M.P.) has introduced a bereavement service at St. Christopher's Hospice which uses responses to the Bereavement Risk Index questionnaire to identify bereaved people in need of support. This questionnaire is completed by nurses who have become acquainted with the family before bereavement and refers to the person thought to be most affected by the death. Most often, of course, this is the widow or widower.

The initial form taken by the questionnaire is given in appendix 5, along with other statistical details of this study. Questions used to measure the variables of appendix 4 have been slightly

221

modified to meet the particular circumstances of a hospice. Thus, in place of the question on duration of marriage we asked for the age of the survivor. This is obviously correlated with duration of marriage, but it also takes into account other studies that included a wider range of ages of bereaved people than did the Harvard Bereavement Study. Some of these studies suggest that younger people suffer relatively more following bereavement than do older people for whom losses are more timely and expectable. The nurses at the hospice did not feel that they could ask family members about their attitudes toward their own deaths, so this question was dropped. Nurses' knowledge of the patients' families did enable them to complete the other assessments in 94 percent of the cases. We also added a question on the amount of family support which seemed likely to be available because two other projects, a study of conjugal bereavement (Maddison, Viola, and Walker 1969) and one of unsupported women in South London (in an adjacent borough to the area served by the hospice; Brown and Harris 1978), had indicated that this was likely to be an important predictor despite the findings of the Harvard Study (see pages 162–163 for a discussion of our own findings on family support).

A "risk score" was obtained by adding together the points gained by each answer. An arbitrary cut-off point of 18 was taken as the risk threshold. Any bereaved person with a risk score of 18 or above was thought likely to require counseling.

Evaluative research in a clinical setting raises some delicate ethical problems. Some nurses at the hospice were opposed to research that would withhold help from bereaved families who were obviously in need of it. But how could we compare the outcomes of widows and widowers at risk who received counseling with those who did not receive counseling if *all* received counseling? The problem was solved by allowing the nurses to decide whether or not an "imperative need" for counseling existed among the bereaved and by only including within our research evaluation those whose need for bereavement support was not seen as imperative. We were aware that in doing this we were reducing the chance of obtaining a positive evaluation. As it happened, only 12 percent of the bereaved were thought to be in "imperative need." This left sixty-seven "high risk" (scoring 18 + on the Index of Bereavement Risk) bereaved who were divided into two groups by tossing a coin. On this basis, thirty-two were selected for support from the bereavement service, and thirty-five made up a control group.

About twenty months after bereavement both the treated and the untreated high risk groups, together with ninety-three low risk bereaved, were visited at home by a research interviewer who used several of the outcome scales from the Harvard Study to measure bereavement outcome. (Further details of the technical aspects of this study are given in appendix 5.) It was found that the high risk bereaved from the control group who had received no support from the bereavement service had significantly worse outcomes than did the low risk bereaved (who received no bereavement support either). This confirmed the value of our Index of Bereavement Risk. More to the point, except during the first year of the project, the high risk controls had significantly worse outcomes than the high risk bereaved who had received the help of the bereavement service. In fact, bereavement support reduced the outcome scores in the high risk group to about the same level as those in the low risk group. Bereavement counseling *did* help.

Although this study showed that our index did predict bereavement risk, our predictions were certainly not perfect. To discover which questions constituted the best predictors of overall outcome in the setting of St. Christopher's Hospice, we carried out a statistical analysis termed "stepwise regression" (see appendix 5). This showed that "clinging or pining," which was our reformulation of the "Intensity of Yearning" measure used in the Harvard Bereavement Study, was the best single predictor, but that the nurses' own educated guess (equivalent to our Coder's Prediction of Outcome) also correlated significantly with outcome. So did "self-reproach," and so, also, did the age of the bereaved person, except that the latter correlated with outcome in a direction opposite from the expected direction. Older bereaved people had poorer overall outcome than did younger. The gender of the client was also relevant, with women having worse outcome scores than men.

The last two variables raise some problems about the outcome measures used in this study. As we can see from the nonbereaved control group in the Harvard Bereavement Study, older people tend to have more symptoms that contribute to higher scores on the health questionnaire than do younger people, whether they are bereaved or not. Similarly, women tend to report more symptoms than do men whether they are bereaved or not. Only when a correction is made to allow for these control group differences does it become clear that the "bereavement effect" is greater in younger rather than older clients and in widowers rather than widows.

Length of preparation for the patient's death was not a predictor of outcome in the hospice study because in this study there were very few among the bereaved who had not been prepared for the patient's death. All the patients in the hospice had died from cancer, and family members had had every opportunity to anticipate their deaths.

The Index of Bereavement Risk we are currently using is a modification of the index developed from our Harvard data. Although based on the Harvard Bereavement Study, this version also draws upon the findings of Brown and Harris's studies of depressed women in the borough of Camberwell, England (1978). They found a high incidence of depressive symptoms among women of low socioeconomic status following losses or other major changes in their lives. Those most vulnerable were women with young children at home, no job outside the home, and no "intimate other" to provide support. The revised version of the questionnaire substitutes questions on the number of children under fourteen at home and anticipated employment outside the home for the omitted questions on age and length of preparation for bereavement. (It is worth noting that children at home are themselves at risk following bereavement and that support given to a bereaved parent may also benefit these children.)

The question on occupational class has been retained, despite the negative results of our regression analysis, because of the importance that Brown attaches to this factor. The wording of the question on present relationships has been changed to take account of Brown's finding that the existence of a close, intimate relationship with another person can protect a woman from the damaging effects of life events. (Brown's examination of this issue was based in part on Weiss's exploration of the nature of loneliness.) This question also takes into account the finding of Maddison, Viola, and Walker (1969) that bereaved people are less likely to be at risk if they perceive their family as supporting the expression of negative feelings rather than as insisting that the bereaved "cheer up" or "pull themselves together."

A study that provided a further check on the predictive power of this revised Index of Bereavement Risk became possible in the course of an evaluation of terminal care in the area served by St. Christopher's Hospice (Parkes 1982). In this study, widows and widowers whose spouses had died at St. Christopher's Hospice were followed up at thirteen months after bereavement. A Bereavement Outcome Score was obtained for each individual by adding together the number of instances of the more common symptoms he or she reported. Although this score lacks the sensitivity of the detailed and lengthy outcome measures used in the Harvard Bereavement Study, it did correlate fairly well with the predictive instrument. Widows and widowers with a low predictive score were unlikely to have a poor outcome, whereas many of those who had higher scores on the risk index reported lasting symptoms of grief (appendix 5).

## Conclusion

The research carried out at St. Christopher's Hospice has confirmed the value of a Bereavement Risk Index based on the findings of the Harvard Bereavement Study as a means of identifying bereaved people in need of counseling. About 600 patients die each year at the hospice, and the use of this method of screening has enabled a group of ten to twelve carefully selected and trained volunteer counselors to offer support to the majority of those family members who are thought to be at risk. We will indicate how they do this in chapter 10.

Despite our progress, it would be wrong to suggest that our work is in any sense definitive. There is every reason to continue attempts to improve both the Bereavement Risk Index and the methods used to support the bereaved. Our ability to predict which of the bereaved are at special risk should be made more accurate, as should our ability to predict such risk before bereavement occurs among spouses of terminally ill patients. And our methods of counseling, like our predictive instruments, should be made more effective through the processes of examination and revision. In the next chapter we discuss approaches to helping the bereaved, but we do not intend by so doing to obscure the need for research on these issues.

# Chapter 10

---

# *Implications for Care*

While the Harvard Bereavement Study was not set up to evaluate any particular form of care, it does, we believe, have important implications for the prevention and treatment of some of the ill-effects of bereavement. In this chapter we shall review these implications and go beyond them to illustrate by means of case examples some of the methods of intervention which we have developed in other settings.

It is convenient to subdivide the implications for prevention and care into those that come into effect before bereavement and those that come afterward. We shall consider in turn implications for preventing or mitigating, at each of these times, the three syndromes that have emerged from the Harvard Bereavement Study: the syndrome associated with unexpected, untimely deaths; that associated with ambivalent relationships; and that associated with undue reliance on the dead person.

Other researchers have spoken of the prevention of "pathological grief" as if this were a single entity and have formulated overall rules for intervention accordingly. We sympathize with this viewpoint and at one time shared it. However, experience has led us to revise our view. It now appears to us that forms of intervention which are appropriate for one type of bereavement may be useless or even harmful in another.

The most obvious example of this kind of problem concerns the eliciting of grieving by the counselor. Much of the literature on helping individuals after bereavement emphasizes the importance of ensuring that grief not be repressed or avoided. It describes cases in which symptoms have arisen because grief has not been expressed to the full. Ever since Lindemann's classical paper was published in 1944, pathological reactions to bereavement have become firmly associated with inhibition of grief. Some counselors have come to think that once they have provoked the expression of tears, their task is over. However, several studies of psychiatric illness following bereavement have shown that delayed or avoided grief is uncommon (Parkes 1964; Anderson 1949). Clayton has shown that by and large the intensity of grieving at the time of bereavement is *directly* and *not inversely* related to poor outcome a year later (Clayton, Desmarais, and Winokur 1968).

Our own study confirms Clayton's findings. Avoidance of grief was only occasionally responsible for poor outcomes. The most frequent problem observed in our sample was not the initiation of grief but its termination. A high level of yearning was often an early indicator of a recovery process which was going badly. It seems unlikely that helpers who confined their activity to eliciting further expression of grief would have achieved very much with these already fully grieving widows and widowers. There is some danger that they would find themselves colluding with the perpetuation of chronic grief.

There were, to be sure, some bereaved people who showed little evidence of grief at the time of our first interview three weeks after the loss, but who showed high levels of emotional distress later. These were the survivors of ambivalent marriages described in chapter 5. It seems very likely that they would have benefited from the kind of intervention described by Lindemann.

The situation is further complicated by the fact that unexpected and untimely bereavements tended to give rise to reactions in which episodes of intense emotional distress alternated with attempts at avoidance of distress by keeping away from reminders of loss. Should we encourage counselors to confront these people with the reality of their loss and by so doing increase their distress? Or should they collude with them in their attempts to keep the distress within tolerable limits by avoiding any reminders of loss?

Clearly it is necessary for counselors to discover what kind of grief they are dealing with if they are to be of help to the bereaved and to adapt their support to the particular needs of particular individuals. Having said this, we must also recognize that it will often be hard for the counselor to find out what kind of relationship the bereaved has had with the deceased and so to anticipate ambivalent grieving. Furthermore, in many instances mixed pictures give rise to special problems. And in dealing with unexpected or untimely bereavement, it may not be easy to find the right balance between eliciting and alleviating distressing emotions.

## Before Bereavement

Clinical experience at St. Christopher's Hospice has convinced us of the value of counseling families before the death of a family member from cancer, and it is important for members of caring professions to learn how to do this. Some research evidence, discussed below, also supports this view (Cameron 1983).

### FOREWARNING AND THE COMMUNICATION OF INFORMATION

Our data regarding the importance of forewarning suggest that we look again at the ways in which doctors inform patients and their families of the course illness may take. The peculiarly traumatic impact of sudden, untimely bereavement—overwhelming, as it so often does, integrative capacities—implies that the possibility of a terminal course must be made known as soon as it is medically recognized. Of course, this information should, if possible, be communicated gradually so that it will not in itself constitute an overwhelmingly traumatic confrontation with impending loss.

Yet even when warnings are given well in advance of bereavement, they are often ignored or misunderstood. In a study of London widows, of the nineteen who said that they had been told early of the seriousness of their husbands' conditions, only six thought that they had fully accepted the situation, and eight reported that they had not believed what they had been told (Parkes 1970). The very natural tendency of families to maintain their optimism in order to encourage the patient may make it more difficult for them to acknowledge that a disease is life-threatening.

Clinical experience suggests that it is more useful for discussion of the course of an illness to take place with physicians (or other professionals) whom the family members already have reason to trust than with strangers whose concern for the family may be in doubt. Yet it is often a specialist who has not previously met the patient or family who is the purveyor of bad news. The specialist's expert knowledge is important to the family; the problem is to provide the family with both the specialist's knowledge and the family physician's ongoing commitment.

How often have we heard such phrases as "the doctors gave her six months to live," as if life was in the gift of the doctors? And how often were such predictions hopelessly wrong? In one study (Parkes 1972a) it was shown that the predictions of length of survival made about patients referred to St. Christopher's Hospice were quite uncorrelated with actual length of survival. All that could accurately be said was that patients with incurable cancers were likely to die within a relatively short or a relatively long period from the time of referral. Any attempt at a more precise estimate of the remaining span of life was worthless.

Given this degree of uncertainty, it is obviously improper for physicians, however clever, to allow themselves to be pressured into giving a precise answer to the question, "How long?" Nevertheless they must be prepared to give *an* answer to the question in general terms and to do everything in their power to communicate news without damage to its recipients.

Doctors may tell too much or too little, too soon or too late. They may use language that is misunderstood and not realize that the message has not been received. Or they may fail to give the emotional support that is necessary if patient and family are not to be overwhelmed in the face of intolerable trauma. Finally they may not acknowledge their own need for support in the face of a distressed family.

It takes time to break bad news, and the setting in which communication takes place will influence how it is received. No doctor should remove a patient's wife from his bedside during visiting hours, tell her that the prognosis is "hopeless," and expect her to return to the bedside as if nothing had happened. Yet this is often done.

Detailed consideration of the management of terminal care and the ways of supporting patients and their families is beyond the scope of this book. Suffice it to say that the first step is not to give information but to find out what the family already knows or imagines and at the same time to assess their capacity to cope with the true situation. By taking an interest in the family and their needs, a basis for a trusting relationship can be developed. This makes it relatively simple to move on to give the information that is needed in a language which will be easily understood. Having done this, the informant must be prepared to stay with the family, to give them time and permission to react to the news, and to answer any further questions they may have. It is often valuable to include other members of the caring team in this meeting or, if this is not possible, to keep them informed of the family's reaction to the news. They can then continue to give support and can periodically assess the extent to which the family has understood and accepted the information.

People absorb information most effectively when the information fits with their existing views. Information that requires radical reorientation and is, in addition, highly unpleasant, is apt to be distorted, suppressed, or exaggerated. It is therefore most important for those providing information to find out if they are being understood. What does the family make of what they have heard? And what further questions do they want to raise?

It is also important for informants to recognize that intense emotional response to threatening news is entirely natural and that the bearers of the news may well become targets, though perhaps in a disguised fashion, for anger that can be directed nowhere else. Or they may find individuals expressing intense guilt or remorse, quite possibly without justification. Those providing information must be able to tolerate in a sympathetic way the expression of these feelings and to remain supportive figures.

The dominant emotion elicited by news that an illness carries a bleak outlook is likely to be fear. Some support can be provided by professionals, but the sustenance the patient and the patient's family can provide to one another is likely to be even more important. Insofar as it is possible, patients and their families should share information rather than deal with the information in mutual isolation. Unfortunately, professionals sometimes encourage families to withhold information from patients, on the grounds that patients would otherwise become painfully anxious; at the same time, patients often withhold from their families their actual awareness of events. It may be that some families manage best with this kind of mutual pretense, but most families will do better if there is opportunity for mutual support based on open communication.

Family members will usually find it easier to come to terms with the threat of loss if the patient has been informed of the true situation and reached a similar degree of acceptance. But the terminally ill may choose not to know. In such circumstances it is unwise and cruel, in our view, to force the pace by breaking down the defenses of denial and expecting the family or the other members of the caring team to then pick up the pieces. Rather, we should permit each person who is facing death to do so in his or her own way. All caregivers can do is to stay close, to make it as easy as possible for information to be obtained, and to respect those whose way of maintaining their morale is to refuse such information.

On the whole, individuals manage more effectively when they recognize a worrisome reality than when they are led to collude in the pretense that all is well. In work with patients undergoing major surgery, Janis (1958) found that those who were given realistic information, together with emotional support in advance of the surgery, adjusted more easily to the trauma than those who had not been warned. To be sure, those given realistic information were more worried and anxious. But their initial distress was in the service of coming to terms with the experience they would undergo and proved in the final analysis to have been of value. Our findings regarding the importance of forewarning suggest strongly that anticipatory guidance would be valuable for men and women facing bereavement as well as for presurgical patients. Those facing death are another matter. Their problem is to achieve as high a quality of life as they can before death takes them. If they can deal with the reality of their condition, so much the better for those close to them. If they cannot, they should not be required to.

## AMBIVALENCE

Our study shows very clearly that people whose relationship with a dying person has been highly ambivalent often find themselves trapped in a state of self-punitive grief: once someone is dead, it is too late to say "I'm sorry." Further, Cameron's research (1983) suggests that anger and guilt are particularly likely to complicate bereavement when the care of the dying patient has been inadequate even when the survivors are clearly not to blame for this failure. Comparing surviving relatives of patients who had died in a hospice-style "palliative care unit" (P.C.U.) in Montreal with a matched group of relatives of patients who had died in other wards of the same hospital, she found not only that the relatives of P.C.U. patients expressed less anger and guilt than did the relatives of patients dying in other wards, but that they also had fewer health problems after bereavement.

It would seem to follow from this research as well as from ours that rather than depriving family members of the opportunity to care for a dying individual, we should do our best to ensure that they remain closely involved. By encouraging the family to care for the patient, we give them the opportunity to make restitution for any failure or lack of care in the past. This applies whether or not we have evidence of ambivalence. Nurses and doctors sometimes think that they are helping the family by reassuring them that they are no longer needed. They may even make family members feel that their presence on the ward is a nuisance and that the patient will suffer if they intrude. Yet the patient is usually far happier if those to whom he or she is most closely attached are near at hand during much of the time. Some fear dying alone and lonely.

Even if the patient is unconscious, the family normally wants to maintain a vigil at the bedside. Hospital staff may feel that this serves no useful purpose and that they should protect the family by assuring them that they are not needed. But this may be the last opportunity that the family will have to care for the person they love, and we think it would be a short-sighted policy to deny it to them. Similarly, doctors sometimes think that they can relieve stress on the family by admitting a seriously ill patient to the hospital. Yet, if a good standard of physical care can be achieved at home (this is important—it can be traumatic for the family to be unable to provide good care) and the family receives the psychological support that they need, they will usually prefer to keep the patient at home, however burdensome that may be.

On the other hand, it is also important for the bereaved that they can feel that death was not the endpoint of a miserable, degenerative process. Parkes carried out a home visit to a middle-aged man in a late stage of abdominal cancer who was refusing admission to the hospital. A report on this experience illustrates some of these points:

It was immediately apparent that the relationship between the patient and his wife had broken down. The patient was obviously very ill and in pain. Like many people who suffer chronic unrelieved pain, he was petulant and complaining, preoccupied with his pain and demanding help. His wife, a big, masterful woman, had dealt with his incessant demands by treating him like a naughty boy. Lacking any means of relieving his pain, she could only try to pretend that it was not as bad as he said it was. By making light of his pain she belittled the patient. Both were clearly at the end of their tethers, but when I suggested that the patient might like to come into the hospital to enable us to get his pain under control, he immediately looked terrified and refused on the grounds that, "I'd never get out of there alive."

The patient, his wife, and the family doctors all needed time to express their feelings of frustration and sadness. Thereafter it took only a few days to get the patient's pain properly controlled at home with a small, four-hourly dose of morphine by mouth and a phenothiazine tranquilizer. A week after my first visit the patient surprised us all by asking to enter the hospice "to give my wife a rest." Clearly the relief of pain and the support that both of them had received had caused him to modify his views of doctors and their intentions. He knew that he might never return home but no longer seemed terrified by the prospect of hospital admission.

235

Visiting the ward a week later, I asked the nurse in charge how the patient and his wife were getting on. "Oh, they're such a couple of love birds," she replied. He lived for another two weeks. His wife seldom left his side, and they sat together in the ward, arm in arm, until he peacefully died.

When I visited his widow a month later, she was still grieving, but her grief seemed very normal and was already beginning to abate. "If he had died the way he was when you first saw him," she remarked, "I'd never have forgiven myself."

LOSSES WITH DEPENDENCY AND YEARNING

It comes as no surprise that women in our study were more likely to have difficulties of this kind than were men, and it may well be that the changes in social attitudes which have taken place in recent years and which encourage women to seek for a greater degree of autonomy within marriage will reduce the risk of chronic grief after bereavement. The chilling statistical probability that most married women will one day be widows should motivate them to avoid too great a dependence on their spouses. The change from the role and the status of married woman to that of widow must be one of the most searching of psychosocial transitions, yet there are no widowhood preparation courses and little in the way of published guidelines for the widow-to-be. The reason is not hard to discover. There are strong psychological reasons for not planning for the death of someone we love—we feel as if any attempt to prepare for this event would cause it to come about.

Of course, it is not always the man who will die first, and there are many situations in which a husband may be aware that he is likely to be the survivor. But again there are strong taboos prohibiting him from making his awareness of this fact explicit.

Nevertheless, there is no doubt that those who are likely to lose a spouse often begin to consider in advance the implications of that event and in some cases their partner may help them to do so. We earlier (in chapter 7) described the consequences of a dying husband's commission to his wife that she not grieve for him. But if commissions can be binding, they can also be liberating. Spouses who explicitly absolve their partners from blame, who express confidence in their spouses' ability to make good lives for themselves, or who give them permission to make new relationships and, possibly, to remarry may help them to move toward new and satisfying identities.

A sixty-year-old woman who had been admitted to St. Christopher's Hospice for terminal care confessed that she had "spoiled" her husband. She had waited on him hand and foot throughout their married life and obtained satisfaction from his dependence on her. Nevertheless, she had realized, as her illness progressed, that he was quite unprepared for life as a widower. With characteristic determination she announced that since she was not going to be around for much longer her husband had better learn to fend for himself. She taught him how to cook and keep house, encouraged him, and, most important of all, gradually withdrew her support from him so that, by the time she was admitted to the hospice, both of them knew that he could cope without her.

## After Bereavement

There are now a number of organizations as well as a wide range of caring agencies, social workers, pastoral counselors, doctors, and the like who can be called on to help the bereaved. The help which they offer ranges from individual therapy to group support, from sophisticated analytical psychotherapy to self-help (mutual aid), and from telephone "hotlines" to home visits. Some make use of tranquilizers or antidepressants; others oppose all use of drugs. Some offer only short-term "crisis intervention"; others provide lasting support regardless of the duration of disability.

Of course, there are few places where all of these different types of help are available and few guidelines to enable us to choose among them. Nevertheless there is evidence that certain types of bereavement support can reduce some of the damaging effects of bereavement (for a review of this evidence, see Parkes 1981a). Several attempts at scientific evaluation have been carried out, and some of them (such as the study described in appendix 5) have demonstrated statistically significant differences between helped and unhelped bereaved people. At the time of this writing it seems that the best results are obtained when individual support is offered early in bereavement to selected widows or widowers who are thought to be at special risk.

Several detailed descriptions of bereavement counseling have been published (for example, Worden 1982; Raphael 1977; and Parkes 1981b); each emphasizes different aspects of the counseling, although most agree on the importance of acceptance of loss and movement beyond loss. However, it is not clear from these reports precisely which components of the interventions proved most beneficial nor, since the counselors obviously tailored their methods to suit the individual needs of their clients, what overall program of intervention might be recommended.

Evaluations of bereavement counseling, such as that conducted at St. Christopher's Hospice, have thus far shown that bereavement counseling is helpful primarily to those among the bereaved selected as at high risk. It is possible, although we cannot yet be certain of this, that counseling with a low risk group would be harmful. If this is the case, an evaluation of counseling with an unselected group might show no effects, since the positive results with the high risk group would be balanced by negative results with the low risk group. With these reservations in mind, we can return to examine the implications of the Harvard Bereavement Study for interventions aimed at reducing the damaging effects of the three types of bereavement from which recovery is most problematic.

UNEXPECTED AND UNTIMELY LOSS

It is very clear from our findings that the impact of an unexpected and untimely bereavement can overwhelm a person's existing ability to cope with stress and trigger reactions that will lead to lasting problems. It follows that any action which reduces that impact could be expected to be of lasting benefit.

We would expect that families faced with sudden bereavements are in immediate need of support, and the way in which news is broken and support given could be of crucial importance. Even though the bereavement is an established reality, the bereaved still need time and the chance to talk through the implications of their loss and to react emotionally. They have to prepare themselves for an event that has already occurred. One of the functions of rituals of mourning may well be to aid this process.

To suggest how ritual may be useful, we might consider the comments made by one widow. Mrs. Baker's husband had died during the night from an illness that no one had taken seriously.

> I never thought that I would appreciate one . . . but actually, I think the wake was a good thing because I was able to talk about his dying and it became more of a reality. And I saw so many people that I hadn't seen in years and everyone that we'd ever been nice to, and people that I didn't even know, and I learned so many things about my husband that I hadn't known [*cries*]. . . . Everyone would ask what happened, and then, and I, I mean when something cataclysmic happens you can't help but talk about it.

For Mrs. Baker the wake was an event that helped her to take in the reality of her husband's "cataclysmic" death. Another such event was the conversation she had with a young priest the afternoon of the day on which her husband died.

239

My oldest daughter was very, very upset. . . . When she came home
that night we went down to Holy Name Church, and I went with
her, and . . . my daughter went to confession. I didn't go to confession, but I went in and spoke to the priest, and then I broke down
and told him that I, you know, I just couldn't understand it. My
husband and I had lived such a good life that it just seemed like such
a senseless thing. And he was very kind. . . . I was really crying
buckets by this time and he came out of the confessional and he
spoke to us outside, my daughter and I, and then he said that he'd
come up later on. . . . And he came up about nine-thirty or ten and
he stayed until eleven-thirty.

These opportunities to share her feelings and to make real the
event of her husband's death, together with a network of family
and friends (who provided support when it was needed but also
made demands upon Mrs. Baker which she was constrained to
meet), seem to have enabled her to grieve in a healthy way.
During the days following her husband's death, Mrs. Baker was
careful not to cry in front of the children or in public. When
alone, she cried a great deal. And yet, although she described
herself as normally very emotional, someone who could cry
over anything, she now cried without collapsing and without
relinquishing her responsibilities to her family.

I cry at night. I cry in the bathroom usually and I cry in the bathtub
[laughs] and when I'm putting in the laundry. But not uncontrolla-
bly.

I've had a great deal of things to do with the baby, the house, and
my mother sick. One reason I am so calm is because I am nursing
the baby and I just know that I can't fall apart. I'll lose the milk and
we'll all be in trouble.

Mrs. Baker was aware that too much control might be a bad
thing. She did not repress her feelings all the time. Rather, she
achieved a balance between control and expression of feelings
in which recovery from her loss was not impeded while she
continued to meet her responsibilities. "I'm going to show ev-

erybody that I can come up fighting," she said. And despite the way in which her husband had died, she did. At the time of our follow-up interview, she was doing well in terms of all our criteria of outcome.

### THE LOSS OF AMBIVALENT RELATIONSHIPS

Some of the widows and widowers who suffered unexpected bereavements were so shocked that they were unable to express grief. Superficially they resembled the ambivalent grievers whose early reaction to their loss was also minimal. However, those who suffered unexpected bereavements were manifestly distressed, whether in shock or not.

The group of widows and widowers whose marital relationships had been contentious conforms most closely to the clinical picture of "delayed grief" which has received so much attention in psychiatric studies. And it is this group that can be expected to respond to interventions aimed at promoting the overt expression of grief, such as those proposed by Lindemann and reformulated, using the language of learning theory, by Ramsay (1979) and, in psychoanalytic terms, by Volkan and Sarvay (1975). These approaches share the object of provoking in full the expressions of sadness, rage, guilt, and shame, which are all appropriate reactions to the loss in question. When this catharsis has been achieved it is assumed that the course of grief, which has up until that time been blocked by repression, will proceed to take its normal course towards resolution.

Mawson et al. (1981), who carried out a random allocation study of a mixed group of psychiatric patients whose illness had been attributed to pathological grief, found that the group who had been treated by means of "forced mourning" did in fact show some reduction in measures of avoided grief but the overall improvement was only marginally significant. It appears that only a subgroup of the sample were greatly helped by this technique. If, as seems likely, that subgroup were the ones who

241

suffered from delayed or ambivalent grief, then Mawson's study will have confirmed the findings of our study.

Why should it be that ambivalence gives rise to delayed or avoided reactions, and why should the promotion of a painful grieving process help? Our data suggest some answers to both these questions.

The literature on bereavement lays great stress on the social pressures that currently are said to favor the repression or avoidance of grief. We are all said to be members of a "death-denying" society, and writers such as Gorer have pointed to the decline in rituals of mourning as evidence of this. We accept that, to an extent, this is true. Bereaved people are no longer expected to wear black or to withdraw from society for great periods of time, and the funeral is no longer an opportunity for the unrestrained exhibition of public grief. Nevertheless, the bereaved are expected to express sadness, and our data made it clear that grief is still seen as a duty to the dead. Widows and widowers were very conscious of the expectations of their peers, and those who did not grieve overtly expected criticism. It seems, then, that some additional factor is needed to explain the relative lack of initial mourning in the ambivalent group.

Our data lead us to suspect that this factor was a repudiation of attachment. That is to say, our respondents often gave as their reason for not grieving the assertion that they had not loved the deceased or that he or she had not loved them. This assertion was backed by the evidence of conflict within the marriage. Despite these assertions, there is every reason to believe that these widows and widowers had been strongly but insecurely attached to their spouses, and the strength of that attachment explains the difficulties that subsequently arose when their initial attempts to avoid grieving failed.

Ambivalence complicated the course of mourning. It made expression of great grief seem hypocritical, so that even while they were immersed in grief, widows or widowers might feel forced to say, "Of course, we didn't have the greatest marriage in the world." But the grief nevertheless would exist so long as there had been attachment to the other. Indeed, ambivalent attachments can be harder to dissolve than unambivalent attachments because there is not the memory of a loving other to support continued feelings of worth. Furthermore, it is difficult to mourn wholeheartedly when there was anger toward the dead as well as attachment, and difficult to understand one's own feelings when they are so mixed.

Yet the problems of facing a new world, however unsatisfactory the old one may have been, inevitably taxed the resources of the bereaved and increase their wish for an attachment figure. The needs met in the marriage, if only partially and reluctantly, did not cease to exist. By the time a year had passed the ambivalent mourners in our study were pining for the lost person, whereas grief had now abated among widows and widowers whose recovery was going well.

We suspect that actions aimed at facilitating mourning in this group succeed for several reasons. First, they initiate reality testing, the process by which the bereaved become aware of what they have lost and begin the painful relearning of a new set of assumptions about the world. Second, they facilitate this process by providing a source of emotional support, the therapist/counselor, who can be treated for a limited period of time as an attachment figure. Third, they mitigate feelings of guilt and reduce self-punitive tendencies by combining the functions of confession and ordeal. That is to say, by encouraging the bereaved to share feelings of self-reproach and to experience the pain of grief to the full, they go some way toward absolving the bereaved from their obligation to the dead. While the confession of guilt does not necessarily remove that feeling, it may enable the bereaved to consider more creative ways of bringing something good out of the bad thing that has happened. Those who work with bereaved people are often impressed by the concern they show for others and the lengths to which they will go to turn their own experience to good use. The widow whose husband has died from cancer raises money for cancer research; the widower offers help to his local hospital; each finds his or her own way to justify the fact that, while another has died, he or she has survived.

People will often choose to admit guilt to a clergyman even if they do not make a formal act of confession. Because of this, clergy may have a special role to play in helping the bereaved to forgive themselves. In some societies the bereaved engage in self-flagellation, cut themselves with knives or otherwise punish themselves. In our own society, the bereaved tend to dislike sympathy, which often leaves them feeling that they are obtaining credit under false pretenses.

Raphael's (1977) study suggests that some of the factors which lead to problems in recovery from bereavement may do so by impairing family ties. It is obvious that one correlate of a conflict-filled marriage may be poor relationships with the spouse's family. The end of the marriage is then likely to bring about a decided diminution in contacts with the in-laws. But there can be less obvious connections as well.

It is seldom that bereavement affects the life of only one survivor. Rather, the entire social network around the dead person must change—and especially the dead person's family. If all goes well, there will be a restructuring that will produce a new family as supportive to its members as the old one had been. If all does not go well, the trauma of the loss and the emotions it unleashes may create violent estrangement between family members or impose intolerable pressures on them.

The self-protective reactions of the family's members can further threaten the integrity of the family. For example, the defensive reaction in which the surviving spouse feels and behaves as if the dead person were still present and resists any attempt at replacement can impede the family's efforts to establish new, realistic alignments among its members. Or, to give another example, ambivalent spouses may visit their anger and pervasive anxiety on those closest to them. It should be small wonder if fellow members of such a family, themselves shaken by grief, feel threatened and doubt their own abilities to manage.

The family system, unable to deal with all this, may cease to act as a support to its members. It may even become destructive. Some of the very resources that enable a family to support its members—closeness, the sharing of resources, and the intimate knowledge each member has of the strengths and weaknesses of the others—can also be used to hurt and to disrupt. The family that goes out of balance can become a monster.

Outsiders—be they therapists, other members of the care-giving professions, or simply friends and neighbors—because they are not caught up in the dynamics of the family, are sometimes able to give support at the very moment when the family is most incapacitated and, though more rarely, to move the family toward healthy reorganization. By replacing the family's lack of confidence with their own confidence, by providing their strength, by displaying to the family their genuine respect, these outsiders can reintroduce safety and order into what has become, for the family, an unsafe and chaotic world.

THE LOSS OF RELATIONSHIPS OF DEPENDENCY

The particularly disabling effect of an unexpected and untimely loss seems to arise from its transformation of the world into a frightening place, a place in which disaster cannot be predicted and accustomed ways of thinking and behaving have proven unreliable and out of keeping with the actual world. The person is forced to distrust the model of the world that has previously made sense of things. Where there has been security, there is now anxiety; where there has been assurance, there is now disorganization. One way the suddenly bereaved individual may nevertheless manage is to hang on to the now discredited assumptions about the world. The widow or widower can maintain a sense of an ongoing relationship with the dead person and from this sense of continuity derive feelings of security and continued meaning.

In this respect the unexpectedly bereaved in our study resembled some of the dependent widows and widowers who had organized their lives on the assumption that they were helpless and unable to cope with life without the support of their partner. When the partner died, they clung to the role of mourner, from which they could derive a sense of ongoing relationship with the dead person as well as find sanction for continued helplessness. Any movement away from grief, among these dependent widows and widowers, exposed them to the dangers of a world with which they could not cope. They were then compelled to turn again to the partner who had protected them. But doing so brought them face-to-face with their loss. Hence their grief was endlessly renewed.

To be successful, any intervention among the dependent grievers must address these problems. It must increase their security, improve their self-esteem, and reduce their helplessness in the new circumstances of life in which they now find themselves.

Parkes, working with people who seek psychiatric help after bereavement, has developed a therapeutic approach to the treatment of chronic grief aimed at fostering and rewarding autonomy among the bereaved and discouraging their tendency to cling to the past. In this approach, movement toward increased autonomy is a condition of continued treatment and the likelihood of the therapist becoming a party to a life of social withdrawal with excessive attachment to the therapist is minimal.

Attachment to the therapist is not discouraged; in fact, the security that arises from such an attachment is essential if the bereaved are to find the confidence and motivation to relinquish helpless grieving. How then can the therapist encourage a secure, healthy attachment (which, as in the growing child, can be expected to lead to autonomy) and avoid fostering an insecure, unhealthy attachment and a new dependency? The answer must be the same as that which is offered by a wise parent —the promise of whole-hearted support when it is needed but on the clear and explicit understanding that support will be withdrawn when it is no longer needed, together with the confident anticipation that, in the long term, the bereaved person is good enough, strong enough, and clever enough to cope without support.

In order to build a relationship of trust, it is at first important to offer unqualified support. The bereaved need to believe that here is one person who truly wants to understand their situation and who will permit them, if they wish it, to cling immoderately for a while. By showing interest, listening carefully, avoiding judgment, and encouraging positive attitudes, the therapist helps to bring about a mutually respectful relationship in which both parties can begin to trust each other. In this context, expressions of grief are neither encouraged nor discouraged. They are permitted, but they are not seen as a sacred duty to the dead nor as the key to therapy. At the same time, they are not treated as discreditable signs of weakness which must be given up at once if the bereaved are to take their place in the world. Rather they are a valid expression of feelings and experiences which must be acknowledged if they are to be made part of the person's past and no longer the focus of the person's present.

Once a therapeutic relationship has been established, the emphasis is gradually and gently shifted from support to encouragement. The therapist begins to direct attention to the steps that must be taken if the bereaved are to discover their own potentialities. Small successes can do a lot to improve the self-esteem of the bereaved person, and the therapist recognizes and rewards with pleasure every independent effort that is made by the bereaved. The therapist's confidence in the ability of the bereaved to grow and to begin to rebuild his or her life can be conveyed directly by exhortation and indirectly by a tacit assumption that the need for support is diminishing over time.

Bereaved men and women who have for a long time believed themselves crippled by their loss are not easy to help. They are doubtful of their own capacities and distrustful of the world. There is always danger that they will become excessively reliant on the therapist. But setting clear targets and expecting that they will be met, mobilizing encouragement from the family, and fostering feelings of autonomy while discouraging tendencies to cling to the role of mourner all help direct the chronic mourner away from reliance on protective grief.

A rather different situation obtains in the case of the newly bereaved person who is at risk of chronic grief but for whom mourning has not yet become a way of life. Here a little help may go a long way. It is much easier to prevent chronic grief than it is to alter it when it has become established. The newly bereaved may feel helpless and inadequate, but they are still open to conviction that there is a place for them in the world, and the understanding and reassurance of another person may give them the courage to take the first steps into that world.

A counselor—who may be either a professional or a friend— can be helpful by recognizing that grieving takes time and that there are some who need permission to grieve. The counselor ·hould also recognize that sympathy is not incompatible with optimism. Optimism is essential but must be judicious: expectations too far ahead of what the bereaved can accept may feel to the bereaved like rejection. (There are, it must be noted, dangers in friends attempting to act as bereavement counselors. Working with someone whose grief has become chronic will overtax the resources of any but the most heroic friends. Friends are invaluable just in providing friendship and all this implies: people to talk to, reassurance that the world is friendly, things to do, actual help. But friends can become exhausted by the stubbornness of chronic grief. It is unfortunate for the bereaved individual if someone tries to be available and helpful and then, discovering that he or she cannot continue, rejects the bereaved person.)

Sadness, anger, and self-reproach may all need to be expressed by the bereaved as they feel them. As the intensity of their grieving declines, widows and widowers can be helped to find more satisfactory directions for their energies. This is important. The therapist who is content to facilitate the expression of grief but does not insist on forward movement will end up colluding with angry or self-punitive behavior which only succeeds in isolating the widow or widower.

It is commonly supposed that therapists should be value-free in reacting to clients. Yet the therapist is constantly feeding back to the client reactions of agreement or disagreement, approval or disapproval. In dealing with clients disabled by bereavement, it may be especially important that therapists acknowledge that they are not value-free but are instead committed to the clients' return to effective functioning. The therapists, while ready to hear confessions without appropriating the priestly right to forgive sins or prescribe penances, should make clear that some actions are to be preferred to others. Nor is the therapist passive. The bereaved need an active ally, someone who will not only provide approval for movement toward independence but may indeed participate in developing goals and making decisions.

Among the most important gifts a therapist can make to a client is respectful interest. The very act of giving unqualified attention to another person goes some way to convincing that person that he or she is worthy of the attention. And for a widow or widower, who may feel that in some occult way misfortune has been deserved, the contrary opinion of the therapist can be reassuring.

By drawing on therapist's understanding of their suffering, the bereaved may gain compassion and forgiveness toward themselves. Beyond this, although they will not expect it, they may discover respect for their abilities to come through and from this respect may gain the further confidence in themselves they will need to fully inhabit the lives that lie ahead for them.

## General Conclusions

In light of our findings, it seems reasonable for programs to seek out people who are at special risk in bereavement in order to give them the emotional support they will need if they are to review and accept the reality of loss and move with hope rather than dread into the world now opening to them. These principles of care in the practice of bereavement counseling have been used at St. Christopher's Hospice, and there is evidence from systematic random-assignment studies that they are effective (see appendix 5). Counseling at St. Christopher's takes place with all widows and widowers identified as "high risk," using criteria we have described. It is provided by volunteers, selected as having stability and sensitivity, who are carefully trained in counseling techniques. They visit all high risk widows and widowers in their homes ten days to two weeks after the bereavement. They then provide whatever support seems to be needed. A detailed description of this program has been published in a counselor's manual (Dyne 1980).

The research reported in appendix 5 indicates that counseling of this kind does improve outcome on several of our measures. There is also reason to believe that bereavement counseling may reduce the incidence of suicide among the bereaved. In St. Christopher's Hospice, bereavement counseling was introduced in 1974. In the six years preceding 1974, six bereaved relatives of individuals who had died in St. Christopher's are known to have committed suicide. In the eight years between 1974 and 1982, only two bereaved relatives, as far as we know, have committed suicide.

A one-to-one relationship of counselor and client is only one approach to helping widows and widowers return to effective functioning. One of us (R.S.W.) has explored the usefulness of educational groups as devices for facilitating widows' reorganization of their lives. In these groups, meeting one evening a week for a total of eight meetings, widows heard a lecturer talk about the issues they might be confronting and then participated in discussions with each other. The first meeting, no matter the topic, seemed uniformly difficult; simply joining with a group of others who had lost husbands imposed on each participant recognition of the reality of her own loss. But it proved helpful, as the meetings went on, for widows to be able to share experiences and to consider together the problems they encountered in the attempt to redirect their lives. For most of the participants, a group experience of this sort seemed helpful in the process of "getting used to it" and moving on to a new life with new goals.

Still, it must be kept in mind that a group does not initially provide a therapeutic alliance such as can be formed with a personal therapist. By the third meeting, no later than the fourth, the widows or widowers in a group are likely to become allies, but until this happens the members of the group will doubt the safety of a setting in which they are among strangers. The group may at first make them more, not less, anxious. Those who are unprepared for this might do well to establish a personal counseling relationship before entering a group.

Other approaches to helping widows and widowers have also been developed. One approach, to which our colleague Phyllis Silverman (1970; also, Silverman et al. 1974) has contributed, is the linking of bereaved individuals together into a kind of self-help network. This approach, usually limited to widows, is in wide use in the United States, often under a name such as "The Widow-to-Widow Program." In it, women who themselves have been widowed several years make contact with new widows to offer whatever help may prove useful. A visiting widow may provide the new widow with an opportunity to talk about her loss, offer her advice about housing, children, jobs, or benefits, reassure her that she will be able to manage despite her currently distraught state, or encourage her to resume her usual responsibilities. New widows are also invited to attend meetings in which such issues as financial planning are discussed, and where they may meet others in the same situation as themselves. The underlying premise of the program is that new widows can be effectively helped to re-establish themselves by women who have shared and dealt with the experiences they are now having.

Finally, mention must be made of Cruse, the main national organization in Britain for widows, widowers, and their families, which provides individual and group counseling using mutual support groups, networks, and professional counselors. From its government-supported headquarters, Cruse provides a wide range of literature and advice for its members as well as training courses for doctors, social workers, and other members of the caregiving professions.

All these approaches stress coming to terms with loss and getting on with life. Personal therapy provides a professional ally; groups that have an educational emphasis provide a kind of temporary community, together with information which, among other things, may communicate that the individual is dealing with issues that are well known and that have been dealt with by many others; Cruse and widow-to-widow programs provide information, support, and linkages to others, all aimed at a restructuring of life.

Bereavement care is a new field of study, though not a new field of service. The plight of widows and widowers has always been recognized. Every marriage that has not ended in divorce or in the simultaneous deaths of the marital partners has produced a widow or widower, and in virtually all times and places they have been socially marginal and emotionally distressed. Insofar as men, more than women, have been able to find a meaningful community through their work or through civic activity, the *social* situation of men may have been less bleak. And insofar as remarriage is more easily available to men, their tenure in the status of the widowed may be shorter. But men seem as desolated emotionally by the loss of their marriage partners as do women; and, because men's lives are on the whole emotionally more constricted than are women's, men may rely more on their marriages as sources of intimacy and be the more isolated should the marriage be lost.

Because husbands are, on the average, older than their wives and because men die at younger ages, widows outnumber widowers at every age level. In most "developed" countries the widow is often roleless, an object of pity, a fifth wheel, a living reminder of the now dead spouse. Widows who pursue active civic lives often do so primarily as "representatives" of their husbands. (This is the role adopted by Coretta King, to name one.) Many widows, lacking a social system that welcomes them, roles to occupy them, status to preserve their self-esteem, or beliefs to give them hope, are often lonely, adrift, self-doubting, and hopeless. Widows can usually find sympathy, though not without risk: to ask for sympathy too often may lead to becoming a target for irritated impatience. And sympathy, helpful as it can be, rarely fosters movement toward renewed functioning.

It is a sign of our times that problems of living, which might previously have been resolved within the family or the extended network of the village, have become matters for organized care on a much larger scale than ever before. Whether we like this tendency or not, we cannot deny that it is happening. It is futile for doctors to say that it is not their job to treat grief if the bereaved and their relatives continue to see grief as an illness. It is pointless for social workers to suggest that the elderly widowed live with their children if there is no place for them in the children's homes or lives. And it is fruitless for clergy to throw up their hands and blame our problems on the current decline in religious faith if the churches remain empty and the faith they proclaim is unbelieved. Social problems require social solutions.

## Other Losses

Bereavement is only one of the many kinds of loss of person or function or basis for confidence that occur from time to time in all our lives. Not only are we vulnerable to a wide range of loss of relationships, but also to accidental injuries, sudden illnesses, and damage by violent or nonviolent crimes.

Unexpected reverse, no matter its form, turns out to have consequences similar in many ways to those of unexpected bereavement. The "Unexpected Loss Syndrome," as described in chapter 4, resembles the "Disaster Syndrome" described by Wallace (1956) and others. Wallace describes as the first phase of reaction to disaster a syndrome quite similar to the shock and numbness of the unforewarned bereaved: "Absence of emotion, lack of response to present stimuli, inhibition of outward activity, docility, undemandingness." Lifton (1967) has spoken of the "psychic numbing" characteristic of this early reaction, and Wolfenstein, in her classic review of the literature (1957), describes how, as time passes, the disaster victim may remain preoccupied by tormenting memories of the disaster and angrily question why it happened.

Similarly, victims of muggers, and others who have been subjected to sudden violence, often speak of their sense of shock, numbness and disbelief. They display still other similarities to the suddenly bereaved, including subsequent withdrawal from social interaction with a tendency to idealize the past and to denigrate the present and future.

Just as some unexpected bereavements could have been anticipated if those in possession of essential information had been able to communicate that information effectively, so the literature on disaster is filled with accounts of warnings which were never given or which were given in so guarded a fashion that they could be shrugged off by listeners who were, on their part, loath to understand.

There is a growing literature on the value of preparation in dealing with inescapable pain and loss. We earlier noted that surgical patients, if provided with accurate information and emotional support, can better weather the pain of recovery and whatever loss of function may have occurred (Janis 1958; Lazarus and Hagen 1968; and Egbert et al. 1964). Patients who have suffered injuries or diseases necessitating limb amputation can be helped to accept the eventual prosthesis if, for example, before amputation of a leg they are taught to walk on an artificial leg fitted over the bent knee. Being able to anticipate the limitations and potentialities of life after loss means that when the loss actually occurs, it makes a kind of sense, it is not out of the blue, and adaptation need not combat the need to repudiate the reality of change.

Even with preparation, there is trauma in loss. Numbness and disbelief may make it hard for some people to accept services aimed at introducing them to the skills and outlooks appropriate to their changed realities. They must first be given support and time to grieve for the loss of the cherished past. When crippled patients refuse to accept a wheelchair, or old people who are a danger to themselves at home refuse to accept the need for institutional care, or seriously ill patients refuse to agree to an operation that may save their lives, similar approaches may be justified. In each case, before an individual is asked to take an unavoidable step, it may be necessary to offer that individual emotional support to help him or her express rage, sorrow, and shame.

It is worth noting that in the impact phase of a disastrous loss, people sometimes seek escape from pain through drugs, requests for euthanasia, or suicide, and that their families and even, at times, their professional caregivers may collude in this. It is sometimes tempting for us to put patients out of *our* misery. This is not to say that a professional caregiver would deliberately encourage a patient's suicide. Withdrawal of investment, however, perhaps by taking the position that nothing more can be done and perhaps accompanied by a disowning of responsibility, may accomplish the same end.

Whenever a person is faced with the loss of another person to whom he or she has become intensely and insecurely attached, the loss is likely to be preceded by intense clinging and followed by chronic grief. This can be the case in the ending of a relationship in psychotherapy and may become especially important in working with those who have dependency problems. The termination of therapy is, then, particularly tricky, involving as it does the loss by these individuals of a person whom they had begun to trust.

In working with dependent patients or clients, a contract for ending therapy should be drawn up and agreed to. From the very beginning, the patient should be aware that the aim of therapy is the achievement of autonomy. Patients' confidence in themselves will be undermined if therapists allow themselves to be persuaded to extend the contract.

Inevitably, the dependent patient will have a hard time after therapy has ended and may need brief help from another therapist at this time. It may sound strange to suggest that one should use psychotherapy to treat the end of psychotherapy but a short-term intervention of this kind may well help to get someone through the severe grief that can follow termination of a therapy on which he or she has become heavily dependent.

If dependency is sometimes an issue in working with individuals who have suffered other losses as well as in working with those who have suffered bereavement, so may be ambivalence. Ambivalence is especially likely to be present when loss has come about through marital separation or divorce.

The experience of those whose marriages end in divorce has emotional similarities to that of widows and widowers whose marriages were conflict-laden. In divorcing couples, too, husband and wife will have provided each other with ample reason for anger. Even more frequently than in the high-conflict marriages that ended with bereavement, marriages that end in divorce will have had occasions of verbal and perhaps physical assault and instances of betrayal of trust; the escalating mutual misuse of the marriage itself, followed by almost inescapable conflicts over property division, support payments, custody, and visitation will have seen to that. Yet in marriages that end by divorce as well as in conflict-laden marriages that end with the death of the husband or wife, there continues to be mutual attachment; each partner continues to feel the other to be a figure who is still connected to the self, who in some way completes the self (Weiss 1976a). Thus divorce, like the death of a spouse after a thoroughly unhappy marriage, is often followed by an extended interval in which the husband or wife by turns denies sadness and yearning ("It was the best thing I ever did; I feel as if I'm starting a new life.") and expresses these same emotions in tears, depression, and gestures toward reconciliation. It is quite common among those whose marriages have ended by separation and divorce to feel bewildered by their own reactions and to find it most difficult to achieve either satisfactory intellectual acceptance or satisfactory emotional acceptance of the loss of their marriages. Indeed, the early suppression of grief (perhaps accompanied by denial of its existence) followed by failure to recover, while a relatively uncommon consequence of the loss of marriage by death, may be a more frequent consequence of the loss of marriage by divorce.

The processes of recovery from bereavement and the ways in

which these processes can be impeded may provide a model for recovery from any irremediable loss. Awareness of these processes and of how to facilitate them may be helpful not only in relation to bereavement.

The world contains many sources of security and satisfaction, but none of them is imperishable, and we all need to be prepared for the losses that will surely come. One way to prepare for loss in our own lives is to make contact with others who are facing loss in theirs. By doing so, we help to create a community that cares and can be trusted. In time we, too, will need the presence of others, if not their active help, as well as trust and confidence and hope. Trusting each other, we can trust in life and in ourselves.

# Appendix 1

# *The Health Questionnaire*

The full version of the health questionnaire as used in the Harvard Bereavement Study contains a number of questions which are not relevant to the measurement of outcome after bereavement. Some of these are omitted in the reproduction of the health questionnaire that follows. Those questions that were thought relevant, together with a number thought to reflect relatively unchanging aspects of personality, making 272 in all, were scored and the results subjected to a factor analysis. The factor analysis made it possible to subdivide the health outcome and personality measures into clusters of intercorrelated variables.

The clusters were named according to the most appropriate overall description of the questions which made them up:

I.    Depression (twenty-four questions)
II.   Compulsive Self-Reliance (eleven questions)
III.  Stimulus-Seeking (nine questions)
IV.   Autonomic Reaction (twelve questions)
VII.  Worry (fourteen questions)
VIII. General Health (seven questions)
IX.   Shyness (ten questions)

The questions which make up these clusters are indicated in the text by the appropriate Roman numeral.

It will be seen that clusters I, IV, and VIII reflect psychological and somatic symptoms likely to be affected by bereavement. Clusters II, III, VII, and IX, however, reflect personality variables that are unlikely to be greatly affected by bereavement. Other clusters not here listed (labeled V, VI, and X in our system) had relatively low factor loadings and did not make much logical sense when lumped together. Consequently they were excluded from further analyses.

A shortened version of this questionnaire has been used at St. Christopher's Hospice (see appendix 5) and in other settings to evaluate recovery outcomes. It contains only those questions marked with Roman numerals I, II, III, IV, VII, VIII, and IX.

The "Ten Best Questions"—that is, questions that best distinguished the one-year bereaved from the control group—are indicated by B.Q. in the margin. These, too, are included in the shortened version of the questionnaire. A score derived from them has also been used by itself as an outcome measure.

## The Health Questionnaire

COMPLAINTS AND SYMPTONS

We'd like to know about your health—I have here a list of ailments I'd like to ask about.

[For each symptom ask:]

1. Have you ever had _____ (or have you ever had trouble with _____)?

   [Mark an "x" in column "yes" or "no."]

2. About when did it start?

   [Mark an "x" in column that is appropriate, and write in the figure the respondent gives in the empty column. The figure should be identified as "age" or "years ago."]

[IN THE CASE OF CHRONIC OR RECURRING PROBLEMS THAT *DID NOT* START DURING PAST YEAR, ASK:]

3. During the past year, would you say your condition has improved over what it was the preceding year; has it been decidedly worse than it was over the preceding year; or has it been much the same as it was the preceding year?

Scoring. The following are scored:

1. Acute condition arising during past year.
2. Chronic condition worse during past year.

## Complaints and Symptoms

| Remarks | When? Yes | No | During Past Year[a] | During Past Two Years | Write in Answer[a] | If Chronic—During Past Year: Improved | Worse | Same | No Problem for Years |
|---|---|---|---|---|---|---|---|---|---|
| **Eyes:** | | | | | | | | | |
| 1. Any blurring? | | | | | | | | | |
| 2. Watering? | | | | | | | | | |
| 3. Other trouble? | | | | | | | | | |
| 4. Headaches? | | | | | | | | | |
| 5. Migraines? | | | | | | | | | |
| | Score 1[a] → | | | | | Score 1[a] → | | | |
| **Ears:** | | | | | | | | | |
| 6. Hear well? | | | | | | | | | |
| 7. Infections? | | | | | | | | | |

[a] A check in these columns scores one point.

## Complaints and Symptoms

| Remarks | Yes | No | When? During Past Year | During Past Two Years | Write in Answer | If Chronic—During Past Year: Improved | Worse | Same | No Problem for Years |
|---|---|---|---|---|---|---|---|---|---|
| **Nose:** | | | | | | | | | |
| 8. Trouble with breathing? | | | | | | | | | |
| IV 9. Runny nose/clogging? | | | | | | | | | |
| 10. Hay fever? | | | | | | | | | |
| 11. Nosebleeds? | | | | | | | | | |
| | | | | | ↑ Score 1 | | | | |
| **Mouth:** | | | | | | | | | |
| 12. Cold sores? | | | | | | | | | |
| 13. Bleeding gums? | | | | | | | | | |
| 14. Excessive cavities? | | | | | | | | | |
| | | | | | | ↑ Score 1 | | | |

## Complaints and Symptoms

| Remarks | Yes | No | When? During Past Year | During Past Two Years | Write in Answer | If Chronic—During Past Year: Improved | Worse | Same | No Problem for Years |
|---|---|---|---|---|---|---|---|---|---|
| **Throat:** | | | | | | | | | |
| 15. Difficulty swallowing? | | | | | | | | | |
| IV 16. Feel lump in throat? | | | | | | | | | |
| VIII 17. Sore? | | | | | | | | | |
| | | | | | | Score 1 | | | |
| **Chest:** | | | | | | | | | |
| 18. Asthma? | | | | | | | | | |
| 19. Coughing? | | | | | | | | | |
| 20. Cough blood? | | | | | | | | | |
| 21. Shortness of breath? | | | | | | | | | |
| IV 22. Pain in chest? | | | | | | | | | |
| | | | | | | Score 1 | | | |

## Complaints and Symptoms

| Remarks | Yes | No | When? During Past Year | During Past Two Years | Write in Answer | If Chronic—During Past Year: Improved | Worse | Same | No Problem for Years |
|---|---|---|---|---|---|---|---|---|---|
| **Heart:** | | | | | | | | | |
| IV 23. Palpitations? | | | | | | | | | |
| 24. Heart condition? | | | | | | | | | |
| **Stomach:** | | | | | | | | | |
| IV 25. Sick feeling? | | | | | | | | | |
| 26. Indigestion? (gas, heartburn) | | | | | | | | | |
| 27. Stomach ulcers? | | | | | | | | | |
| 28. Vomiting? | | | | | | | | | |
| | | | Score 1 | | | Score 1 | | | |

265

## Complaints and Symptoms

| Remarks | When? | | Write in Answer | If Chronic—During Past Year: | | | |
|---|---|---|---|---|---|---|---|
| | Yes | No | During Past Year / During Past Two Years | Improved | Worse | Same | No Problem for Years |

**Bowel:**

29. Constipation?
30. Diarrhea?
31. Blood appear?

Score 1

**Urine:**

IV 32. Too frequently?
33. Blood appear?

Score 1

## Complaints and Symptoms

| | When? | | | | If Chronic—During Past Year: | | | |
|---|---|---|---|---|---|---|---|---|
| Remarks | Yes | No | During Past Year | During Past Two Years | Write in Answer | Improved | Worse | Same | No Problem for Years |

**Skin:**

34. Hives or rashes?

35. Itching?

36. Tumors or growths?

37. Loss of hair?

**Musculature:**

38. Swollen or painful joints?

VIII 39. Pains in the back?

40. Pains in the face?

41. Paralysis?

Score 1          Score 1

*Complaints and Symptoms*

| Remarks | Yes | No | When? | | | If Chronic—During Past Year: | | | |
|---|---|---|---|---|---|---|---|---|---|
| | | | During Past Year | During Past Two Years | Write in Answer | Improved | Worse | Same | No Problem for Years |
| **Blood:** | | | | | | | | | |
| 42. Diabetes? | | | | | | | | | |
| 43. Anemia? | | | | | | | | | |
| 44. High blood pressure? | | | | | | | | | |
| IV 45. Dizziness or fainting? | | | ↑ **Score 1** | | | | ↑ **Score 1** | | |

## Complaints and Symptoms

|  | Yes | No | When? During Past Year | During Past Two Years | Write in Answer | If Chronic—During Past Year: Improved | Worse | Same | No Problem for Years |
|---|---|---|---|---|---|---|---|---|---|
| **Nervous System:** | | | | | | | | | |
| IV 46. Nervousness? | | | | | | | | | |
| IV 47. Trembling/twitching? | | | | | | | | | |
| IV 48. At times feel hot all over? | | | | | | | | | |
| IV 49. Sweat when you haven't been doing anything? | | | | | | | | | |
| 50. Have you damp hands? | | | | | | | | | |
| | | | **Score 1** | | | **Score 1** | | | |

Remarks

## Complaints and Symptoms

| Remarks | When? | | | | If Chronic—During Past Year: | | | |
|---|---|---|---|---|---|---|---|---|
| | Yes | No | During Past Year | During Past Two Years | Write in Answer | Improved | Worse | Same | No Problem for Years |

**[For women only]:**

Menstrual periods:

51. Cramps?

52. Excessive bleeding?

53. Irregularity of periods?

54. Have you stopped having periods?

Score 1 ↑          Score 1 ↑

*Complaints and Symptoms*

| Remarks | When? | | During Past Year | During Past Two Years | Write in Answer | If Chronic—During Past Year: | | | |
|---|---|---|---|---|---|---|---|---|---|
| | Yes | No | | | | Improved | Worse | Same | No Problem for Years |

**Sleep:**

VIII 55. Have you ever had trouble falling asleep?

56. Have you ever found yourself awakening in the middle of the night?

57. Have you ever had nightmares?

Score 1   ↑                                         ↑   Score 1

58. How much do you sleep now?

Code:   1. Less than five hours a day
        2. Five to seven
        3. Eight to nine
        4. Ten to eleven
        5. More than than eleven

[Circle correct number.]

271

## Complaints and Symptoms

| | | | When? | | | If Chronic—During Past Year: | | | |
|---|---|---|---|---|---|---|---|---|---|
| Remarks | Yes | No | During Past Year | During Past Two Years | Write in Answer | Improved | Worse | Same | No Problem for Years |

**Sleep (contd.):**

59. Have there been periods when you got much more or much less sleep?

B.Q. 60. Have you ever taken tranquilizers?

61. Have you ever taken sleeping pills?

Score 1        Score 1

62. How about such things as appetite, would you say your appetite is: [Circle correct number.]

1. POOR
2. FAIR
3. GOOD
4. TOO GOOD

63. Have you noticed any changes in appetite over the past year?

1. YES
2. NO

64. If "yes": What kind of change—better or worse than before?

1. BETTER
2. WORSE

65. We were talking about your weight a little while ago. How is your weight now compared to year or so ago?

1. MORE
2. LESS
3. SAME

66. Have there been any big ups and downs in your weight throughout the past year?

1. YES
2. NO
3. GRADUAL CHANGE

B.Q. 67. Do you smoke? Has the amount you're smoking changed over the past year?

1. SMOKES MORE
2. SMOKES SAME
3. SMOKES LESS
4. NONSMOKER
0. NOT KNOWN

68. Would you say you smoke more than is good for you?

1. NO
2. YES
3. OTHER [Record]:
4. NONSMOKER

69. Do you drink coffee? Has the amount you drink changed over the past year?

1. DRINKS MORE COFFEE
2. THE SAME
3. DRINKS LESS COFFEE
4. DOES NOT DRINK COFFEE
0. NOT KNOWN

70. Like a lot of people, do you sometimes drink more coffee than is good for you?

1. NO
2. YES
3. OTHER [Record]:

B.Q. 71. Do you drink spirits, beer or wine? Has the amount you drink changed over the past year?

1. DRINKS MORE ALCOHOL
2. DRINKS SAME ALCOHOL

273

3. DRINKS LESS ALCO-
HOL
4. TEETOTAL
0. NOT KNOWN

III 72. Like a lot of people, do you sometimes   1. NO
drink more than is good for you?   2. YES
3. OTHER [Record]:

Here are some things that doctors hear about all the time. As I read each statement, please tell me whether or not it has been true for *you* during the past year. Just answer "yes" if it is true for you, "no" if it is not true.

Ring Scores

|  |  | YES | NO |
|---|---|---|---|
| I | 73–1. During the past year I have felt weak all over much of the time. | 1 | 0 |
| I | 73–2. During the past year I have had periods of such great restlessness that I could not sit long in a chair. | 1 | 0 |
|  | 73–3. During the past year my memory has seemed to be all right. | 0 | 1 |
|  | 73–4. During the past year I have got some exercise every day. | 0 | 1 |
| I | 73–5. During the past year I have had periods of days, weeks, or months when I couldn't take care of things because I couldn't "get going." | 1 | 0 |
| I | 73–6. During the past year I have spent more days sick in bed than is usual for me. | 1 | 0 |
| I | 73–7. During the past year I often have a hard time making up my mind about things I should do. | 1 | 0 |

| | | |
|---|---|---|
| 73–8. During the past year I thought my general health was what it should be. | 0 | 1 |
| 73–9. During the past year I have tended to feel tired in the morning when I wake up. | 1 | 0 |

[Questions 74 to 88 are general questions concerning family background and education.]

I am going to read you some things about which husbands and wives sometimes agree and sometimes disagree. Would you tell me which of these caused differences of opinion or have been a repeated problem during your marriage?

CODE: Yes = 1, No = 0

YES    NO

89–1. Time spent with friends?

89–2. Household expenses?

89–3. Being tired?

89–4. Being away from home too much?

89–5. Disciplining children?

89–6. In-laws?

89–7. Not showing love?

89–8. Your (husband's/wife's) job?

89–9. How to spend leisure time?

89–10. Religion?

89–11. Irritating personal habits?

90. Taking all things together, how would you describe your marriage?
1. VERY HAPPY
2. PRETTY HAPPY
3. NOT TOO HAPPY
0. NOT KNOWN

I would like your opinions on a number of different things. I'm going to read you several statements. Some people agree with these statements; some people disagree with them. As I read each one, will you tell me whether you *more or less agree* with it, or *more or less disagree* with it?

CODE: AGREE = 1, DISAGREE = 0

AGREE          DISAGREE

91–1. These days a person doesn't really know whom he can count on.

91–2. What young people need most of all is strict discipline.

91–3. Most public officials are not really interested in the problems of the average man.

91–4. Nowadays, a person has to live pretty much for today and let tomorrow take care of itself.

II  91–5. There are two kinds of people in this world: the weak and the strong.

91–6. Immigration to Great Britain should be stopped except from one or two countries.

91–7. Any good leader should be strict with people under him in order to gain their respect.

91–8. Prison is too good for sex criminals: they should be publicly whipped, or worse.

91–9. In spite of what some people say, the lot of the average man is getting worse, not better.

91–10. The most important thing to teach children is absolute obedience to their parents

276

91–11. Most people don't really care
what happens to the next fellow.

91–12. It's hardly fair to bring a child into
the world with the way things
look for the future.

B.Q. 91–13. It's safer not to fall in love.

[Questions 92 to 99 cover religious faith and observance.]

[ASK EVERYBODY, INCLUDING MARRIED, CHILDLESS RESPONDENTS.]
We have talked about parents and children. I have here words of advice parents
often give their children or to young people. Please tell me whether you *would*
or *would not* give a child this advice.

Score: Yes = 1, No = 0

YES     NO

II 100–1. Whatever you do must be done
perfectly.

II 100–2. One drink is one too many.

II 100–3. Never show your feelings to others.

II 100–4. Once your mind is made up, don't
let anything change it.

II 100–5. Always be on guard with people.

100–6. Choose your friends only from people of your own religion.

100–7. Very often, the old ways of doing
things are the best ways.

Here are some other questions to consider. Would you answer "yes" or "no"
to each one?

Score; Yes = 1, No = 0

YES     NO

101–1. Are you the worrying type?

277

101–2. When you go out, do you usually prefer to go by yourself?

IX 101–3. Do you feel somewhat apart or remote even among friends?

101–4. To avoid arguments, do you usually keep your opinions to yourself?

IX 101–5. Do you sometimes feel people are against you without any good reason?

101–6. Do you feel you have had your share of good luck in life?

I 102. In general, would you say that most of the time you are in high spirits, good spirits, low spirits, or very low spirits?

1. HIGH
2. GOOD
3. LOW
4. VERY LOW

[Questions 103 to 120 cover income, housing, neighbors, and friends.]

Here are some ideas that people have expressed. Would you tell me whether you *agree* or disagree with each one?

Score: AGREE = 1, DISAGREE = 0

AGREE DISAGREE

I 121–1. On the whole, life gives you a lot of pleasure.

121–2. Behind your back people say all kinds of things about you.

I 121–3. Nothing ever turns out for me the way I want it to.

121–4. In going into marriage a larger sacrifice is made by the woman than the man.

121–5. A person has moments when he feels he is a stranger to himself.

121–6. The unmarried person can be just as contented as the married one.

121–7. Most people think a great deal about sex matters.

121–8. I have personal worries that get me down physically.

121–9. A person should have a physical check-up at least once a year.

B.Q. I 121–10. You sometimes can't help wondering whether anything is worthwhile any more.

121–11. Next to health, money is the most important thing in life.

121–12. Children give their parents more trouble than pleasure.

121–13. I can't really enjoy myself when I am alone.

121–14. Certain kinds of places make me tense or nervous such as high buildings, tunnels or bridges.

122–A. Everybody these days has some things he worries about—some big and some small. What about the big things? What would you say has worried you or been on your mind most *in the past few weeks?*

122–B. Now what about small things? What has bothered you or been on your mind most *in the past few weeks?*

VII 122–C. In general, do you worry *a lot* or *not very much?*

1. A LOT
2. NOT VERY MUCH

3. NEVER WORRIES

0. NOT KNOWN

122–D. Would you say you worry more now than you used to or not as much as you used to?

1. MORE

2. ABOUT THE SAME

3. NOT AS MUCH

4. NEVER WORRIES

0. NOT KNOWN

Almost everybody has personal worries these days. Here is a list of worries that people all over the country have. I will read each one, and would you tell me whether it is something that worries you: *often, sometimes,* or *never?*

Code: OFTEN = 1, SOMETIMES = 2, NEVER = 3, N.K. = 0.

OFTEN   SOMETIMES   NEVER

VII   122–1. Not having enough money.

VII   122–2. Financial debts.

122–3. Getting along with someone.

III   122–4. Moving ahead in the world.

II   122–5. How your work is going.

I   122–6. Loneliness.

VII   122–7. Your children.

122–8. Sex problems.

122–9. Personal enemies.

VIII 122–10. Your health.

122–11. Growing old.

122–12. The world situation.

II   122–13. Criticism from others.

122–14. Marriage problems.

122–15. Other [Write in.]

[Questions 123 to 131 cover problems with children.]

Now here are a few general opinions people have expressed. Would you indicate whether you *more or less agree* or *more or less disagree* with the following opinions?

Score: AGREE = 1, DISAGREE = 0

AGREE   DISAGREE

132–1. As a rule, it's much better to do things on the spur of the moment than to think and plan ahead.

132–2. Showing feelings of grief and sorrow is all right for children, but not for adults.

IX   132–3. A person does better for himself by keeping away from his family.

132–4. A person's emotions can affect his health.

133. How often have you seen a doctor during the past year?

1. ONCE A MONTH/ MORE OFTEN
2. 6–10 TIMES
3. 3–5 TIMES
4. LESS THAN 3 TIMES

134. Part of every health history covers the time a person has been in a hospital. Altogether, how many different times have you been a patient in a hospital either in your home town or elsewhere except to give birth?

1. NEVER
2. ONCE OR TWICE
3. 3–4 TIMES
4. 5–7 TIMES
5. 8–10 TIMES
6. 11 plus TIMES

135–1. What hospitals were you in? [Record below.]

135–2. About when were you there? [Record below.]

135–3. What was the thing you went to the hospital for? [Record below.]

VIII 136–1. During the past year, have you had occasion to go to a hospital or clinic either for yourself or a member of your family?

1. YES
2. NO

136–2. [For each clinic named:] What was the condition you went to the clinic for? [Record below.]

B.Q. 137–1. During the past year, have you seen anyone about any emotional problems you may have—such as a minister, social worker, psychologist, or psychiatrist?

1. CLERGYMAN
2. SOCIAL WORKER
3. PSYCHOLOGIST
4. PSYCHIATRIST IN A CLINIC
5. PRIVATE PSYCHIATRIST
6. OTHER [Specify:]
7. HAS SEEN NO ONE

137–2. How often have you seen him? [If more than one person, code the one most frequently seen.]

0. NONE
1. 1–3 TIMES
2. 4–8 TIMES
3. 2–6 MONTHS
4. 7–10 MONTHS
5. MORE THAN 10 MONTHS

137–3. Had you seen this person or someone like him before this past year? [Record the nature and duration of previous help.]

1. HAS HAD CONTINU-

OUS RELATION
WITH SOME THERA-
PIST *FOR MORE
THAN ONE YEAR*
2. HAS SOUGHT HELP
INTERMITTENTLY
IN THE PAST
3. HAS SOUGHT HELP
PREVIOUS TO THIS
YEAR *AT LEAST
ONCE BEFORE.*
4. NO
5. D.N.A.

138. If person does not mention hospitalization for nervous breakdown, ask:
Have you ever had a nervous breakdown:

1. YES
2. NO
3. DON'T KNOW
4. D.N.A.

139. If "yes": When was this?

1. NO
2. DURING PAST YEAR
3. MORE THAN A YEAR
AND LESS THAN 3
YEARS AGO
4. 3–6 YEARS
AGO
5. MORE THAN 6 YEARS
AGO
6. NOT KNOWN

140. What kind of treatment did you receive? [Code all that apply.]

1. SHOCK
2. PSYCHOTHERAPY
3. DRUGS
4. REST
5. SUPPORTIVE THER-
APY (e.g. social worker,
clergyman, etc.)

**283**

6. NONE
7. D.N.A.

Here are some statements people make about themselves. Please tell me if they
are *mostly true* of you or *not true* of you.

Score: Mostly true = 1 Not true = 0

|  | MOSTLY TRUE | NOT TRUE |
|---|---|---|

141–1. People often ask me for advice.

VII 141–2. At times I have been worried beyond reason about something that
really didn't matter.

II 141–3. I've found that it doesn't pay to
put yourself out for other people.

141–4. I'm frequently sorry about decisions I have made.

141–5. Most of the time I don't care what
others think of me.

141–6. When problems come up I'm generally able to find out how to solve
them.

VII 141–7. I am the kind of person who takes
things hard.

141–8. When I want something very
much, I want it right away.

B.Q. 141–9. Life is often a strain for me.

III–141–10. I suppose I am a gambler at heart.

141–11. I am very confident of myself.

IX 141–12. I sometimes feel that no one un-
derstands me.

141–13. I tend to go to pieces in a crisis.

IX 141–14. Some people don't have as much
respect for me as they should.

141–15. I get discouraged easily.

141–16. I always take good care of my health.

141–17. On the whole I'm satisfied with myself.

142. Apart from your husband/wife, has any other member of your immediate family died in the past year or so? If "yes": Who?

1. MOTHER
2. FATHER
3. CHILD
4. AUNT/UNCLE
5. GRANDPARENT
6. SIBLING
0. NONE

143. Have you faced any other major upsets during the past year or so (e.g., fire, thefts, job loss, problems)? [Record below.]

During the past few weeks, did you ever feel:
Score: Italicized answers score 1.

| | | | |
|---|---|---|---|
| III | 144–1. Particularly excited or interested in something? | Yes | *No* |
| I | 144–2. Bored? | *Yes* | No |
| | 144–3. Proud because someone complimented you on something? | Yes | *No* |
| B.Q. I | 144–4. Depressed or very unhappy? | *Yes* | No |
| | 144–5. Pleased about having accomplished something? | Yes | *No* |
| | 144–6. Upset because someone was unkind? | *Yes* | No |
| I | 144–7. That things were going your way? | Yes | *No* |

145. In the past few weeks, did anything happen to make you angry? If "yes": What happened? [Record below.]

B.Q. I 146.    Taken altogether, how would you say things are these days—
would you say that you are *very happy, pretty happy,* or *not too happy?*

1. VERY HAPPY
2. PRETTY HAPPY
3. NOT TOO HAPPY
   Score 1

B.Q. I 147.    Think of how your life is going
now. Do you want it to *continue in
much the same way as it's going now;* do
you wish you could *change some
parts of it;* or do you wish you
could *change many parts of it?*

1. CONTINUE IN MUCH
   THE SAME WAY
2. CHANGE SOME
   PARTS Score 1
3. CHANGE MANY
   PARTS Score 2

I    148.    When you think of the things you
want from life, would you say that
you're *doing very well; doing pretty well,*
or you're *not doing too well* now in getting the things you want?

1. DOING VERY WELL
   NOW
2. DOING PRETTY
   WELL NOW
3. NOT DOING TOO
   WELL NOW Score 1

We are almost finished now, I just have a few more statements which I'd like
*you* to read. Circle whether each statement is either *mostly true* for you or *mostly
false* for you. [Hand respondent SELF-RATING LIST. After taking back list,
thank the respondent for his or her cooperation and emphasize how much help
he or she has given.]

Self-Rating List

Score: Italicized answers score 1.

1. I am easily awakened by noise.

*MOSTLY TRUE*
MOSTLY FALSE

I   2. My daily life is full of things that keep me interested.

MOSTLY TRUE
*MOSTLY FALSE*

3. I am about as able to work as I ever was.

MOSTLY TRUE
*MOSTLY FALSE*

I   4. At times I have fits of laughing and crying that I cannot control.

*MOSTLY TRUE*
MOSTLY FALSE

5. When someone does me a wrong, I feel I should pay him back if I can, just for the principle of the thing.

*MOSTLY TRUE*
MOSTLY FALSE

I   6. I find it hard to keep my mind on a task or job.

*MOSTLY TRUE*
MOSTLY FALSE

7. I have had very peculiar and strange experiences.

*MOSTLY TRUE*
MOSTLY FALSE

8. At times I feel like smashing things.

*MOSTLY TRUE*
MOSTLY FALSE

9. My judgment is better than it ever was.

MOSTLY TRUE
*MOSTLY FALSE*

VIII 10. I am in just as good physical health as most of my friends

MOSTLY TRUE
*MOSTLY FALSE*

VII 11. I prefer to pass by school friends or people I know but have not seen for a long time, unless they speak to me first.

*MOSTLY TRUE*
MOSTLY FALSE

III 12. I am a good mixer.

*MOSTLY TRUE*
MOSTLY FALSE

13. Parts of my body have feelings like

burning, tingling, crawling, or like
"going to sleep."

*MOSTLY TRUE*
MOSTLY FALSE

14. I sometimes keep on at a thing until
others lose their patience with me.

*MOSTLY TRUE*
MOSTLY FALSE

I   15. I wish I could be as happy as others
seem to be.

*MOSTLY TRUE*
MOSTLY FALSE

16. I am easily downed in an argument.

*MOSTLY TRUE*
MOSTLY FALSE

17. It takes a lot of argument to convince
most people of the truth.

*MOSTLY TRUE*
MOSTLY FALSE

18. I blush as often as others.

*MOSTLY TRUE*
MOSTLY FALSE

19. I have quarrels with members of my
family.

*MOSTLY TRUE*
MOSTLY FALSE

I   20. I don't seem to care what happens to
me.

*MOSTLY TRUE*
MOSTLY FALSE

21. Some people are so bossy that I feel
like doing the opposite of what they
request, even though I know they are
right.

*MOSTLY TRUE*
MOSTLY FALSE

22. I seem to be about as capable and
clever as most others around me.

MOSTLY TRUE
*MOSTLY FALSE*

VII  23. Often I can't understand why I have
been so cross and grouchy.

*MOSTLY TRUE*
MOSTLY FALSE

24. I do not worry about catching diseases.

MOSTLY TRUE
*MOSTLY FALSE*

25. I like collecting flowers or growing house plants.

*MOSTLY TRUE*
MOSTLY FALSE

VII 26. I am more self-conscious than most people.

*MOSTLY TRUE*
MOSTLY FALSE

II 27. I like to cook.

*MOSTLY TRUE*
MOSTLY FALSE

I 28. I certainly feel useless at times.

*MOSTLY TRUE*
MOSTLY FALSE

VII 29. I cry easily.

*MOSTLY TRUE*
MOSTLY FALSE

30. I cannot understand what I read as well as I used to.

*MOSTLY TRUE*
MOSTLY FALSE

VII 31. I feel anxious about something or someone almost all of the time.

*MOSTLY TRUE*
MOSTLY FALSE

III 32. When I get bored I like to stir up some excitement.

*MOSTLY TRUE*
MOSTLY FALSE

III 33. I like to flirt.

*MOSTLY TRUE*
MOSTLY FALSE

34. I believe my sins are unpardonable.

*MOSTLY TRUE*
MOSTLY FALSE

35. Some of my family have habits that bother and annoy me very much.

*MOSTLY TRUE*
MOSTLY FALSE

III 36. I like to talk about sex.

*MOSTLY TRUE*
MOSTLY FALSE

37. I have at times stood in the way of people who were trying to do something not because it amounted to much but because of the principle of the thing.

*MOSTLY TRUE*
MOSTLY FALSE

38. I get mad easily and then get over it soon.

*MOSTLY TRUE*
MOSTLY FALSE

I 39. I brood a great deal.

*MOSTLY TRUE*
MOSTLY FALSE

40. I dream frequently about things that are best kept to myself.

*MOSTLY TRUE*
MOSTLY FALSE

IX 41. My way of doing things is apt to be misunderstood by others.

*MOSTLY TRUE*
MOSTLY FALSE

42. I have had blank spells in which my activities were interrupted and I did not know what was going on around me.

*MOSTLY TRUE*
MOSTLY FALSE

43. I can be friendly with people who do things which I consider wrong.

*MOSTLY TRUE*
MOSTLY FALSE

44. When I leave home I do not worry about whether the door is locked and the windows closed.

MOSTLY TRUE
*MOSTLY FALSE*

IX 45. I do not blame a person for taking advantage of someone who lays himself open to it.

*MOSTLY TRUE*
MOSTLY FALSE

46. At times I am all full of energy.

MOSTLY TRUE
*MOSTLY FALSE*

VII 47. Once in a while I feel hate toward members of my family whom I usually love.

*MOSTLY TRUE*
MOSTLY FALSE

48. Once in a while I laugh at a dirty joke.

*MOSTLY TRUE*
MOSTLY FALSE

49. I have periods in which I feel unusually cheerful without any special reason.

*MOSTLY TRUE*
MOSTLY FALSE

50. I have certainly had more than my share of things to worry about.

*MOSTLY TRUE*
MOSTLY FALSE

IX 51. Often I cross the street in order not to meet someone I see.

*MOSTLY TRUE*
MOSTLY FALSE

52. Sometimes I enjoy hurting persons I love.

*MOSTLY TRUE*
MOSTLY FALSE

53. When someone says silly or ignorant things about something I know about, I try to set him right.

*MOSTLY TRUE*
MOSTLY FALSE

54. I am often said to be hotheaded.

*MOSTLY TRUE*
MOSTLY FALSE

55. People often disappoint me

*MOSTLY TRUE*
MOSTLY FALSE

IX 56. I feel unable to tell anyone all about myself.

*MOSTLY TRUE*
MOSTLY FALSE

57. I would certainly enjoy beating a crook at his own game.

*MOSTLY TRUE*
MOSTLY FALSE

III   58. I am attracted by members of the opposite sex.

*MOSTLY TRUE*
MOSTLY FALSE

59. I am often sorry because I am so cross and grouchy.

*MOSTLY TRUE*
MOSTLY FALSE

II   60. I pray several times every week.

*MOSTLY TRUE*
MOSTLY FALSE

61. Dirt frightens or disgusts me.

*MOSTLY TRUE*
MOSTLY FALSE

62. My skin seems to be unusually sensitive to touch.

*MOSTLY TRUE*
MOSTLY FALSE

I   63. I feel tired a good deal of the time.

*MOSTLY TRUE*
MOSTLY FALSE

IX   54. I shrink from facing a crisis or difficulty.

*MOSTLY TRUE*
MOSTLY FALSE

65. I have often been frightened in the middle of the night.

*MOSTLY TRUE*
MOSTLY FALSE

# Appendix 2

# *Symptoms Reported by Bereaved and Non-bereaved Respondents*

As described in chapter 2, there was a marked difference between fourteen-month bereaved respondents and the matched group of married men and women in our comparison group with respect to the Autonomic Reaction score of the Health Questionnaire (see appendix 1).

Table A2.1 shows how these two groups replied to each question which made up this score.

Clearly the largest differences were in trembling/twitching, sweating, nervousness, dizziness or fainting, palpitations, pain in chest, and feeling lump in throat—all reflections of the somatic effects of anxiety.

There was no excess of chronic symptoms which had become worse in the bereaved group when compared with the non-bereaved. Among the thirty-five physical symptoms that were not included in the Autonomic Reaction group, there were only six that were reported by 10 percent or more of the combined sample as having come on for the first time or grown worse during the preceding year, and no significant differences were

TABLE A2.1

*Autonomic Reaction—Number and Percentage of Bereaved and Nonbereaved Respondents Reporting Each Symptom*

| (Number in Sample)<br>Question | Bereaved Group<br>68 | | Non-bereaved Group<br>68 | |
|---|---|---|---|---|
| | N | % | N | % |
| Nose running<br>or clogged | 7 | 10 | 6 | 9 |
| Feel lump in<br>throat | 6 | 9 | 2 | 3 |
| Pain in chest | 9 | 13 | 3 | 4 |
| Palpitations | 6 | 9 | 3 | 4 |
| Sick feeling | 11 | 16 | 12 | 17 |
| Urinates too<br>frequently | 5 | 7 | 5 | 7 |
| Itching | 6 | 9 | 5 | 7 |
| Dizziness or<br>fainting | 10 | 14 | 3 | 4 |
| Nervousness | 16 | 23 | 9 | 13 |
| Trembling/<br>twitching | 10 | 14 | 3 | 4 |
| At times feel<br>hot all over | 8 | 12 | 9 | 13 |
| Sweat when<br>you haven't been<br>doing anything | 8 | 12 | 2 | 3 |
| | 102 | | 62 | |

found between the groups. Likewise, there were no significant differences between the bereaved and the comparison group on self-estimates of "general health," "health worries," or "physical health compared with that of most of my friends."

Figure A2.1 shows the changes in the Autonomic Symptom score in the three subgroups who were followed two years (N = 13), three years (N = 31), and four years (N = 15) after bereavement.

*Symptoms Reported by Bereaved and Non-bereaved Respondents*

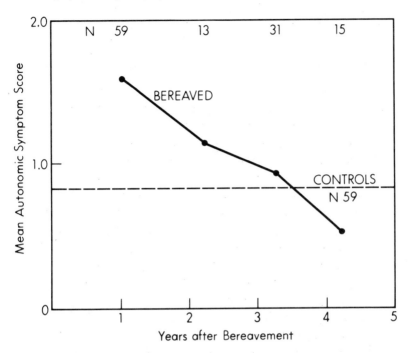

FIGURE A2.1

*Changes in Autonomic Symptom Score in Bereaved Respondents Who Were
Followed Up*

NOTE: There was no significant difference between bereaved and comparison groups after the first year.

# Appendix 3

# *Intercorrelation of Outcome Measures*

To examine the interrelationship of the outcome measures we can study table A3.1 which gives correlation coefficients between each of the eleven principal outcome measures.

In this table any correlation higher than 0.23 is significant at the 5 percent level. This means that there is some significant interrelationship between practically all of our outcome measures.

The largest cluster of outcome indicators, all of which intercorrelate quite highly, include: "Functioning," "Movement toward Improved Adjustment," "Acceptance," "Attitude toward the Future," "Anxiety/Depression," "Guilt/Anger," "Self-Evaluation," and "Resilience." It follows that people who are coping well a year after bereavement are likely to be moving toward a satisfactory adjustment to life, to be accepting of their loss, positive about their future prospects, emotionally calm, resilient, and with high self-evaluation. Despite all this there is not a strong tendency for them to be either socially active or physically healthy although our figures do suggest a trend in this direction.

"Social Activity" was, in fact, the measure that correlated least strongly with other measures, and this seems to reflect the fact that although some people were socially withdrawn because they were unhappy or maladjusted, there were others for

TABLE A3.1.

*Intercorrelations of Outcome Measures*

| | Functioning | Movement toward Adjustment | Acceptance | Social Activity | Attitude toward Future | Physical Health | Anxiety/Depression | Guilt/Anger | Self-Evaluation | Resilience | Health Questionnaire Score |
|---|---|---|---|---|---|---|---|---|---|---|---|
| Functioning | | *0.65* | *0.53* | 0.22 | *0.48* | *0.33* | *0.69* | *0.51* | *0.57* | *0.74* | *0.42* |
| Movement toward Adjustment | *0.65* | | *0.40* | *0.25* | *0.57* | *0.33* | *0.45* | *0.34* | *0.61* | *0.60* | *0.24* |
| Acceptance | *0.53* | *0.40* | | *0.39* | *0.42* | 0.13 | *0.52* | *0.47* | *0.49* | *0.58* | 0.17 |
| Social Activity | 0.22 | *0.25* | *0.39* | | *0.46* | 0.05 | 0.06 | *0.27* | *0.30* | *0.37* | 0.12 |
| Attitude toward Future | *0.48* | *0.57* | *0.42* | *0.46* | | *0.32* | *0.49* | *0.47* | *0.65* | *0.60* | *0.27* |
| Physical Health | *0.33* | *0.33* | 0.13 | 0.05 | *0.32* | | *0.46* | *0.36* | *0.39* | *0.31* | *0.39* |
| Anxiety/Depression | *0.69* | *0.45* | *0.52* | 0.28 | *0.49* | *0.46* | | *0.76* | *0.61* | *0.76* | *0.64* |
| Guilt/Anger | *0.51* | *0.34* | *0.47* | *0.27* | *0.47* | *0.36* | *0.76* | | *0.45* | *0.39* | *0.54* |
| Self-Evaluation | *0.57* | *0.61* | *0.49* | *0.30* | *0.65* | *0.39* | *0.61* | *0.45* | | *0.77* | *0.50* |
| Resilience | *0.74* | *0.60* | *0.58* | *0.37* | *0.60* | *0.31* | *0.76* | *0.39* | *0.77* | | *0.51* |
| Health Questionnaire Score | *0.42* | *0.24* | 0.17 | 0.12 | *0.27* | *0.39* | *0.64* | *0.54* | *0.50* | *0.51* | |

NOTE: Significance levels after Fisher and Yates. $r > 0.23$ means that $p < 0.05$; $r > 0.30$ means that $p < 0.01$; $r > 0.38$ means that $p < 0.001$. All correlations in which $p < 0.05$ are italicized.

whom solitude was a chosen way of life. They could remain alone at home without undue depression and were functioning well in their life spaces and moving toward a satisfactory adjustment. True, they tended to have a less positive attitude toward the future than those who were actively committed to society, but there must be many widows and widowers who choose not to turn outward toward society after their bereavement, and our figures seem to indicate that this does not necessarily mean that they are maladjusted.

"Social Activity" showed no correlation (r = 0.05) with "Physical Health." This indicates that those with health problems were neither more nor less socially isolated than the general run of bereaved respondents. We can guess that while there may have been some whose health prevented them from going out, there were others whose illnesses engendered a supportive reaction in others and that these two effects canceled each other out in the final analysis.

"Physical Health" status correlated most highly with "Anxiety/Depression" and at a lower level with most other outcome measures. Presumably the anxiety/depression resulted from the poor health, but it is also interesting to note how poor health also seemed to correlate, though not strongly, with low self-esteem and the expression of anger and/or guilt. The low correlation between health and "Acceptance" probably means that repudiation of widowed status is not a major cause of illness among the bereaved, but it is necessary to emphasize the "catch-all" character of the "Physical Health" measure. We have no good reason to believe that "general health" is, in fact, a satisfactory general indicator of anything, and we tend to regard it as a rag-bag of unrelated conditions (see pages 293–294).

The "Health Questionnaire Score," it should be remembered, is another assemblage of questionnaire items which was intended as a general outcome measure rather than a measure of a particular type of outcome. Perusal of table A3.1, however, reveals it to be especially highly correlated with measures of emotional disturbance (anxiety/depression, guilt/anger, low self-evaluation, and resilience). That this should be the case is not surprising if we examine the questions asked (appendix 1), many of which are concerned with feelings. It cannot be regarded as an index of acceptance or social activity, and it gives little indication of movement toward better or worse adjustment.

One further point is worth noting before we leave the "Health Questionnaire Score." This score is the only one of those listed in table A3.1 which was obtained directly from the respondents rather than being made by the coders at the end of an evaluation of the third interview. The fact that it was made at a different interview that was carried out a month after the third interview by a different interviewer who was unknown to the respondent makes it an important check on the reliability of our assessments. The fact that the "Health Questionnaire Score" correlates so highly with four of the coders' outcome ratings of emotional disturbance reassures us that these ratings are not unduly biased by the coders' emotions or by day-to-day fluctuations in the respondent's emotional state.

The general conclusion that emerges from this phase of the analysis is that, despite the differences between individual outcome measures, there is sufficient overlap between them to allow us to speak of a single outcome rather than having to consider separately emotional outcome, outcome in relation to role functioning, physical outcome, feelings of internal comfort, and so on. The rather simplistic division of respondents into "good," "intermediate," and "bad" general outcomes, which it was necessary to adopt for purposes of statistical analysis, is thus found to have some empirical justification. This does not prevent us from also studying particular types of outcome, but it does make it unlikely that we shall find big differences between the determinants of these.

The independent contribution that each predictive variable in our short list made to our main outcome variable ("Overall Outcome") is shown in the right column of table A3.2. Fifty-seven percent of the group difference can be predicted, and this difference is significant at a probability of 0.029. The value of "eta," the predictive coefficient, for the lower ten variables in this table is so low that it is reasonable to omit them from the Predictive Index without serious loss of predictive power.

Table A3.2 also shows how each of our main outcome variables was predicted by the same eighteen predictive variables. In general, there were no big differences between the constellations of predictive variables which predict each type of outcome. Thus, the first four variables listed—the "Coder's Prediction of Outcome," "Yearning at Interview I," "Wish for Death at Interview I," and "Duration of Terminal Illness"—were among the first six predictors for all these outcome measures and each predicted outcome at a significant level.

"Social Class" was a good predictor of "Guilt/Anger" but a borderline or poor predictor of other variables. "Alcohol Consumption" was a good predictor of the "Ten Best Questions Score" but a poor predictor of everything else.

This last finding is not hard to explain. "Has the amount of alcohol you drink changed over the last year?" was included among the questions that best discriminated bereaved from nonbereaved respondents (the "Ten Best Questions"), and it was no surprise to find that people who drank before bereavement tended to drink more after bereavement.

"Duration of Marriage" was a borderline predictor of "Overall Outcome" but a poor predictor of everything else. The borderline "eta" is probably a "freak" finding, and for this reason this variable has been omitted from the Index of Bereavement Risk described in appendix 5. "Anger" and "Guilt" at Interview I, however, are found among the best eight predictors of most types of poor outcome and have been retained.

The overall discriminant score would have enabled significant predictions to be made of all forms of outcome except

TABLE A3.2

*Values of Eta for Eighteen Predictive Variables and Six Outcome Measures*

|  | Ten Best Questions | Social-izing | Guilt/ Anger | Funct-ioning | Psychological Adjustment | Overall Outcome |
|---|---|---|---|---|---|---|
| Numbers with Good/ Bad Outcome | 26/22 | 12/28 | 21/23 | 33/14 | 36/12 | 27/22 |
| % of Group Difference that Can Be Predicted | 63% | 47% | 68% | 60% | 62% | 57% |
| p | .008 | N.S. | .007 | .021 | .009 | .029 |
| **Predictive Variables at Interview I** | | | | | | |
| Coder's prediction | *.39* | *.39* | *.48* | *.44* | *.50* | *.49* |
| Yearning | *.45* | .23 | *.49* | *.32* | *.31* | *.46* |
| Wish for death | *.35* | .29 | .29 | .21 | *.50* | *.45* |
| Duration of Terminal Illness | *.37* | *.35* | *.42* | *.40* | .24 | *.44* |
| Social Class | .00 | .18 | .21 | *.40* | *.30* | *.30* |
| Duration of Marriage | .03 | .04 | .15 | .17 | .02 | .26 |
| Anger at Interview I | .27 | .07 | *.39* | *.30* | .17 | .26 |
| Guilt at Interview I | *.38* | .23 | *.33* | .21 | .28 | .25 |
| Insomnia | .16 | .01 | .25 | .22 | .20 | .21 |
| Emotional Upset at Interview I | .25 | .07 | .27 | .20 | *.30* | .20 |
| Number of Children | .10 | .22 | .13 | .21 | .06 | .18 |
| Race | .00 | .04 | .08 | .23 | .19 | .11 |
| Siblings Near | .16 | .20 | .14 | .00 | .20 | .10 |
| Alcohol Consumption | *.50* | .13 | .19 | .18 | .17 | .08 |
| Numbness | .06 | .06 | .01 | .15 | .16 | .04 |
| Religion | .04 | .13 | .14 | .06 | .19 | .04 |
| Number at Home | .09 | .20 | *.30* | .08 | .10 | .03 |
| Age | .05 | .23 | .12 | .02 | .00 | .02 |

NOTE: Figures in italics are significant at p < .05

301

"Socializing." In this instance only 47 percent of the group difference could be predicted and the difference did not reach the 5 percent level of significance. The only two variables that significantly predicted "Socializing" were the "Coder's Prediction of Outcome" and the "Duration of Terminal Illness." Although unforewarned bereavements seem to be given to social withdrawal, there is little reason, from this study, to regard social withdrawal as a necessary indicator of bad outcome, and for some people a degree of withdrawal at thirteen months after bereavement may be a satisfactory way of coping.

The other outcome assessments are less equivocal. "Guilt/ Anger," which, on grounds of psychoanalytic theory, would be regarded by some as the most ominous combination of affects, is also the most readily predicted. Sixty-eight percent of the group difference could be predicted, and this was significant at less than the 1 percent level ($p = .007$). Six variables contributed significantly to this prediction, and five of them were among the eight best predictors of "Overall Outcome." Understandably, "Guilt at Interview I" and "Anger at Interview I" were significant predictors of "Guilt/Anger" at Interview III, but it is worth nothing that "Yearning," "Duration of Terminal Illness," and "Coder's Predictions" were even better indicators of "Guilt/Anger." An odd finding that is less easy to explain is the association between "Guilt/Anger" and "Number at Home." While this may have been a chance association, it also seems possible that, since anger normally arises in interaction with others, the more people there are close by the greater the opportunity for anger. Conversely, the person who remains isolated and alone after bereavement may find that occasions for anger are few; a general state of irritability may exist, but it takes people to set it off. The fact that others around are also likely to be affected by the bereavement sometimes leads to a reciprocal build-up of bitterness and enmity between the very people who ought to be supporting each other. Despite this finding, it is worth remarking that "Number at Home" was not a significant predictor of any other type of poor outcome, and this would seem to indicate that there are compensations in having people around which make up for any increased danger of quarrels which may exist.

# Appendix 4

---

# *Discriminant Functions Analysis*

In this study eighteen predictive variables, selected on the grounds that each was reliable and representative of other variables of its type, were intercorrelated with a measure of outcome using the form of multivariate analysis, discriminant functions analysis. It was possible to optimize the discriminating power of each predictive variable by confining the analysis to those respondents who had clear-cut "good" or "bad" outcomes and by omitting any whose outcome was intermediate or uncertain.

The figure "eta" gives a good idea of the contribution which each predictive variable makes to the total variance. If all eighteen variables were to be used as a predictive index, it would be necessary to multiply the score for each individual question by "eta" in order to obtain a weighted score. This would give the best possible prediction of outcome.

The measure of "Functioning" would be regarded by some as the most important single measure of outcome. Focusing as it did on the effectiveness with which the respondent was able to fulfill his or her life tasks—to work, to undertake household responsibilities, to manage money, to rear children, and so forth —it was essentially concerned with practical matters. It was also a relative measure and was assessed not in absolute terms but in terms of the ability with which the respondent had coped

## TABLE A4.1

### Influence of Eighteen Predictive Variables on Overall Outcome

| Predictive Variables from Interview I | Mean Value | | Eta | Probability |
|---|---|---|---|---|
| N | Good Outcome 27 | Bad Outcome 22 | | |
| Coder's Prediction | 1.07 | 1.73 | 0.492 | 0.00041 |
| Yearning | 3.78 | 2.82 | 0.458 | 0.001 |
| Wish for Own Death | 1.07 | 1.82 | 0.445 | 0.0015 |
| Duration Terminal Illness | 2.19 | 3.77 | 0.442 | 0.0016 |
| Socioeconomic Status | 3.37 | 4.23 | 0.300 | 0.034 |
| Duration of Marriage | 2.93 | 4.55 | 0.263 | 0.065 |
| Anger | 1.78 | 2.18 | 0.257 | 0.071 |
| Self-Reproach | 1.33 | 1.77 | 0.254 | 0.074 |
| Insomnia | 4.37 | 3.77 | 0.208 | 0.15 |
| Emotional Upset | 3.04 | 2.55 | 0.120 | 0.17 |
| Number of Children | 2.78 | 3.55 | 0.184 | 0.20 |
| Race | 1.22 | 1.32 | 0.108 | 0.47 |
| Siblings Near | 1.26 | 1.64 | 0.098 | 0.51 |
| Alcohol Consumption | 1.67 | 1.82 | 0.080 | 0.59 |
| Numbness | 0.59 | 0.64 | 0.045 | 0.75 |
| Religion | 1.44 | 1.41 | 0.036 | 0.80 |
| Number at Home | 1.78 | 1.73 | 0.031 | 0.82 |
| Age | 36.90 | 37.10 | 0.023 | 0.85 |

with these same life tasks prior to bereavement. A high score on the "Functioning" scale, therefore, indicated that the respondent was now less effective than before bereavement.

On analysis there were hardly any differences between the factors which predicted "Functioning" and those which predicted "Overall Outcome." The five significant predictors of "Functioning" were all among the seven best predictors of "Overall Outcome," and there were no discrepancies worth noting. "Psychological Adjustment" is also predicted by more or less the same variables that predict "Overall Outcome." The exception here is the measure of "Emotional Upset Observed at Interview I," which significantly predicts "Psychological Adjustment" a year later but does not correlate significantly with any of the other outcome measures. This finding confirms our view that emotional disturbance in the post-bereavement period does foreshadow emotional disturbance later, but the level of significance is not sufficiently high to make this particular measure a reliable predictor of outcome as a whole, and it is not sufficient for interviewers to take only the mood of the moment into account when making such predictions.

The "Ten Best Questions Score" is the only outcome measure that we can be sure is independent of coder or interviewer bias. It will be recalled that this score was derived from the ten questions that best distinguished bereaved respondents from nonbereaved controls on answers to our Health Questionnaire fourteen months after bereavement. It can, therefore, be taken as a measure of the damaging effects of bereavement. The questions were asked by an independent interviewer who knew nothing of the content of the first three interviews. It is reassuring to find that among the five variables which significantly predicted "Overall Outcome," four also predicted a high score on "Ten Best Questions."

"Overall Outcome" is by no means the most readily predicted of outcomes: only 57 percent of the group difference was predicted from the eighteen predictive variables. But this level of predictive power is significant at the $p = 0.029$ level. Other forms of outcome which are rather more easily predicted were "Guilt/Anger" (68 percent predictable at $p = 0.007$), "Ten Best Questions" (63 percent predictable at $p = 0.008$), "Psychological Adjustment" (62 percent predictable at $p = 0.009$), and "Functioning" (60 percent predictable at $p = 0.021$).

# Appendix 5

---

# *Development of a Bereavement Risk Index at St. Christopher's Hospice*

The assessments that emerged from the multivariate analysis described in appendix 4 have been used as a means of identifying people in need of the help of the Bereavement Service at St. Christopher's Hospice. The first Bereavement Risk Index that we used is given in table A5.1.

These questions reformulate the assessments of outcome-relevant antecedents discussed in chapter 9 in the form of a questionnaire to be answered by the nurses who care for cancer patients and their families at the hospice (see p. 221). Each question A through H contributes a part of the total score which is entered on the reverse of the card. Any person having a score of 18 or more was rated as "high risk" for the purposes of assigning support, and people with a score of 4 or 5 on question "H" were always offered the help of the Bereavement Service regardless of their total score. (They comprise the "Imperative Need" Group.)

Three hundred and two respondents were approached for our

TABLE A5.1

*First Bereavement Index: Ring one item in each section. Leave blank if not known.*

......  Check here if key person not well enough known to enable these questions to be answered.

**A.**

*Age of key person (applies only if key person is spouse)*
1. 75+
2. 66–75
3. 56–65
4. 46–55
5. 15–45

**B.**

*Occupation of principal wage earner of key person's family.*
1. Professional and executive
2. Semi-professional
3. Office and clerk
4. Skilled manual
5. Semi-skilled manual
6. Unskilled manual

**C.**

*Length of key person's preparation for patient's death*
1. Fully prepared for long period
2. Fully prepared for less than 2 weeks
3. Partly prepared
4. Totally unprepared

**D.**

*Clinging or Pining*
1. Never
2. Seldom
3. Moderate
4. Frequent
5. Constant
6. Constant and intense

**E.**

*Anger*
1. None (or normal)
2. Mild irritation
3. Moderate— occasional outbursts
4. Severe—spoiling relationships
5. Extreme—always bitter

**F.**

*Self-Reproach*
1. None
2. Mild—vague, general
3. Moderate—some clear self-reproach
4. Severe— preoccupied with self-blame
5. Extreme—major problem

G.

*Family*

1. Warm, will give full support
2. Doubtful
3. Family supportive but lives at distance
4. Family not supportive
5. No family

H.

*How will key person cope?*[a]

1. *Well*—normal grief and recovery without special help
2. *Fair*—probably get by without special help
3. *Doubtful*—may need special help
4. *Badly*—requires special help
5. *Very badly*—requires urgent help

---

[a]All ringed four or five on question H will be visited.

research evaluation, of whom sixty-one (20 percent) could not be traced; nineteen (6 percent) were dead or too ill to be interviewed; and forty-one (13 percent) declined an interview.

The 181 who were followed up were distributed as follows:

|  | N |
|---|---|
| Group A: "Imperative Need" Group | 21 |
| Group B: Predicted "High Risk" Group, having scores of 18+ (These had been assigned at random to "Supported" Group BH = 32 and Control Group BT = 35.) | 67 |
| Group C: Predicted "Low Risk" Group | 93 |
|  | 181 |

Although the sexes were analyzed separately, there were few differences between them, and in the final analysis we lumped the ninety-two widowers and eighty-nine widows together. The mean age for the group was 66 years ($\pm$ 11).

For the purposes of measuring outcome in this study, we used the following scales from the Health Questionnaire (see appendix 1):

310

1. Autonomic Symptoms (thirteen questions)
2. Depression (twenty-four questions)
3. Habit Change (four questions measuring increase in consumption of tranquilizers, sedatives, alcohol, and tobacco)
4. Health Care (three questions on use of health care systems during the preceding year)
5. Worry (ten questions)
6. Physical Symptoms (ten questions)

An "Overall Outcome Score" was obtained by assigning more or less equal weight to each of these scales and adding them together (scores for scales 1, 2, 5, and 6 were each divided by 10). To test the predictive value of the index we compared the outcome scores of Group C (Predicted "Low Risk") with Group BT (Control Group "High Risk"). We took an arbitrary cut-off score of 3.0 as our measure of good or poor outcome.

Table A5.2 shows that there was a significant (p < .02) association between predicted outcome and actual outcome. Respondents in the "High Risk" group were twice as likely to have four or more autonomic symptoms and almost twice as likely to have increased their consumption of drugs, alcohol, and tobacco as were the "Low Risk" group (both significant p < .01).

TABLE A5.2
*Overall Outcome and Predictive Groups*

|  | High Risk Group (BT) Predictive Score 18+ 38 | Low Risk Group (C) Predictive Score < 18 93 |
|---|---|---|
| Poor Outcome (Overall Outcome Score 3.0+) | 22 (57%) | 30 (32%) |
| Good Outcome (Overall Outcome Score < 3.0) | 16 (42%) | 63 (68%) |

NOTE: Yates' $\chi^2$ = 6.37, 2 d.f., p < .02.

But our predictions were far from perfect. Thus, nearly a third of those expected to do well had a poor outcome, and 42 percent of those expected to do poorly had a good outcome.

To see whether these predictions could be improved upon, we carried out a stepwise regression analysis on data from fifty-six respondents from groups BT and C. This showed that the best predictor of outcome from the questionnaire was "Clinging or Pining." This score correlated r 0.37 with our outcome score (p < .01). Allowing for intercorrelation between variables, it was also worth including sex (females scored higher than males), age (older scored higher than younger respondents), and the nurse's estimate of the respondent's ability to cope (Question H). This last question was, in fact, the best predictor of the depression score as indicated by a repeat run of the computer program using depression score as the outcome variable.

In interpreting these findings, it is important to consider the influence that variables have on each other. Thus "Self-Reproach" (Question F), which did not reach a useful level of prediction in its own right, nevertheless correlated r 0.25 with outcome (p < .10). However, it also correlated with "Clinging or Pining" and with the nurse's estimate of coping ability, and these proved to be more powerful predictors of outcome.

Older age and female sex, as we have seen, are likely to affect psychosocial adjustment scores in married controls as well as bereaved respondents. The above findings, therefore, cannot in themselves be taken as indicating that older people and women have more difficulties *as a result of bereavement* than do younger people and men.

"Clinging or Pining," which was correlated highly with "Self-Reproach" (r 0.47) and "Anger" (r 0.34) as well as with the nurse's prediction of ability to cope (r 0.55), remained our best individual indicator of outcome. Question C, on length of preparation for death, did not prove predictive. Presumably this was due to the fact that all the respondents had lost spouses from cancers in the special circumstances of care provided at St.

Christopher's Hospice. Consequently, there were only two who were thought to have been less than fully prepared and even those scored only 2 on this question.

As a result of these findings, the Bereavement Risk Index has been modified as shown in table A5.3. This revised index has now been tested in the course of replication of an earlier study of surviving spouses of patients who died from cancer in two of the boroughs served by St. Christopher's Hospice. In this replication no unsupported control group was included. Seven widows and widowers who were identified as especially high risk in that they had scores of 18 or more on the Bereavement Risk Index were offered counseling. Four of them accepted this offer. This means that the outcome scores of the entire high risk group may have been lowered to some degree by counseling of these four.

Table A5.4 shows the distribution of good and poor outcomes among respondents having predictive scores of 0 to 14 and those having predictive scores of 15 or more. There is a significant association between predictive score and outcome.

### TABLE A5.3.
### *Second Bereavement Risk Index*

| | CONFIDENTIAL | | Case Note: |
|---|---|---|---|
| Name of Patient (surname first in capitals) | Age: | | Number: |
| | Date of Admission: | | Date of Death: |
| Surname of Key Person: | First Name: | | |
| Address: | | Telephone: | |

Relationship to patient:       O.P. Yes/No
Do you think key person would object to follow up?    Yes/No/Not known
Staff member(s) most closely involved:

313

# RECOVERY FROM BEREAVEMENT

Other family members in need of help:
Comments: (include details of help already being given):

Questionnaire: (Ring one item in each section. Leave blank if not known.)
. . . . . . . . . Check here if key person not well enough known to enable these questions
to be answered.

| A. Children under 14 at home | B. Social class— Occupation of principal wage earner of key person's family * | C. Anticipated Employment of key person outside home | D. Clinging or Pining | E. Anger |
|---|---|---|---|---|
| 0. None | | 0. Works F/T | 1. Never | 1. None (or normal) |
| 1. One | 1. Professional and executive | 1. Works P/T | 2. Seldom | 2. Mild irritation |
| 2. Two | | 3. Retired | 3. Moderate | |
| 3. Three | 2. Semi-professional | 4. Housewife only | 4. Frequent | 3. Moderate— occasional outbursts |
| 4. Four | | 5. Unemployed | 5. Constant | |
| 5. Five or more | 3. Office and clerical | | 6. Constant intense | 4. Severe— spoiling relationships |
| | 4. Skilled manual | | | 5. Extreme— always bitter |
| | 5. Semi-skilled manual | | | |
| | 6. Unskilled manual | | | |

*If in doubt, guess.

F.
*Self-Reproach*
1. None
2. Mild—vague and general
3. Moderate—some clear self reproach
4. Severe—Preoccupied with self-blame
5. Extreme—major problem

G.
*Relationship now*
1. Close intimate relationship with another
2. Warm supportive family permitting expression of feeling
3. Family supportive but live at distance
4. Doubtful
5. None of these

H.
*How will key person cope?†*
1. *Well*—normal grief and recovery without special help
2. *Fair*—probably get by without special help
3. *Doubtful*—may need special help
4. *Badly*—requires special help
5. *Very badly*—requires urgent help

†All scoring 4–5 on H will be followed up.

**314**

TABLE A5.4.

*Replication of Predictive Study: Overall Outcome and Predictive Groups*

|  |  | Predictive Scores | |
| --- | --- | --- | --- |
|  |  | High Risk Group | Low Risk Group |
|  |  | 15+ | 0–14 |
|  | n. | 20 | 16 |
| Poor Outcome |  | 11 (55%) | 1 ( 6.25%) |
| Good Outcome |  | 9 (45%) | 15 (93.75%) |

Yates $\chi^2$ = 5.6, 2 d.f., p < .02

# References

Abraham, K. 1924. A short study of the development of the libido. In *Selected papers on psycho-analysis*. New York: Basic Books, 1953.

Ainsworth, M. D., and Wittig, B. A. 1969. Attachment and exploratory behaviour of one-year-olds in a strange situation. *Determinants of infant behaviour,* ed. B. Foss, vol. 4. London: Methuen.

Anderson, C. 1949. Aspects of pathological grief and mourning. *International Journal of Psycho-Analysis* 30:48–55.

Bowlby, J. 1960. Separation anxiety. *International Journal of Psycho-Analysis* 41: 89–113.

―――. 1969. *Attachment and loss.* Vol. 1: *Attachment.* New York: Basic Books.

Bowlby, J., and Parkes, C. M. 1970. Separation and loss. In *The child in his family,* vol. 1. of International Yearbook of Child Psychiatry and Allied Professions, eds. E. J. Anthony and C. Koupernik. New York: John Wiley.

Breuer, J., and Freud, S. (1895). *Studies on hysteria.* Standard edition of *The complete psychological works of Sigmund Freud,* vol. 2. New York: W. W. Norton.

Brown, G. W., and Harris, T. 1978. *Social origins of depression: a study of psychiatric disorder in women.* London: Tavistock.

Cameron, J. and Parkes, C. M. 1983. Terminal care: evaluation of effects on surviving families of care before and after bereavement. *Postgraduate Medical Journal* 59: 73–78.

Clayton, P. J., Desmarais, L., and Winokur, G. 1968. A study of normal bereavement. *American Journal of Psychiatry* 125: 168–78.

Clayton, P. J., Halikas, J. A., Maurice, W. L., and Robbins, E. 1973. Anticipatory grief and widowhood. *British Journal of Psychiatry* 122:47–51.

Cumming, E., and Henry, W. E. 1961. *Growing old.* New York: Basic Books.

Darwin, C. 1872. *The expression of the emotions in man and animals.* London: Murray.

Deutsch, H. 1937. Absence of grief. *Psycho-Analytic Quarterly* 6:12–22.

Dohrenwend, B. P., and Dohrenwend, B. S. 1969. *Social status and psychological disorder.* New York: John Wiley.

Dyne, G. 1981. *Bereavement visiting.* London: King Edward's Hospital Fund for London.

Egbert, L. D., Battit, G. F., Welch, C. E., and Bartlett, M. K. 1964. Reduction of Post-operative Pain by Encouragement and Instruction of Patients: A Study of Doctor/Patient Rapport. *New England Journal of Medicine* 270:825–27.

Engel, G. L. 1961. Is grief a disease? *Psychosomatic Medicine* 23:18–22.

# References

Fisher, R. A., and Yates, F. 1963. *Statistical tables for biological, agricultural and medical research.* 6th ed. Edinburgh: Oliver and Boyd.

Fitzgerald, R. 1970. Reactions to blindness: an exploratory study of adults with recent loss of sight. *Archives of General Psychiatry* 22:370–79.

Freud, S. (1917). *Mourning and melancholia.* Standard edition of *The complete psychological works of Sigmund Freud,* vol. 14. New York: W.W. Norton.

Glick, I. O., Weiss, R. S., and Parkes, C. M. 1974. *The first year of bereavement.* New York: Wiley Interscience.

Gorer, G. 1965. *Death, grief and mourning in contemporary Britain.* London: Tavistock.

Hart, J. T. 1971. The inverse care law. *Lancet.* 1:405–12.

Holmes, T. H., and Rahe, R. H. (1967). The Social Readjustment Rating Scale. *Journal of Psychosomatic Research* 11:213–18.

Janis, I. L. 1958. *Psychological stress: psycho-analytic and behavioral studies of surgical patients.* London: Chapman and Halland. New York: Academic Press.
———. 1962. Group identification under conditions of external danger. Paper read at Medical Section of British Psychological Society, 23 May 1962.

Kay, D. W., Roth, M., and Hopkins, B. 1955. Aetiological factors in the causation of affective disorders in old age. *Journal of Mental Science* 101:302–16.

Klein, M. 1940. Mourning and its relationship to manic-depressive states. *International Journal of Psycho-Analysis* 21:125–53.

Krupp, G. R. 1962. The bereavement reaction: a special case of separation anxiety. In W. Muensterberger & S. Axelrad (Eds.) *The Psychoanalytic Study of Society,* Volume II. New York: International Universities Press.

Kval, V. A. 1951. Psychiatric observations under severe chronic stress. *American Journal of Psychiatry* 108:185–92.

Lazarus, H. R., and Hagens, J. H. 1968. Prevention of psychosis following open heart surgery. *American Journal of Psychiatry* 124:1190–95.

Lear, M. W. 1979. *Heartsounds.* New York: Simon and Schuster.

Lehrman, R. 1956. Reactions to untimely death. *Psychiatric Quarterly* 30:567–8.

Lifton, R. J. 1967. *Death in life: the survivors of Hiroshima.* New York: Random House.

Lindemann, C. 1944. The symptomatology and management of acute grief. *American Journal of Psychiatry* 101:141–9.

Longford, E. 1964. *Victoria R.I.* London: Weidenfeld and Nicholson.

Lopata, H. Z. 1973. *Widowhood in an American city.* Cambridge, Mass.: Schenkman.

Lynch, J. J. 1977. *The broken heart: the medical consequences of loneliness.* New York: Basic Books.

Maddison, D. C., and Walker, W. L. 1967. Factors affecting the outcome of conjugal bereavement. *British Journal of Psychiatry* 113:1057–67.

Maddison, D. C., and Viola, A. 1968. The health of widows in the year following bereavement. *Journal of Psychosomatic Research* 12:297–306.

Maddison, D. C., Viola, A., and Walker, W. L. 1969. Further studies in bereavement. *Australia and New Zealand Journal of Psychiatry.* 3:63–6.

Marris, P. 1958. *Widows and their families.* London: Routledge and Kegan Paul.

Mawson, D., Marks, I. M., Ramm, L., and Stern, L. S. 1981. Guided mourning for morbid grief: a controlled study. *British Journal of Psychiatry* 138:185–93.

Multivariate Research, Inc. 1969. *The multivariate statistical analyzer.* Dover, Mass: Multivariate Research, Inc.

317

# References

Oman, C. 1936. *Henrietta Maria.* London: Hodder and Stoughton.

Parkes, C. M. 1962. Reactions to bereavement. M.D. thesis. University of London.

———. 1964. The effects of bereavement on physical and mental health: a study of case records of widows. *British Medical Journal* 2:274–79.

———. 1965. Bereavement and mental illness. *British Journal of Medical Psychology* 38:1–26.

———. 1970a. The first year of bereavement. *Psychiatry* 33:442–67.

———. 1970b. "Seeking" and "finding" a lost object: evidence from recent studies of the reaction to bereavement. *Social Science and Medicine* 4:187–201.

———. 1971. Psycho-social transitions: a field for study. *Social Science and Medicine* 5:101–15.

———. 1972a. Accuracy of preditions of survival in later stages of cancer. *British Medical Journal.* 2:29–31.

———. 1972b. *Bereavement: studies of grief in adult life.* New York: International Universities Press.

———. 1972c. Components of the reaction to loss of a limb, spouse or home. *Journal of Psychosomatic Research.* 16:343–49.

———. 1975. What becomes of redundant world models? a contribution to the study of adaptation to change. *British Journal of Medical Psychology.* 18:131–37.

———. 1976. Determinants of outcome following bereavement. *Omega* 6:303–09.

———. 1979. Evaluation of a bereavement service. In *The Dying Human,* ed. André de Vries and Amon Carmi. Ramat Gun, Israel: Turtledove.

———. 1980. Terminal care: evaluation of an advisory domiciliary service at St. Christopher's Hospice. *Postgraduate Medical Journal.* 56:685–89.

———. 1981a. Bereavement counselling—does it work? *British Medical Journal.* 281:3–6.

———. 1981b. Evaluation of a bereavement service. *Journal of Preventive Psychiatry* 1:179–88.

———. 1982. Determinants of disablement after loss of a limb. In *Emotional rehabilitation of the physical rehabilitation patient,* ed. David W. Krueger. Forthcoming.

Parkes, C. M., Benjamin, B., and Fitzgerald, R. G. 1969. Broken heart: a statistical study of increased mortality among widowers. *British Medical Journal.* 1:740–43.

Parkes, C. M., and Brown, R. 1972. Health after bereavement: a controlled study of young Boston widows and widowers. *Psychosomatic Medicine* 34:-449–61.

Parkes, C. M., and Parkes, J. L. N. 1983. "Hospice" versus "hospital" care: re-evaluation of ten years of progress in terminal care as seen by surviving spouses. In press.

Ramsay, R. W. 1979. Bereavement: a behavioral treatment of pathological grief. In *Trends in behavior therapy,* ed. P. O. Sioden, S. Bates, and W. S. Dorkens III. New York: Academic Press.

Raphael, B. 1977. Preventive Intervention with the Recently Bereaved. *Archives of General Psychiatry* 34:1460–64.

Rees, W. D., and Lutkins, S. G. 1967. Mortality of Bereavement. *British Medical Journal* 4:13–16.

318

Silverman, P. R. 1970. The widow as caregiver in a program of preventive intervention with other widows. *Mental Hygiene* 54:540–47.

Silverman, P. R., MacKenzie, D., Pettipas, M., and Wilson, E. 1974. *Helping each other in widowhood.* New York: Health Sciences.

Stein, Z., and Susser, M. W. 1969. Widowhood and mental illness. *British Journal of Preventive and Social Medicine* 23:106–10.

Stern, K., Williams, G. M., and Prados, M. 1951. Grief reactions in later life. *American Journal of Psychiatry* 108:289–94.

Stroebe, M. S., Stroebe, W., Gergen, K. J., and Gergen, M. 1981. The broken heart: reality or myth? *Omega* 12:87–106.

Thomas, C. 1957. *Left-over life to kill.* London: Putnam.

Tisdall, E. E. P. 1952. *Queen Victoria's private life, 1877–1901.* London: Jarrolds.

Vachon, M. L. S., Lyale, W. A. L., Rogers, J., Freedman-Letofsky, K., and Freeman, S. J. J. 1980. Controlled study of self-help intervention for widows. *American Journal of Psychiatry* 137:1380–84.

Volkan, V. 1970. Typical findings in pathological grief. *Psychiatric Quarterly* 44:-231–50.

Volkan, V., Cillufo, A. F., and Sarvay, T. L. 1975. Pre-grief therapy and the function of the linking object as a key to stimulate emotionality. In *Emotional flooding,* ed. Paul Olsen. New York: Human Sciences Press.

Wahl, C. W. 1970. The differential diagnosis of normal and neurotic grief following bereavement. *Archives of the Foundation of Thanatology* 1:137–41.

Wallace, A. F. 1956. *Tornado in Worcester: an exploratory study of individual and community behavior in an extreme situation.* National Academy of Science Disaster Study no. 3. Washington, D.C.: National Research Council.

Weiss, R. S. 1973. *Loneliness: the experience of emotional and social isolation.* Cambridge, Mass.: M.I.T. Press.

———. 1975. *Marital separation.* New York: Basic Books.

———. 1976a. The emotional impact of marital separation. *Journal of Social Issues* 32:135–45.

———. 1976b. Transition states and other stressful situations: their nature and programs for their management. In *Support systems and mutual help: multidisciplinary explorations,* ed. Gerald Caplan and Marie Killilea. New York: Grune and Stratton.

Wolfenstein, M. 1957. *Disaster: a psychological essay.* New York: Free Press.

Worden, W. 1982. *Grief counseling and grief therapy.* New York: Springer.

Wretmark, G. 1959. A study in grief reaction. *Acta Psychiatrica et Neurologica Scandinavica Supplement* 136:292–99.

Yamamoto, T., Okonogi, K., Iwasaki, T., and Yoshimwa, S. 1969. Mourning in Japan. *American Journal of Psychiatry* 125:1600–65.

Young, M., Benjamin, B., and Wallis, C. 1963. Mortality of widowers. *Lancet* 2:454–56.

# Index

Abraham, Karl, 10

Acceptance of loss, 32–33; anticipated grief and, 78; bereavement counseling and, 238; in chronic grief, 140; in delayed grief, 112; in divorce, 257; emotional, 157–59, 164, 167; identity and, 161; intellectual, 156–57; in unexpected loss syndrome, 63, 65, 74, 85, 88, 90–91, 93; unresolved grief and, 195; yearning versus, 144

Accidental deaths, 59; case illustration of, 83–92

Acute grief, 15; anger expressed during, 22

Affect, disturbance of, 145

Age factors: in pathological grief, 18–19, 23; as predictive variable, 53

Agnostics, 53

Ainsworth, Mary D., 124, 135, 136

Albert, Prince, 129–30, 134, 135, 153

Alcohol consumption: in chronic grief, 210; conflicted grief and, 108; increase in, 39–40, 191; as predictive variable, 54; for tranquilizing effects, 177–78; unresolved grief, 170

Alcoholism: marital conflict and, 99–100, 102, 112; unresolved grief and, 192–200

Ambivalence, 20; in chronic grief, 19; in depressive illness, 10, 11; and intervention before bereavement, 233–37; in losses other than bereavement, 256–57; *see also* Marital conflict

Amputation, preparation for, 255

Analytical psychotherapy, 237

Anderson, C., 13–14, 228

Anger: in acute stage of grief, 22; assessment of, 29, 33; in chronic grief, 14; in conflicted grief, 110, 116, 121; expression of, 249; in grief reaction, 3–4; impact on family of, 246; and inadequate care during final illness, 234; level of, as predictive variable, 47, 51, 52; during terminal illness, 100; in unanticipated grief, 63

Animals: distress signals of, 4; mourning behavior in, 3

Anna O. (case), 9

Anniversary reactions, 24

Anticipated grief: case illustration of, 74–83; unanticipated grief compared with, 69–79, 92–96

Anticipatory grief, 57, 58

Antidepressant drugs, 191, 237

Anxiety: aroused by grief reaction, 4; assessment of, 33; in chronic grief, 131; in conflicted grief, 104, 107, 110, 116; dependency and, 139; impact on family of, 245; in pathological grief, 14; in unanticipated grief, 60, 69, 73, 93; yearning and, 145

Appetite loss: incidence of, 39; in unanticipated grief, 88

Arteriosclerotic heart disease, 7–8

Assessment of outcome, 29–33; reliability of, 28

Atheists, 53

Attachment, 3; anticipated grief and, 81, 94, 95; autonomy and, 152; con-

# Index

# Index

Maddison, D. C., 6, 17, 18, 23, 222, 225
Manic-depressive illness, 11; hospitalization for, 37
Marital conflict: assessment of, 97–103; divorce and, 257; outcome and, 106–11, 164; questionnaire items on, 27, 275; and reaction to bereavement, 103
Marital relationship: growth in, 127; unanticipated grief and, 61, 72, 94; variables based on, 45, 47, 51–52
Marris, P., 14
Martin, Sir Theodore, 130
Maudsley Hospital, 14
Mawson, D., 241, 242
Medical history, 27
Melancholia, 10–11
Mother, loss of, 11, 20
Motteville, Madame de, 56–57
Mourning: Freud on, 2; guided, 17–18; identity based on, 160; perpetual, 19; resemblance to depressive illness, of, 10; rituals of, 239, 242; in social animals, 3; social attitudes toward, 18
"Mourning and Melancholia" (Freud), 2, 10, 121
Multiple bereavements, 20
Mutual aid, 237, 251–52
Myocardial infarction, 8

Neilson, Mr. (case), 170, 192–300, 215
Neurotic illness, history of, 21
Norton, Mrs. (case), 146–49, 162
Numbness, 55; absence of, in delayed grief, 111; in disaster syndrome, 254; and resistance to intervention, 255; of victims of violence, 254

Object: loss of, in depressive illness, 10, 11; withdrawal of libido from, 2
Obligation to deceased, feelings of, 69

"Old sergeant's syndrome," 20
Oman, C., 57
Oral incorporation, 11
Other-esteem, 173
Outcome: assessment of, 29–33; intercorrelation of measures of, 296–303; marital conflict and, 106–11; overall, 42–43; predictors of, 45–55, 216–26
Over-dependence, see Dependency

Palliative care unit (P.C.U.), 234
Parents, 11; insecure attachment with, 123
Parkes, Colin Murray, ix, x, 2, 6–8, 10, 14, 17, 21, 23, 25n, 51, 58, 63, 70, 172n, 217, 225, 228, 230, 235, 238, 308, 321–13
Pathological grief, 9–22; causes of, 15–22; see also specific syndromes
Personality factors: in conflicted grief, 122–23; in pathological grief, 20–21
Physical trauma: body's reaction to, 2; recovery from, 5
Post-partum depression, 175
Prados, M., 18
Predictors of outcome, 45–55
Prohibition of grieving, 165–67
Protestants, 54
Psychiatric illness: incidence in bereaved people of, 8; significance of grief syndromes in, 171–74
Psychic numbing, 60, 254
Psychological trauma: defense against, 2; hysterical symptoms and, 9
Psychosocial transitions, 70–71, 236
Psychosomatic disorders, 15
Psychotherapy, 237; termination of, 256

Questionnaire, see Health Questionnaire

326